Door in
Dark Water

The Gulf of Maine

Vinalhaven Is.

Seal Is.

South
Bristol

Monhegan Is.

PORTLAND

Inner
Fall

Toothacher
Ridge

Jeffreys Ledge

Cashes Ledge

PORTSMOUTH

Isles of Shoals

Annisquam

G U L F   O F   M A I N E

Gloucester

BOSTON

Cape Cod Canal

Door in Dark Water

P. D. Callahan

Nightwood Press

Published by Nightwood Press, Carlisle, Massachusetts 01741.

Printed in the United States of America.

Portions of this book have appeared in different forms in
The Molotov Cocktail and *Black Heart Magazine*.

Book design, cover design, art, and ink-wash drawings by
Jon Albertson, Albertson Design, www.albertson-design.com.

Author's photograph by
Nancy Pattison Roberts, www.nancyrobertsphotography.com.

Maps by the author.

ISBN-13: 978-0-9665609-2-3

For Nancy and Joy

And for Sydney and Owen

The South Bristol Area

Damariscotta

Damariscotta River

Muscongus Bay

South Bristol

Boothbay
Harbor

New Harbor

Johns Bay

Rutherford Is.

Pemaquid Pt.

Thrumcap Is.

Outer Heron Is.

Damariscove Is.

CONTENTS

Part Three: **Normie & Candy B**

Part Four: **All Anyone Needs**

PROLOGUE

SOMETIMES, working on the water was about increasing your tolerance for fear, raising the bar. And later, after the bar had been raised and the stories had been told (and they would be told because they served the purpose of making the new threshold evermore permanent), what you had feared in the past often seemed trivial or nonsensical.

And, in some cases, fear was about nothing at all. Purely imaginary.

But *experiencing* the fear could be paralyzing and nearly heart stopping, just the same.

This happened to me one beautifully calm night in July of 1975, six miles from Monhegan Island at about 3:30 am.

I was on watch outbound on the *Miss Angel* with everyone else turned in below, including the skipper, Arthur "Mr. P" Poland. The fishing was very heavy just southwest of the island — big cod and pollock coming over the rail alive and shining like newborns. But we had been going for thirty days without a break and everyone was cranky and tired. It was one of those runs when you are making the bulk of your money for the whole year, but you wished the fish would stop being there and give you a break.

It was my day to take the morning watch: two hours at the helm making sure we didn't run anybody down, staring at the eerie green sweep of the radar screen and looking around, taking a tour of the deck, watching the gauges, listening to the FM radio chatter and the recorded NOAA (National Oceanic and Atmospheric Administration) weather. The autopilot was making its *shish-ting, shish-ting* noises as it micro-adjusted the rudder, and the yellow Caterpillar turbocharger whistled a constant and penetrating high-pitched note. It was Sunday morning and all of us had been drinking on the Saturday night and some, including Mr. P, had kept pounding the booze and not gone to bed at all. Now he was in his bunk like the rest of the crew.

Miss Angel made an easy sixteen knots, which was very fast for a fishing boat. In truth, she was a wild plastic horse wrapped around a roaring diesel, much too lively in any sea action, and as loud as a bass drum. It was dark, of course, and the moon had already set. Making sure you didn't run anything down was mostly looking out the forward windows to see if what you picked up on the radar matched what you saw out the window. Green blip on the radar should match up with red or green running lights, or 360-degree white masthead light, or both.

We knew the schedule for the oil barge from Portland to Searsport. Always worth watching for, since the tug had a very long cable out to the barge-in-tow and you didn't want to run between the tug and the barge. If you did, the taut cable would rip your wheelhouse off in a half-second and probably cleave you into two or more ugly pieces. But the probability of that happening was very low since the tug sported a vast array of vertical white lights and was very hard to miss.

Not running down other boats was always paramount. But equally important was making sure that there were no changes to the engine speed whatsoever. In other words, when a lowly deckhand draws the short straw for the watch in the wee hours, the last thing he ever wants to do is change the throttle the slightest, even fifty or a hundred rpm, unless he has a real problem. If he does, everybody sleeping down below is immediately in the mad scramble: out-bunk, on-boots, and poking their hung over and groggy-looking faces up through the companionway to see what is going on. Why'd you slow down? What's going on, Cappy?

Miss Angel was fast because she had a big engine; so we were all in the process of going deaf listening to it whether we liked it or not. And when you turned in on a boat like that, you actually didn't sleep — you rested and pretended to sleep, because you were lying in bunks next to a screaming six-cylinder Caterpillar diesel with a turbocharger that whined and whistled like a jet plane through a fiberglass bulkhead less than a quarter-inch thick and no more than ten or fifteen feet away. Some guys wore the aircraft headphones, but they were a pain to sleep in, even if you were pretending, and the only alternative was plastic earplugs, which eventually made your earholes hurt.

That particular morning, there was a traditional sailboat race — the Portland to Monhegan race — that had started the previous day. We knew about the race and we knew that the course of the race crossed our own course for that morning, so we were watching for sailboats so as not to hit anyone.

After an hour on watch, I could see a line of sailboats on the radar that was clearly identifiable as the Monhegan race. All the boats were strung out in a line, but they were fairly close together, so I picked a sailboat target and adjusted the autopilot to point the *Miss Angel* directly at it.

That was standard practice. Once you lined up the target, you could then pick out the sailboat by the lights through the forward window — right off the bow — and you could keep your eye on it. If the sailboat kept moving, which it should, and you stuck to your course line, you would go safely astern the target boat. I picked the boat out and I could see his red port-side running light. Everything was fine.

The sailboat, of course, could hear us coming, since it was so quiet under sail, and as was usually the case he got a little excited as we got closer.

The guy at the helm, the skipper or whatever, started waving a flashlight at me hoping someone was at the wheel on this boat bearing down on them (like that was going to wake me up if I was asleep) and I'm sure the *Miss Angel* was making plenty of noise with a straight pipe of wet exhaust roaring out through her stern, so I turned on the big searchlight to let the guy know that I knew that he was there and then I carefully shone the light astern of his sailboat because I didn't want to run down his dinghy if he had one in tow.

Everything was cool, and I didn't have to slow down and get all the hungover guys jumping out of their bunks below and bumping into each other or banging into the galley stove and raising hell over nothing.

We passed by the stern of the sailboat and didn't run down any dinghy in tow, because he wasn't towing any stupid dinghy because he was in a race, I guess, and that would slow him down or something, so I went out and stood at the port-side rail and felt the breeze on my face and listened to the *Miss Angel* growling and listened to the water *hissing* and *shooshing* rhythmically off the hull, off the spray bars on her forward cheeks. Then, I waved a flashlight back at the sailboat as we passed. The world was in order.

But when I got back in the wheelhouse, I suddenly saw a bright white light out the forward window right off the port bow. Heartbeat escalation. Had to be a masthead light.

Holy shit. How the fuck could I have missed that? I didn't understand, but I didn't have a lot of time to think. If a masthead was that close, I was right on top of a sailboat, twenty or thirty seconds away from a collision. I couldn't see any running lights, so it must be hove to or at anchor. But why would it be at anchor? Glanced at the depth recorder. Jesus, we were in seventy or eighty fathoms of water. I suppose you could anchor up in at that depth, but that doesn't make any sense. What the fuck is going on, what is he doing? Maybe he's running but his running lights are out. Shit. I stepped over to the radar. I don't think I was breathing at this point. I was going to run this guy down. How could I have missed him? Mr. Smartass flashing the big spotlight and showing off coming too close to the stern of that other boat, what a fucking idiot I am, a smartass idiot. The radar gain was turned up high and there was greenish white clutter around the center of the screen. Maybe he's too close to see, I thought, so I turned down the range to five hundred yards. I still couldn't see him. I must be right on top of him. I was going to run him down, for fuck's sake. That would wake everybody up, all right. I had this heavy clutch in my stomach and I reached for the throttle. One last look. Got to be sure. I ran back out on deck to see if I could see him from the port side. I was about to turn this guy's boat into matchwood and chop him up into bloody pieces of arms and legs. I had to see him.

By now, it was almost four o'clock so there was a modicum of first light starting to show in the east and on the horizon. From the port side with a clear view, I could see under the masthead light now. I could see the line of the horizon where the shadow of the boat should be.

There was no boat sitting under the masthead light. Just the horizon. It was the morning star, Venus. Maybe the masthead light of the galaxy. I had never seen it so bright.

JUVENILE ATLANTIC HERRING *(Clupea harengus)*

Part One

SOUTH BRISTOL

HENRY

FORTY YEARS AGO I FELL IN LOVE WITH a place of great beauty and way of life that is now gone.

My infatuation lasted ten years. And in the end, I was defeated by the impossibility of that love. But nothing could have kept me from it.

Nothing.

It was where I had to go, a door I had to open. The story is worth listening to, I promise you.

It starts in 1972 in South Bristol, Maine, a town of five hundred souls.

"Them zincs was all dis-immigrated," Henry says, "every bit of 'em was gone."

Henry is the king of malaprops, but he doesn't care what anyone thinks. Something close to the right word is good enough for him; and besides nobody dares correct him.

In the forecastle of the *Alice M*, six of us crammed in there for coffee at five am, the light dim and the air thick with cigarette smoke, listening to sixty-four-year-old Henry Jones. Nobody dares because this is his boat, and most everybody (except me) is on his herring crew and they have been with him for most of their fishing lives.

I am visiting my friend, Gladden Schrock, playwright and fisherman on Henry's crew, who has lived in South Bristol for fifteen years. Fresh from college, I have no plan. I don't know it yet, but I have stepped into a reality that will change my life forever, walked through some secret doorway to a place where career path and credentials and a map of the future are irrelevant, where the physical world is everything (all anyone thinks about and

Henry Jones, South Bristol

talks about): the corrosive and creative force of the sea, catching something alive and selling it for food and money, living to the next day and the next day.

This place will soon invade and permanently alter my educated head, and Henry Jones will become an irreplaceable touchstone for the ten years I plunge headlong into fishing.

But hell, I don't know any of this. I am clueless. And beautifully stupid of this place.

I can make out the shapes of stuff taking place in front of me, though; like I can see that the guys sitting in this galley *really* don't care that I don't know anything. Ha, that's pretty clear. And I'm thinking that maybe they prefer it that way.

Get this. They find it amusing (hell, they find it hilarious at times) that I am such a dope about their world. That's kind of a cool thing, and it even seems to have some kind of redeeming value. Maybe because I'm so foreign it doesn't matter? Either way, they appear to extend a level of forgiveness to my stupid questions that would never be extended to the kids who grew up in South Bristol (because those kids should know better).

And something else. It feels to me like they say—and mostly do—whatever they want. They take whatever they need, work only when they need to work, do what needs to be done. Not on anybody else's time schedule; operating only on a clock that is based on the pure necessity to catch and kill wild fish.

Back to Henry—he is interrupted as a yellow beam of daylight cuts down through the smoke like a spotlight from above. The short and roly-poly Mr. P has opened the companionway hatch to the morning sunrise and jumps down the ladder with a thud.

"Jesus Christ, boys, I thought the galley was all afire down here, they's so much fucking smoke," he booms as he waves his hand at the smoke.

Henry stops, "That's the smoke comin' out your ass, Mr P. At least that's what Missus P tells me. Ha ha."

"Now get ye coffee would ye? And stop making such a Christly commotion."

"Don't mind me, Henry, you just keep on talking. I'm sure I've heard it before."

"No, you ain't heard it before—you know better than that." Henry waits while Mr. P pours a coffee, and then restarts his story about the iron fastenings that had melted away on a boat that wasn't properly grounded.

"Roy has heard this one," Henry nods to Roy Vose, his old friend and spotter pilot. Henry never tells the same story twice without first acknowledging those who have heard the story previously.

"You remember this one too, Glad," now looking at Gladden sitting across from me.

"So, then. They said she was wired up so fucking wrong, so completely ass-backwards, that the boat was hot as hell. So they couldn't keep no amount of zincs on her. All of 'em was eaten up almost immeejetly. Eaten up in a week's time, or thereabouts.

"So what do they do? Well. The owner just gives up on her completely and stops replacing zincs altogether. And them iron fastenings just dis-immigrated in no time. No time at all.

"It was so bad, that when they brought her in, the boys at the shipyard said you could lean over the side and see the Christly bubbles from the 'lectrolysis coming off of her right there in the water. They said it was like the bubbles you sees inside of a glass of ginger ale."

Henry goes on about how the rampant electrolysis had dissolved all the iron screws and then how a few of the boat's planks had even fallen off when they hauled her out on the shipyard railway, once the outside water pressure against the hull wasn't holding them against the frames anymore.

Sitting there, I am flashing back to how I got here. How I met Gladden in my last year at Hampshire College, far away from here. Like another planet, really.

How I'm sitting on the floor in the theater, sporting a giant bird's nest of a red beard that I haven't cut in four years, an old limpy tee shirt and jeans, and I'm walking two actors through a one-act play I've written about a homeless man living on a park bench. The man is assaulted by an amorphous force (a character costumed in a giant gray sack), a force that periodically pummels him as he tries to ask questions and reason through his life. Gladden's arrival in the experimental amphitheater stops the rehearsal as he reaches down with this maw of a hand — more like a baseball mitt — and introduces himself as both a one-term visiting playwright and a herring fisherman. We become friends throughout the term. Then, in the spring, when he is leaving for home, he invites me for a visit, says he is thinking of starting a theater in Maine.

For my part, all I can think about is how little I know about surviving on my own, how the Vietnam War has us all circling the drain, how I need to feel the heat and the sweat of the world and learn something — anything — about how to survive there. Then I'm thinking all manner of romantic tripe, like why not touch the sea, the primordial source of all life, and the unpredictable master of danger? Yeah, that should fix us right up. And the fact that Gladden lives there and works on the water is perfect.

In June my girlfriend, Joy Vaughan, and I drive to South Bristol.

We rent a yellow house just across the drawbridge on Rutherford's Island looking out on the shipyard and the western gut, the center of town at the tip of the bare peninsula. I start working as a carpenter in the day and searching for herring at night with Henry and Gladden and riding out with the mackerel trappers on weekends to see what that is like. Joy begins waitressing in Damariscotta.

But some form of reality jolt has already happened, some knot's been broken open, untwisted, just by making the decision to move.

Like I said, I don't really know what is going on. I'm twenty-four, for Christ sake. Nobody knows what they're doing at that age. Joy has three years on me in age, at twenty-seven, but we're both of us just out of our minds.

One day, still in the early summer of our first year, I burst into the kitchen in the yellow house, back from a morning ride with Junior Farrin and his trapping crew, and I'm telling Joy how I ended up standing in a dory up to my thighs in these beautiful mackerel, how we had rolled a huge hoop net full of them over the rail, how they thundered aboard in a shower of water and tiny scales, slapping their last gasp all around us.

Hands on her hips, cigarette in hand curling smoke, and looking at me with wondrous amusement, she interrupts me and says, "You are absolutely in love, aren't you?"

(Never one to mince words, Joy.)

"You're in love with the ocean, with the sea."

I'm kinda stunned, speechless for a minute.

Then I say, "Naw, it's the fish. I'm in love with the fish."

Truth is, I love them both.

I love Joy, too. She is the love of my life. But now I have this competing romance that's making my heart race, I have to admit it.

Growing up in the suburbs of Boston, I have never witnessed creatures with such wildness and innocence combined. And, over time, I will discover that pulling fish out of the water and over the rail never gets old. Never.

Being poor does get old, though.

I can say that with great certainty, because we are dirt poor for all of the ten years I chase fish, winter and summer, up and down the Gulf of Maine.

But touching the lives of creatures that live in the ocean — that feeling of surprise and the look in their eyes — never does.

RENTAL ON THE GUT

OUR LANDLORD WAS A RETIRED ARMY colonel in Damariscotta, Mr. Fixit, with a lot of time on his hands. He liked projects but they didn't always come out right. He told me that he bought wrecked cars for next to nothing, bent them back into shape and sold them, and couldn't understand why people would give away a good wreck. I suppose, he'd bought the yellow house on the island thinking he could apply the same method. I only hope his refurbished wrecks turned out better than the yellow house.

The plumbing fixtures were cobbled together with mismatched handles held on by big wood screws, dripping faucets were stopped with homemade washers made from cut up garden hoses, and the furnace was a rescue-job from the Bristol dump. Just enough of the yellow house worked to live in it day to day. But each day held a new surprise.

"This yellow house is held together with old string and rubber bands, for God's sake," Joy commented one night when the bathroom faucet handle came off in her hands.

We didn't care because it was summer — and it was heaven, especially for two kids who had lived in city apartments and college dorms. The economics? Squarely in the scraping-by category.

My work as a carpenter paid $2.75 an hour, and Joy took the car every morning to drive to Damariscotta where she made minimum wages plus tips waitressing the six am shift at the Damariscotta Diner. Not much money between us, but our rent was seventy-five dollars a month and if we kept to eating fish, food was cheap and sometimes free: clams, mussels, smoked herring, fresh mackerel and haddock, wind-dried salt hake and pollock hung on a clothes line, and plenty of crabs.

Visitors would show up with food, too. Herb Kelsey, one of the drawbridge tenders, a heavy man in his fifties with a broad face and a Cheshire cat smile, knocked on the door one night around five with a six-pack of beer and a peck of clams. We cooked the clams and drank all the beer, all the while Herb quizzing us for the raw details of our previous life.

People would just show up unannounced to get to know you, to hear your story. The fact that someone new had moved into town was a big deal. Everyone had to know what we were about, and visitors got the word out.

A few weeks into July, Gladden and Henry Jones shut off some herring one night in McFarland's Cove and invited me along the next day to see them load the catch onto a sardine carrier — a single boatload of herring, around nine hundred bushels.

Henry explained, "Stop-seine herring keep the cans from splodin. If the fish is feedy, then the sardine cans'll splode in the cooker. Stop-seine fish is clean of the feed. That's why the canneries like 'em."

Canneries up and down the coast packed juvenile herring as sardines and preferred fish caught with stop-seines, a long straight net that shut off the herring in a cove and kept them until they were nearly empty of feed.

"When the sardine carriers come to pump out the fish and haul 'em back to the factry, they check the bellies of a few fish to see how much feed is in 'em. They squeeze 'em to see if they'se clean, like." Henry made a motion with his hands as if he were squeezing the length of an imaginary fish.

The following day aboard the *Alice M* we are slurping coffee while we wait for the sardine carrier.

"They's about nine hundred bushel swimming in the pocket, so I told them to send just the one boat," Henry says.

"How can you tell?" I ask, and you can hear a pin drop as the veteran crew look to one another for a moment, and then erupt in a chorus of laughter and smoker's coughs at the shocking naïveté of my question.

Amid the hilarity, Henry grins as he pulls on his cigarette, "You run across 'em with a sound machine in the workboat, of course," and then he pauses for quiet.

"But that ain't such a stupid question, really. Even from someone who went to college."

More laughter.

"So I'll tell ye how we used to do it. They was quite a few men in the days before we had sound machines and electronics, who was quite accurate at telling how many fish you had using a feeling pole. A man like that would have hisself a long thin pole and could get quite good with it. But the pole was kind of flat-like, don't you know, not so much a rounded pole as it was flat and thin, so'se it would go easy through the water." Henry draws his hand along like a fin to demonstrate.

"He would have someone paddle him across the pocket in a skiff while he held this long feeling pole overboard, and down into the fish. An' he could feel the herring rubbing down there agin the pole and he'd tell you how many fish you had by the feel of it."

Henry looks down at his watch and says, "Must be time, boys." The big man is up the ladder, the *M*'s diesel grumbles to life, and we cast off for McFarland's Cove.

After the years of abstract reflections on human development, poetry, and experimental theater that had been my college life, watching those herring get seined up and pumped aboard a carrier will throw internal switches and breakers I don't even know I have. Nothing in the closed and imaginary world I have come from will hold a candle to it. That event, that day in particular, will send me down a path from which no amount of logic can sway me left or right. It seems crazy, but I will feel as if my beating heart is immersed in a broth of love and light (or magically injected with the most powerful haze-inducing, love and sex drug ever invented.) Flooded with feeling and barred from analysis, I will yield to the events in this cove as they strip away everything that isn't pure emotion. I am completely disarmed by the moment — like holding a baby in your arms for the first time or touching the muzzle of a horse.

Sunday afternoon, not a breath of air in the cove, the water as quiet as a millpond. When we get there, the big sardine carrier from Stinson Canning, the seventy-five-foot *Joyce Marie*, is already nestled in, tied to the corks of the pocket, water sluicing across her decks and out of her scuppers as they wash out the fish pump with the deck hose and get the scale baskets ready to collect the herring scales.

Stop-seine crew drying fish, Vinalhaven Island

With the *Alice M* shut down and tethered on a corner of the pocket, all of us get aboard the small seine boat, a heavily built double-ender with a gas-powered two-headed winch to purse the seine with. The winch is silent as we pull the little seine boat around the perimeter of the pocket, leaning over the gunwale pulling the corks hand over hand and slapping them rhythmically against the side of the seine boat to keep the fish in the middle of the pocket while we set the seine around them. It is so quiet that the *chock, chock* of the seine corks echoes off the trees on the shore.

We cut halfway across the pocket so as to not take too many in the first set. Then, when we have come full-circle back to the carrier, someone starts the winch, runs the purse line through the double davits and on to the heads of the winch, *chug, chug, chug*, such a sweet sound pursing the seine, closing it across the bottom. The sound of business, the sound of money. Then the purse is closed and the bronze purse rings are winched all the way up and dropped in a neat row below the davits for the next set.

The pocket seine feels like silk on our hands as we haul back and crowd the fish against the big carrier. The twine is not tarred black like running twine or pocket twine; it is soft. Soon the fish begin to rise as we dry them up, eight-or-ten-inch fish, called fours or fives, for the fact that they would be packed four or five to a can at the factory by snipping off the heads and tails with scissors. The carrier skipper dip nets a few fish — checking them by squeezing them from the head down their bellies to the anus — to push out any feed they might have. But they are clean. The feed they were chasing has moved on, left them caught behind the twine and hungry. The herring continue to rise and begin to roil in an iridescent mass of silvery scales all rainbow colors on the back, flying now from the lightly flapping herring to our hands and faces.

The *Joyce Marie* starts to pump them up through the big green hose, then through the scale box, and then pouring into the hold. The deckhand cracks open a salt bag on deck, stabbing it with a grain shovel and throwing an occasional half shovel of salt into the hold as she loads.

Everyone lights up a smoke as we watch the big boat settle with her load, the herring scales pour into scale baskets on the deck of the carrier like a shiny porridge, and a pink foam from the pump runoff hugs the corks and broad hull of the carrier as we smoke and continue to gently dry up the fish.

I realize that Joy is right — it is a moment of love. I am hooked. To make money this way in the midst of so much beauty seems simultaneously dreamlike and real. I don't know how that can be, but I am in both places at once.

NOVEMBER FISH

BY NOVEMBER I WAS STILL WORKING as a carpenter. I took evening rides with Henry and Gladden looking for stop-seine herring, but the sardine season was essentially over. Leathery brown oak leaves swirled in roadside ditches as winter began to claw its way in.

Dead to the world, and spooned together for warmth in our tiny double bed, the old black phone on our bedside table jarred us both awake on Election Day at five am.

In the edgy voice of someone who has been up all night, Gladden said, "Get down to Henry's right away, and bring your boots. We've got fish at Outer Heron." I grabbed my oil clothes and boots, downed a soggy leftover sandwich, and lit out for the wharf.

Crisp day, but unsettled with a lot of dark-bodied clouds scudding overhead. During the night, Gladden and Henry had shut off a good bunch of herring on the southern end of Outer Heron Island. It was a monster set — Henry pegged it at north of seventeen thousand bushels — but it was late in the season. Most of the sardine factories were closed and Henry had to talk the owner of Port Clyde Packing into opening one of them up for this set of fish. Carriers were on the way, but it would be a scramble to get the fish out before the weather shut us down.

A few inches of snow the week before had turned the rocks soft white all the way to the water's edge. Looking out the big window from the yellow house was like looking at a black and white photograph.

Down at Henry's wharf that morning, we set off for Outer Heron in the *Alice M*, towing a big seine boat equipped with the hydraulic power block and the little seine boat carrying the pocket purse-seine. Gladden took the *Frances*, Henry's open workboat. The water was quiet on the way out of the river, only light air, but a big offshore storm was making up a long sea out of the south.

By the time we reached the cove on the southern end of Outer Heron, the mounting seas were already surging in deep enough to create a white line of breakers on the shore. The running twine that Gladden and Henry had used to shut off the cove had small seine anchors tied along on the corks to keep it stable against the weight of the fish and the tide, but the cove was huge and opened to the southeast, so the big southerly swells were rolling in there almost unimpeded from deep water offshore.

Even at a conservative sixty-five pounds per bushel, Henry's estimate of seventeen thousand bushels put the weight of the fish at over a million pounds. Of course, the herring were swimming, but they would get pushed around by the tide and the heavy swells, so there was enormous pressure on the twine that was stretched from shore to shore. Running some of the fish into a pocket would help, but it was not clear that the gear could hold such a big set of fish in this heavy surge for very long.

We anchored up the *Alice M* and Henry took the rest of the crew aboard the *Frances* to set up the pocket, leaving me aboard the *Alice M* to keep the big seine boat and the little seine boat from riding up on her in the heavy swells. With only a light breeze, and a strong tide running in the cove, the two seine boats would not trail off the *Alice M* nicely as they did when being towed. Instead, they were pushed around in a confused dance, and without intervention all three boats would inevitably come together and chew each other up. On one side, I had the big seine boat, thirty-six feet and ponderously heavy with a mast and a big hydraulic power block. On the other side, the small seine boat, low in the water and cranky. My job as a greenhorn was to keep them apart with an oar when they threatened each other and the *Alice M*.

After cruising around all summer in flat calm weather I was still very much a landlubber, so it was the first time I had spent any time rolling around on a swell. In the end, I gave in to the motion and let it wash over me. After a while, my brain was swimming and dizzy like the first buzz from a good shot of whiskey. Not a bad feeling if you let it go and didn't fight it.

By the time Henry and crew were finished setting the pocket, and running half the fish into it as a holding pen, we had three sardine carriers standing off Outer Heron Island Ledge ready to start loading, but the seas

Bobby Warren's crew loading a carrier, Vinalhaven Island

were continuing to build. The wind was beginning to pick up as well out of the southeast and blowing straight into the big cove. Henry brought the *Frances* back to the *Alice M* and picked me up along with the little seine boat so the whole crew could start the process of purse-seining and pumping the fish aboard the carriers.

First up was the *Delca*, a seventy-eight-footer converted by Port Clyde Packing after WWII from minesweeper to sardine carrier. With twin diesels, she was the fastest carrier on the water and was known to beat anyone to fish. We put the *Delca* on the east side of the pocket with the pocket's corks tied through her starboard scuppers and her nose to the swell, and ran out two of the *Delca*'s massive kedge anchors to the southward in the *Frances* to keep the much heavier carrier from dragging the pocket's lightweight anchors in the building seas. This would put the little seine boat at the same heading when we were drying fish and the *Delca* was pumping; both boats nose to the swells.

Standing in the little seine boat and drying fish against the *Delca* in the heavy swell was like playing music with two different rhythms. The seventy-eight-foot *Delca* rose and fell with a slow and ponderous heave, while the little seine boat rode the swells up and down like a cork. This differential became even more pronounced as the *Delca* loaded. As the stream of luminescent herring poured in, the *Delca* settled deeply and became as steady as a ledge against the swells. In the little seine boat, we bobbed up and down, pushing off the big dayglo pink balloons on the side of the *Delca* as we got close to the end of drying each set.

We made two sets with the pocket purse-seine and flattened the *Delca* with fourteen hundred bushels, all she could carry, but it was getting very tough to handle the little seine boat. She had no power and so had to be towed by hand around the pocket while we set — with some of us leaning out and hauling corks at water level — and we were beginning to take on more and more water every time we set. She was only twenty-two feet, but was very broad-beamed and heavily built, so she held the pocket seine and four or five men easily and was normally wonderful to work out of because she sat so low in the water, but she was too low to be much of a sea boat.

We cast off the *Delca* and watched her climb the hill on each of the big seas as she left the cove. The *Frances* towed the little seine boat back to the *Alice M* and we hopped aboard to take stock of the situation.

The wind was continuing to freshen out of the southeast, and now the long rollers were shifting to the southeast too, and in the range of six to eight feet, as they washed high on the smooth rock face at the head of the cove.

In good weather, we would have taken up the running twine with the big seine boat. Then we might have doubled up the anchors on the pocket, and held all the fish in the pocket. But it was too rough to work out of open boats, so we put on every anchor we had, leaving the running twine in place still tied to the pocket, and had to just hope for the best.

If the weather didn't worsen, we could come back tomorrow and take more fish out. If the seas continued to build, the combination of the heavy seas surging a million pounds of herring forward and back, would tear the gear apart. But we couldn't work. We had to leave them.

Henry made a call over the radio to the two remaining carriers. "It's no good in there, boys, no good. Even if we dared to put another carrier in there, by Jesus, I'm not sure as she'd hold in that surge. Besides, it's getting so'se we'd get in a mess, the way things are jumpin' in there."

"I get it, Henry. Well I guess we'll just have to try it again tomorrow."

"Yes, tomorrow then. We'll see you boys tomorrow and hope for the best.

I do'ne see any other way for it."

Gladden jumped aboard the *Frances* and pointed for home. The rest of us straightened up the deck on the *Alice M*, lengthened out the towlines on the big and little seine boats, as Henry steered for South Bristol.

Back at Henry's wharf, we got in our cars for home. Gladden poked his head in my passenger side window, breathing cigarette smoke with the smell of chewing gum, "Say a little prayer that the sea lets go in the night."

I nodded, "I'm so dizzy, I'm just waiting for the ground to stop heaving up and down."

He laughed.

Since it was Election Day, I stopped at the elementary school on my way home and voted for George McGovern. Standing there with a stubby yellow pencil in the fold-up wooden booths with curtains, I could feel the long swell in my head and feel myself sway with the imaginary wash. I was in the fishing life; at least enough to feel that voting in a national election was somewhat strange.

The next day, the wind had let go to a whisper, but the sound of the big seas breaking still rumbled a dull thunder in the distance as we stood on Henry's wharf in the shelter of the gut. We rode out to Outer Heron Island around eight or nine in the morning, seine boats in tow. In the long ride, we could see that the seas had not gone down very much. As we approached the cove the southern end was white with spray and huge rollers were still charging into the cove itself — mad gray hills, pushing tons of leaden water.

As we rounded the southern point of the cove, there was not much to see. The cove had reverted back to the raw and open place it had always been — smooth granite washed clean by the merciless weight of long southeasterly swells. Every offshore storm that roared its way up the coast from the Gulf of Mexico to Sable Island had driven its unfettered heave into that cove for millions of years, and last night had been no different.

There was nothing left of Henry's gear — all three hundred fathoms of running twine, the pocket, the anchor rodes, anchors, buoys, the two twenty-four-foot seine dories we had left at anchor — everything was gone. Erased. The only visible sign that we had been there at all, and that seventeen thousand bushels of shining herring had been shut off behind a stop-seine in that cove, was a small piece of twine twenty or thirty fathoms long, about the size of a skiff. In a small heap, this sole remaining ball of black twine and brown corks sat high on the broad forehead of the granite face, right at the edge of the scrub roses and gnarly junipers.

In the wheelhouse of the *Alice M*, it was quiet. There was nothing to say. A few of us went on deck. Shortened up the boats-in-tow to keep them out of each other's hair. Smoked and looked for signs of our gear as we circled the cove. After one sweep of the cove, Henry got on the radio and called the carriers from Port Clyde Packing — two of them lay off the Outer Heron Island Ledge buoy waiting to hear the news.

"That's it, boys. Nothin' there but a junk of twine up on the shore. Nothin' at all."

"Okay, Hen. That's it then. Sorry to hear that. We couldn't see much from out here, but we thought we would wait until you went in to check it out."

Clearly, both carrier skippers had seen the destruction. It was plain as day, but out of respect for Henry they had remained silent on the radio while they waited for him to arrive and make the call.

"I know. We was lucky to get the *Delca* loaded and get her out of there in one piece yest'dy."

"That's right, you takes what you can git."

"Yes, I guess that's the truth of it, you takes what you can git."

Henry signed off. We had all heard the radio conversation. Henry pointed the *Alice M* for the barn as we took a long last look at the cove.

How strange it was that Hen and Gladden had happened on those fish way out at Outer Heron Island was not lost on me, and how difficult it must have been in the dead of night to be running — and I'm sure it was nothing less than at full throttle — to fetch the gear from Henry's wharf, and then the rest of the crew coming down from their cozy warm beds in the morning to feast on the spoils of the frantic high drama of their chase. And I learned how Henry could tear around when he got excited, how he could rip against the grain, like a violent thief smashing the jewelry case to grab the diamonds, when there was fish.

Henry had been raised on Damariscove Island, a bald island five miles offshore from Boothbay Harbor. His family spent winters on the mainland, but lived spring, summer, and fall on the island. One of the first fish camps in America, Damariscove was prized by British fishermen for its abundant codfish, its windy space to salt and dry the fish before transport back to England, and being far enough offshore to afford some protection from Indian attack. Damariscove was a fishing settlement long before the arrival of John Smith and the establishment of the Mass Bay Colony.

Not much for school, Henry quit after fifth or sixth grade and started fishing.

"When we were little, we'd catch lobsters with a hoopnet. Take the iron rim of a wagon wheel, tie a few lines crisscross-like to hold the bait in the center, and lace on a mesh bag all around the rim. Then you'd drop the hoopnet down out of your peapod or your dory or whatever, wait a few minutes, and then haul like the bejesus so'se the catch would drop down into the mesh bag. You could get cunners or codfish, if you hauled fast enough, and lobsters."

Henry had probably heard about the fish at Outer Heron, the next island over, through his ancient Boothbay grapevine. We had made some quick money, but it was a big loss of potential fortune. Henry never spoke of it again.

After two days, I was back to work pounding nails. Joy carried on at the diner in Damariscotta. Winter moved in.

A month later, Joy and I cut down a little blue spruce off the main road by the town hall for a Christmas tree. Joy spent thirty dollars on some tree ornaments at a gift store. It was really our first Christmas alone together. We had recently adopted a kitten from a local litter. The mother cat was a beautiful and very smart gray tabby. The owner had taught her to do tricks. He would pat his leg and she would run to him, jump up and do a backflip off of the spot he patted. The kitten's name was George because we thought it was a male. (Six months later we renamed her Georgia when she gave birth to a litter of six kittens.) After Joy trimmed the tree out with her ornaments, George proceeded to knock them off and break them one by one. I laughed and thought it was funny, but Joy cried at how pitiful and out of control our life was.

"I can't believe you think this is funny," she said as she wept.

"What? The cat is just being a cat," I said.

"Yes, but I had to work too hard for those ornaments. I'm working in a diner for Christ's sake. And I wanted to keep them. That's what we do in my family. We keep the ornaments for years."

It suddenly occurred to me how close to the edge we were living, how poor. Maybe Joy sensed the darkness that was to come, the creeping peripheral edges that would eventually dim the sun for both of us. But even if she had, I still would have leapt like a mad flying squirrel at my dream.

By January, the colonel's cobbled together oil pot furnace had given up the ghost. We woke up one morning and it was cold enough in the yellow house to see our breath, so we pulled up stakes and moved to another rental on the south side of Rutherford Island, a house with reliable heat that looked out on Christmas Cove.

BEER STOP

SPRING CAME SLOWLY THAT YEAR. Snow lay rotting on the ground in April but the sun was high enough to raise hell with the small boats hauled out on the shore, so there was work enough getting ready for summer fishing to justify quitting my carpentry job. I was happy to be free again and brimming with promise. One night after supper, I drove to Henry's, near the drawbridge in the center of town to see what was going on.

At the base of the last small hill entering South Bristol was a spot where you could see the harbor (or eastern gut) on the left and the river on the right. Known as the beer stop, it was a longstanding tradition in town. On almost every evening, two or three cars were parked there so the riders could watch the sunset, drink beer, and usually smoke a little weed. They were usually the same six or seven guys, mostly bachelors, and between seventeen and thirty. I joined them on quite a few nights. They welcomed new members easily.

"Ho, ho, come on in and take a seat, take a toke," Lendell called to me through the half-open window. Though it was spring, the cold was snapping back quickly as the sun began to set. Smoke billowed out the windows. "You mean the old lady lets you go out at night?" Lendell asked. The chorus of three others chuckled low and murmured approval of the barb.

"I quit carpentering, so she knows I'm up to no good when I leave the house now," I responded. Lendell, handing me a half-gone joint, said, "Oh, I get it. You're on fishing time now, right?" And then talking over his shoulder to the others said, "That's just about the same, in'it boys?" And then everyone in the car chanted in chorus, "Just about the same," a ritual phrase capturing the fact that nothing much had changed in South Bristol and that in the foreseeable future nothing much was expected to change.

That year, in the spring of 1973, "just about the same" was the answer to almost everything. And it was said in an exaggerated and drawn out Maine accent, usually an imitation of the renowned Maine humorist, Marshall Dodge, who had recorded numerous portrayals of fictional Maine characters. Though he was a Connecticut native, educated at Yale, everyone in Maine loved his recordings and most people liked to imitate his extreme accent.

The beer stop was not only longstanding, but also widely accepted as a local institution. Howard Plummer, the town constable, had set two fifty-five-gallon drums painted green at the beer stop for bottles and trash. As constable, he was considered the point of contact for the county sheriff if anything bad happened, which was rare. The only real law enforcement came via the Maine State Police who drove through town once a week.

That night we got talking about the migration to Connecticut and Florida. For some reason, these two states seemed to attract young working men from Maine. Florida was more obvious than Connecticut because it was said that Maine construction workers moved at twice the speed of Florida construction workers. Maine workers did indeed work faster, but only because the amount of time available to make money, particularly from the tourist trade, was so short. You had roughly three months (a generous estimate), say from June to Labor Day, to make your peak income. The attraction of Connecticut I had never figured out. Anyway, the conversation shifted to a discussion of who had left for what jobs in either of those two places.

Finally, Lendell pointed to the river and said, "Why would anyone want to go to Connecticut? I can make enough to get by, my family is here to help me out if I need it, I don't have to get all stressed out in the city, and this river is the most beautiful place I know."

Broad silence followed as a form of affirmation in the toked-out car.

The peaceful moment of weed-induced contemplation was broken by Benny Upham, a charter member of the beer stop.

"Hey, here's a good one for you, Paulie boy. Two guys came through here about a year ago from Boston or somewhere. Put it this way, they was not from here, if you know what I mean. "

"They were from Chelsea, Benny, you goddamned fool," Lendell chimed in.

"Okay, wherever that is, they was from that place," Benny continued, "and stop messin' up my story you jackass. So they had like these black leather jackets and shit, and they come over to the beer stop and I says to 'em, hey what's up, Cap? They could see we were smoking weed and everything, so then the guy says, we're lost. Where the heck are we? And I says, you're not lost, you're right here Cappy, that's where you are."

"You did get a laugh out of 'em, Benny, I'll give that to you, you fuckin' moron," said Lendell.

"Shut up fatso, let me finish. So I say, wanna hit? And the guys take a hit and then we give 'em a beer, and then one of 'em says hey where can a fella find a place to unload some stuff from a boat, you know, some cargo. What kinda cargo, I says. And he says, like the stuff we're smokin'. That kind of cargo. Jesus Christ, you coulda heard your heart beatin, couldn't you, boys."

"I don't know about that, Benny, but yeah it did get kinda quiet," Lendell quipped.

Undeterred, Benny continued, "So then he says come on guys, we'll pay good money for it. What's good money, I says. And he says fifty grand a pop. Mr. Man, that's a lot of money, I says. And then I says, how you gonna keep from getting caught? Everybody knows everything that goes on around here, for Christ's sake. Not if you don't tell them, the guy says back.

"Jesus Christ, what a pickle. So you know just lookin at them, that these guys don't have a clue. They don't know what it's like here in town and they ain't going to understand it, and we all kinda clammed up. So then this other guy, he's like all serious like he's the one in charge, he says, we'll be back and you guys think about it. And then they drive off. Gawd, what a fucking joke."

"But then tell him what happened, Benny. Come on, finish the story."

"Oh yeah, but you don't know it was the same guys, Lendell, you don't know that. It coulda been some other guys, too."

"Come on Benny. It had to be them guys."

"All right, all right, so then in March, one of the lobster catchers up river, way up above the narrows, sees this like cabin cruiser has gone ashore on the west side of the river, driven way up on the shore and laid right over. So the guy calls the coast guard and says there's a boat gone ashore, you know like a shipwreck. And then he goes in to take a look and sees there are these guys hauling stuff out of the boat and onto a truck with a conveyor belt and then he sees the truck take off."

"Yeah, I remember when that happened," I said, "Henry heard about it on the radio and I drove down to the shore at the mouth of Long Cove and there she was on the other side of the river—this stupid old Chris-Craft laid over bright as day. They caught those guys, didn't they?"

"They run 'em down in Brunswick," Benny said, "truck and all."

"I guess they couldn't get a good spot, so they just run her ashore and hoped nobody would see them. What a bunch of goddamned fools," Lendell offered, "like there is nobody around on the water in the winter or something. Jesus Christ. No common sense whatsoever."

Then came the inevitable chorus of "just about the same," and we all had a good laugh, with a cheery buzz on and hacking from all the smoke.

BIG DORY

YOU WOULD NEVER KNOW from his demeanor that Afton Farrin Jr. had landed in the first wave at Normandy and fought in the infantry all the way to Berlin. He was very quiet and hardly spoke unless spoken to, and though he ran both stop-seining and mackerel trapping crews, he never liked to give anyone direct orders to do anything. He said that there were two kinds of fishing skippers, the ones who yelled and shouted, and the ones who didn't need to. He later told me that the only thing that really bothered him about the experience of fighting in WWII was the fact that pigs would often dine on the corpses, so he didn't care for pigs very much.

Dories hauled out at the gut

I met Junior through Henry and Gladden. It turned out that Henry and Junior teamed up on stop-seining so they could cover more territory: Henry covered the John's Bay side of the island and Junior covered the other, Christmas Cove and the Damariscotta River.

Beginning of May, I was hanging around at Henry's wharf, on the mainland side of the bridge, where we were sloppy-painting his dories with big brushes and pushing them down the bank (still half wet) on wooden rollers and back into the water to get them out of the sun.

Henry knocked off at eleven am — his dinnertime. He fed me every day that I worked, a big meal, usually steak, and a tall glass or two of whiskey and ginger ale. After dinner, Henry napped for two hours, took his dog King for a boat ride in his skiff (often to dig a few clams when the tides were right), and then, edge of dark, Gladden, Henry, and I sailed around on the *Alice M* smoking cigarettes, talking politics, and looking for herring until nine or ten pm.

Wandering across to the island side of the bridge one day, half in the bag after one of our daily dinner-feasts, I discovered Junior sitting in a chair on his wharf, chewing on an unlit pipe as he stared at the ebb tide ripping through the narrow gut. When I asked him what he was up to, he turned to me with a start as though he were waking from a dream.

"Jesus, you got me good, Paul," he said chuckling but not shifting his gaze from the rips.

"Just thinking and watching the ebb. Didn't see you come up."

Then, pointing with his pipe at a heap of black five-gallon cans and white cloth, he said,

"Fiberglass for my old dory. She's awfully big, but they say it'll work."

Then sighing, back to watching the rills in the western gut.

"I don't really know, though. I guess we'll find out."

I offered to help. He nodded.

We started the next morning

Junior's dory was unusual. Built to carry an extra-large load of fifteen thousand pounds of mackerel, she was close to thirty-three feet in length overall, about ten feet longer than usual. She was also built with beefier materials than most seine dories, so as to scale up and hold together as an open boat. This made her much heavier than a seine dory, which could be turned over or run into the water on a few rollers by two men. Unfortunately, she had been on the bank for an entire year and the old girl had dried out and the wood had checked badly. The garboard strake, the lowest plank on the side, had a gash big enough to put your hand through, so Junior had decided fiberglassing was the only way to bring her back to life.

Unlike Henry, Junior was not driven by the need to tell stories (though I imagine his memories were as unrelenting and horrific as anyone else who had lived through the D-Day landing), so I accepted that I might not learn much from Junior's natural state of quiescence. Nor was his crew much different; all of them, outside of Gladden, were family and shared Junior's reluctance to talk.

Maybe, I thought, because I'm green and inured to the embarrassment of asking stupid questions I might try becoming a pest for information — or conversation — whichever is available.

But I soon discovered that once Junior was out of his chair, in motion, and teeth sunk into a project, his responses became even more obtuse. Often, limited to murmurs and nods, his directives devolved to mere hints or clues as to what was required. Surrounded as he was by his like-minded family, Junior's quiet utterance of "can" and a wave in the direction of a tub of fiberglass resin would be translated into a request to fetch the can of resin. Or, when I asked if the new plywood gussets were what he wanted, Junior's attempt at a clear directive to manufacture and install more was a ruminative and noncommittal, "I guess that might be okay."

That's just how he works, I told myself. Pay attention.

Watch what he's doing and sort of...well, you know...read his mind.

Yeah, read his mind. You can do that.

So I downshifted, shutdown my annoying question machine, and opened up a learn-by-doing, and heretofore vacant, region of my brain.

And to my utter amazement, work progressed at a torrid pace...but quietly.

By noon we had patched up the big dory's frames and knees (the bones that held her together), slopped some paint on the interior and heaved her over to fiberglass her bottom. Turning to the cans of resin and fluffy rolls of fiberglass mat, we laid out the mat and poured on great quantities of resin (mixed with double the hardener), and mushed it around with rollers. In three hours the frozen goo was the color of flesh, hard as a rock, and too hot to touch. Undaunted, we slobbered on fresh copper paint, heaved her back over onto her bottom again, and then four of us shouldered her over stones covered with rockweed and flotsam into the western gut at high water.

At some point, I do think I asked myself what I was doing. Something along the lines of, hey what's with all this running around and getting ready? Any idea what are you getting ready for? Apparently, somewhere in the remote corner of my kid-brain a whispering voice had emerged to remind me that I had quit being a carpenter but didn't really have a fishing job. But that wee voice never stood a chance against my blossoming passion for messing with all things boat and sea and fish. None.

I was just there (whatever that meant) and busy as hell.

Moreover, I wasn't particularly savvy when it came to fishing gear. I was good with my hands, and with engines and mechanical stuff, and could work with wood, but the only knots I knew were those I had learned as a cub scout or read about in an old sea scout handbook when I was twelve.

Didn't bother me a bit, though. I was having a blast. I really didn't care what happened because I was having too much fun to worry. At some point, Gladden took pity on me and showed me a bowline and a half hitch and told me I needed to be able to tie them with my eyes closed, so I could do that in the dark. Mostly, he was trying to tell me that I needed to create a permanent memory of the motion so I could tie certain fundamental knots quickly and without thinking.

Why that mattered, I wouldn't find out until much later in my ongoing, and unplanned career.

CREW BY DEFAULT

SINCE I HAD HELPED HIM PATCH up his big dory, Junior thought that I might like to see how the fish trap was set out so he invited me along to help out at Thrumcap Island. Thrumcap had been a productive spot for Junior over the years and a place that his uncle had used before him.

Setting the trap was a quiet but confusing process since everyone else on the crew, Junior's son Michael, his brother Alva, and Gladden, had done it many times before, and there was no reason to talk about it, nor was there much time to explain what they were doing. To my astonishment, most of the trap seemed to flop overboard from the dory in huge tangled lumps.

Who could possibly make sense of this chaotic and snarled mess, I was thinking. But gradually, the black twine spread and relaxed itself into a calm hanging net once it was in the water — almost like a giant dehydrated creature restored to its natural life by immersion in the sea.

Even more amazing was the speed at which everything happened. Combined with my lack of understanding, the whole process of setting the mackerel trap seemed almost comical. In the end, the trap was tied to the frame, leaders designed to guide the fish into the trap were hung in place, and the trap began to fish — calmly suspended underwater — waiting for schools of mackerel and herring to get lost in its dark and enormous room.

I had to laugh. I had some understanding of what had happened, but on the whole I chalked it up as another lesson to be stored in the newly created watch-and-learn location in my brain.

Seated, Michael and Junior Farrin, Standing, Alva Farrin and Ray Lounsbury

The next morning, at about four am, Gladden knocked on my door. As I stood bleary-eyed in the doorway, I looked behind him and noticed that his truck was not in the driveway. Hmm. Then I noticed that he was standing there in his fishing boots. Hmm, again.

Barely able to control his mirth as he watched my face, he told me that he had walked up from the landing at Christmas Cove and that Junior and Michael and Alva were waiting in the boat and wondering if I wanted to go haul the trap with them. He said that Junior had hemmed and hawed — thinking aloud — all the way down the river as to whether he should pick me up or not.

Pipe in hand at the wheel and hunched in the corner as he steers and talks with Gladden.

"Paul was a big help with the dory, don't you think?"

"Yes, he is pretty good with his hands."

"Must be all that carpentering."

"Yes, I expect so."

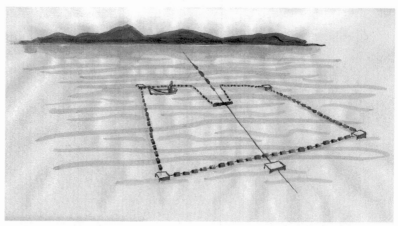

The shape of a mackerel trap

"We could bring him along."

"Yes we could."

"And he did help us set the trap."

"Yes, there is that."

"But it's pretty early. He's probably not up yet, is he?"

"No, but I could go wake him up."

"You could? Yes, I suppose you could do that. I guess I should have called him. Nothing like the first haul of the season. Be a shame to miss that."

"Unhunh."

"I could go into Christmas Cove."

"Yup. He and Joy live just up the street from the Coveside Inn."

"Would you go get him?"

"Be happy to."

Finally, Junior put into Christmas Cove and sent Gladden up the street to fetch me.

Once Gladden explained what was up, I pulled on my boots, grabbed my oil pants and followed him down to the float. It was a short run to Thrumcap, but we could see birds on the trap as soon as we cleared the mouth of Christmas Cove.

Gulls love to watch shiny things. They won't dive on mackerel, but they will on herring, so that indicated a mix of herring and mackerel. As we got closer, the gulls were wheeling and watching, and a raft of swimming cormorants inhabited the interior of the trap. Shags, we called them. Like black snakes with wings, they fly underwater, swallowing the laconic herring whole and gouging the faster swimming mackerel with their hooked beaks, breaking up the schools, and eventually chasing fish out the trap in small bunches. Michael pulled out an old double-barreled ten gauge he kept on the boat — gave them a blast of birdshot. Winged one. The rest of the shags took off lumbering and splashing their feet across the water to get airborne.

The trap was hauled by hand. Very old school. We used the big dory and a skiff — Junior in the skiff and three of us in the big dory. Because the trap had a bottom, like a basket, you couldn't haul it the way you would haul a purse-seine, taking it aboard as you dried the fish. The trap had to be under-run and left in place.

Under-run? Picture a marble on top of a blanket, on a bed. The idea is to get the marble to roll down to the foot of the bed without untucking the blanket. You pinch up a bit of the blanket next to the marble and the marble rolls, let the blanket go, then pinch up the next bit close to the marble again and so on. Because the blanket is tucked in, like the trap is held down by anchors, you continue to move along and pick up a little, but also let go of the previous piece. That's under-running. You haul the twine up and grab a bunch ahead while you let the previous bunch go. The twine goes back into the water and underneath the dory. To seiners, it was a very odd way of drying fish. The twine is taut, not loose like the twine in a seine, so it is much harder to grab a bunch to haul on, and then you have to let it go as you grab another bunch and move ahead. Not exactly intuitive.

But the first step in hauling was closing the door to the trap. Two men in the skiff paddled over to the floating top of the doorframe, hauled the door ropes, and cleated them home to the frame. This stopped the trap fishing, but kept the fish from streaming out the door while we hauled. Closing the door also raised the bottom, the belly of the trap, up a bit. Then, with the skiff and big dory on the north side of the trap, we started under-running the twine north to south.

I was just a kid, twenty-four, and in good shape. But I was unprepared for the workout that was hauling Junior's big trap. Grabbing the first handful of twine was hard enough because it was so taut. The water was cold in June, so I knew it was going to hurt anyway because we couldn't use rubber gloves, but the twine was also heavily tarred and was stiff and coarse, not silky like the little pocket seine. Even with new gloves on, my fingers were quickly burning and stinging.

Then there was the strain. Pulling on that first side of the trap was essentially lifting the whole belly of the trap. And pulling up the belly was like pulling a giant sieve up through the water. The trap's mesh had to be small enough to keep juvenile herring and squid and kyaks (small blueback herring) from getting stuck in the mesh, so the water flowed through it slowly. That coupled with the weight of the double leadlines needed to keep her hanging straight against the sweep of the tide, and it felt like you were trying to pull up the whole ocean bottom.

Progress was very slow. No one was having an easy time. As I looked left and right I thought, if this is just hauling the side, what is it going to take to get all the way across? Sweet Jesus.

With the first haul of the season, everyone had forgotten what a wretched beast she was to haul and there were swears and groans coming from all of us. With this level of unrelenting pull, you also had to be careful of your back when you hauled — step up onto the stringers that ran the length of the dory and keep your back straight, start almost in a crouch and use your legs to haul up, keep steady pressure, and she would keep coming slowly, oh so slowly, sieving the water through, raising the cursed double leads.

After fifteen agonizing minutes of inch-by-inch pulling, we made it down through the first twenty-four feet of the side, reaching the first double leadline where the side met the bottom. My arms were numb and my hands were in deep, aching, icewater pain. We were about a quarter of the way across the trap. At that point, the fish were starting to show some color as they began to run in front of us.

Seeing the color of fish in the water was something that took a lot of experience. I couldn't see it at all. I was told, you had to look though the first color that the water showed you, and then look deeper to the next color — looking through the water all the way to the backs of the fish. As the belly of the trap was coming up, the fish were crowding into the southern end and were beginning to race back and forth. The experienced hands could see them, but we were nearly halfway across before I could see any sign of fish.

Mackerel are tuna family — all muscle — aggressive, powerful swimmers. As they tore back and forth in front of us we could look down on them. See their stripes and their green backs, their eyes. Big fish. Adults, pound or pound and a quarter. Sixteen inches, as big around as your forearm. Some rushed the surface, pushing their silvery heads out of water, foaming the surface and making a *ssshhh* sound.

"Four," Gladden shouted, "maybe, five," meaning four or five thousand pounds. Junior nodded.

From the skiff, Junior cleared the fish out of the southern arm and turned the corner. Then he came aboard the big dory so we could square up, facing west, and dry the fish toward the workboat tied to the corks on the backside of the trap in the southwest corner.

Then the fish disappeared. No more coursing back and forth, anxious eyes and silver faces looking up at us. Just dark water and quiet.

Once mackerel realize that there is no way out, they stop their racing and searching and they dive. The whole school powers straight down. En masse, they put their noses directly against the twine and swim with all they've got.

The twine got immediately heavy and was ripped out of my hand. It was the strangest feeling. I thought something was wrong. The twine I had lost took a dip where I had been hauling, but Gladden covered me on the one side and Michael on the other, both having tied off their twine with straps. I hadn't learned how to tie off yet, or even how to bend the twine over the rail. Bending over the rail meant bringing the twine up and over the rail and pulling down on it for leverage against the diving force of the mackerel.

Michael showed me how to tie off the twine. The stringers we stood on had straps on them, short lengths of pot warp. You tied off the twine with a strap, using a circular motion like tying the feet of a calf in a rodeo. You twisted the bunch of twine in your hands like wringing out a sock, whipped the strap quickly around the bunch, and tied it with a single slip-hitch that could easily be pulled out.

We held there for a minute to let the panicking fish get tired. But it was so strange because we couldn't see them anymore. At least I couldn't.

The feeling of having the twine ripped so suddenly out of my hands — the sudden and impossible weight — was as if someone had suddenly thrown a boulder into the trap. Handling herring was so much easier. Herring were amazingly docile and a lot slower. Hauling five thousand pounds of mackerel was harder than drying fifty or a hundred thousand pounds of herring.

While we took a small breather, we laid out the big bull net — a large dip net with a six-foot wooden handle and an iron hoop three feet across — and got ready to bail the mackerel aboard the big dory where we stood. Then we freed the straps and started to dry the fish again — pulling this time to turn them, to bring them up — to cause the fish to give up. Give up on trying to muscle their way down to freedom.

Now, here is the greatest moment in this drama. And believe me when I tell you that there is not a fisherman alive who doesn't love this moment — or tires of it — no matter how many times he has been through it. It is experiencing a wildness that is both a heart-rending moment and a peak instant of excitement all at once.

The mackerel suddenly decide to give up in one direction, the swimming-down direction, and then decide to go equally hard in the other direction. They come up. It is their last wild attempt at escape.

As you pull, they explode in front of you all at once, four or five thousand leaping bodies in a loud splashing, water flying high enough to rain back down. You are standing in a heavy downpour of seawater and tiny mackerel scales. We know we have them. But it is so loud, you have to shout over the cacophony.

While most are splashing, a few individual fish race across the surface of the thickening pool, defying any understanding of how fish can swim. They scoot quickly along the surface of the other fish with their bodies raised at a forty-five-degree angle, some almost vertical — with three-quarters of their length out of the water. You wonder how they are swimming at all with just their tails in the foaming mass, flying across the fighting bodies of the others. You marvel at the strength that it takes for a fish to almost stand up straight but still swim across the suffocating pack. There seems to be no water. One or two fish even make it over the corks and escape. What is this magical strength, this will to live, that you are a witness to?

You begin the bailing process, dip the big iron bull net and fill the mesh bag. Two of you lift the hoop just over the rail, then put your fingers through the mesh of the bag and pull. They come easily, fish curling and vibrating roll into the dory and thunder drumbeating on the wooden bottom of the boat. Again and again you dip and roll. Water and scales now flying in the dory at your feet but slowing as the fish die. The smell is a light nutmeg. Is that the fish you smell, or is it what they are eating and chasing? It always seems to be there, the sweet smell. There is some blood leaking from gills. Deeper and deeper you stand in the quivering fish until they are up to your thighs.

Someone hops in the skiff, to let the door lines go. The mouth of the trap sags open. She is fishing again. Two of us under-run the leader from the skiff all the way to shore to pick out the occasional meshed dogfish; then it is back to Junior's wharf to take out the fish.

At the wharf, we shipped the mackerel in wooden barrels, placed the barrel on the scales with a block of ice in the bottom, poured in 150 pounds of mackerel, covered the fish with sea water, dropped in another block of ice, then cooped the top with a waxed canvas lid. Very heavy. Then three men horsed each barrel onto the truck. Mackerel had to be fresh to be any good and the entire market consisted of peddlers on the road with pickup trucks and the entire New England market supplied through a broker in Boston. Shipped in barrels it was a great product, but we were lucky to get fifteen to twenty-five cents a pound because it was a dying market. Everyone wanted white fish and mackerel are bloody and strong-tasting. The market was mostly old people who had grown up eating them, and immigrants looking for cheap fish.

My first haul had ripped open my understanding of living in the world. The fury of the mackerel poured in and eliminated the pallid glen of every-day life. I start fishing full time.

Not befuddled anymore, I had crossed over, clear on where I was going: into the heart of this life, stoked with bright blood and the nutmeg odor of gasping fish.

Mackerel trapping is where I learned to tie knots, work out of a dory, and pull until my hands were numb. In a matter of weeks, my forearms became Popeye-sized, and I acquired the fundamental and ancient skills of fish trapping and weirs. Each morning we did our best to beat the shags to the mackerel trap, and at night I kept looking for stop-seine herring with Henry and Gladden. Afternoons were reserved for naps and errands.

STRANGE BEHAVIORS OF SCHOOLS

OVER TIME, I CAME TO UNDERSTAND that Junior's trap was a modernized version of the ancient weir, a fishing method used by native peoples worldwide for thousands of years. A fence, or leader, made from brush or netting extends from shore to direct fish into a big heart-shaped space in which they continue to swim but from which they cannot escape.

And through my insatiable need to ask questions, I also learned that the whole idea of a fish trap is predicated on the strange behaviors of school fish, something that has also not changed for a very long time.

Mackerel and herring and other school fish act like a single organism, but they also act like a fluid. In fact, they act much like the fluid they swim in. When a fluid meets an obstacle it follows the path of least resistance. If the obstacle is a shoreline, the fluid flows along it, providing the entry point of the fluid is not too blunt. For example, if you direct a jet of water at a gentle angle against the wall of a swimming pool, it will flow along it. But if you direct the jet at a ninety-degree angle to the pool wall, the fluid will break up and cause turbulence — spinning eddies and whirls. A school of fish is no different, except that it behaves like a fluid with a collective brain.

The mackerel could easily swim through the big mesh of the leader, but they never do. Instead, the fish at the head of the school see the leader as an obstacle and turn to run along it. This is known as running the twine and is the fundamental reason a fish trap works at all. The fish run the twine of the leader as long as it is set at a graceful angle in the direction of the tide running down the shore, say 110 degrees instead of ninety degrees. But if the backbone and the leader are set too blunt — set perpendicular to the shore — the school will bounce off of the leader, break up or turn back, instead of following along into the trap. Turbulence.

As they run out the length of the leader, they then see the opening of the trap ahead and stream through the door of the trap. Once inside the trap, the school then hits the backside of the trap, and has its first turbulence event. The school either then breaks into smaller eddies and gets chaotic, or it collectively makes a right or left hand turn. Now the school begins to run the much smaller mesh twine of the trap. They stream around both sides or one side of the trap, running the twine all the way up into the arms — the lobes of the heart shape — and are redirected back into the middle. They repeat the same path over and over, but relatively soon the whole school becomes trained into going round and round in the trap, all in the same direction. Sometimes, you can look down on them streaming around the trap, magically swimming past the six-foot opening of the door, trained to the fluid of their school and oblivious to the gaping portal of escape they are passing by.

SWIMMING WAKE

TRAPPING WITH JUNIOR WAS GOOD for a while. The big mackerel kept coming, along with small bunches of squid and butterfish, all of which were good money fish. Prices remained steady and we also caught a fair amount of herring, which we sold for lobster bait. Then in mid-July, the fishing changed abruptly. The tinkers showed up.

Tinker mackerel are juveniles, probably in their second year of existence. About eight to ten inches, they can be good eating but they don't travel very well so the market is soft. Sometimes the tinkers would be mixed with the bigger and more marketable mackerel and we would cull out the tinkers and sell them for lobster bait.

One morning, as we tied the workboat up to the southwest corner of the trap and prepared to board the dories, I saw something strange over the stern. It looked as though Junior had left the boat in gear, but I knew he had already shut the engine down. All quiet. But there it was—a swirling and steady wake streaming out from under the transom of the workboat—as if the boat was idling with the propeller still engaged. Small swirls and eddies were running along the corkline of the trap.

"Hey, Michael, look at this."

"Look at this wake coming from under the boat."

"It's like the boat's still in gear. Junior, check this out."

All around the outside of the trap, a steady flow of water ran like a lazy brook, distorting the water with whirls and ripples. Meanwhile, we could see a huge ball of rockweed and sticks in the center of the trap slowly turning. We stopped our usual routine, donning oil pants and gloves, and watched for a while. Lots of color in the trap.

Then all of us got into the skiff instead of the dories. Stayed very quiet. We had the sense of something present. Something a bit new, and not to

be taken lightly. Arriving at the trap, we generally had a feeling of anticipation, anyway. You never knew what you were going to find. There were
many times when we hauled the trap and found three sea robins and a
green lumpfish. Anticipation was also usually mixed with the sense that it
was not good to make a great deal of noise. No reason to spook, or break
the motion of the school, if there was a school. Best to keep them calm
until we closed the door. No sense in causing a vector of the school to shy
away and sheer off, then find the door opening and lead the rest out to
freedom. No reason to do what shags did underwater — disrupt the fluid
behavior of the school, cause it to go unstable and turbulent.

Today, for some reason, we were walking on eggshells. Once in the skiff,
we pulled quietly hand over hand on the corkline a few feet from the workboat. Junior put his face down to the water, cupping his hands around his
eyes to shade them so he could look down into the darkness of the trap. It
didn't take him long.

"Tinkers. They're all tinkers," he said.

"A whole lot of tinkers."

We all did the same. We looked for a long time. It was a mesmerizing
sight — a steady wall of fish streaming around the trap. They were amazingly close to the surface. They weren't breaking water, but you could look
right down on their green and black backs. Streaming counterclockwise.
Steady, steady, steady. On and on, they went, one behind the other. Endless,
solid fish streaming by without a break. Once your eyes adjusted to what
you were looking at, you could even stand up and still see them clearly.
There was only one reason they were that close to the surface. There was no
where else to go; they were solid fish from bottom to top. Mackerel would
never do that, not unless there was not enough room to go anywhere else.
Each one lazily following the other. The ball of rockweed turned in the
center because the fish had formed a giant whirlpool.

The trap was full.

It was hard to know how many, but there had to be somewhere between
eighty thousand and a hundred thousand pounds of pure tinker mackerel.
With so many fish swimming in a circle, they were also creating their own
wake outside the trap. That was the wake we had seen boiling from under
the workboat. Now we could see that the fish-created current was all
around the trap emanating from the corkline, a swimming wake radiating
outward.

Though it had a gentle rippling sound, we knew that it represented a frightening amount of horsepower.

Standing there, we were in one of those moments when the world is suddenly transformed. We were not thinking of anything but what we had in front of us. Not thinking of what we would have for dinner, or who the Red Sox were playing that evening, or how hot and sleepy it was getting in the afternoons. Our reference points had been altered; the momentum of our day after day sameness, steaming out, hop in the dories, haul the trap, check the leader for dogfish stuck in the big mesh, steam back, sell the fish for bait or ship them to Boston, clean up; all that had stopped and shifted into a unique moment. What we thought about the sameness and routine of our little world, was no longer true.

The week before we had seen a scattering of fish — big mackerel mixed with tinkers and herring. Not enough to ship. We sold them all as lobster bait. Now this.

I think we also knew that we would probably never see anything like this again. There were so many fish in the trap, it was hard to conceive that any more could even fit without some kind of disturbance — a massive die-off, or a rush on the corks.

We also knew that we had more fish than we knew what to do with. It was overwhelming. And disheartening.

We had no market for tinker mackerel. On any given day, you might get away with sending ten barrels (fifteen hundred pounds) to Boston, but that was all they could handle. The weather was too hot in Boston, and tinkers didn't keep well in the stores. They got soft, even shipping them in barrels with seawater and block ice.

And the lobster catchers didn't like to use too many for bait because they had to bag them — stuff them into a mesh bag like herring — because they fell apart so quickly. Lobster catchers wanted big fish they could string on with a bait needle, like hake heads or red fish racks. Some even claimed that mackerel were a physic to the lobsters and that they would shit themselves to death in the holding crates if they ate too much mackerel.

Worse yet, the tinkers were going to be a bitch to handle. We could attach a pocket to the trap and run in ten or twenty thousand, but the shags would clean them out in short order. Left undisturbed, shags could easily eat a bushel of herring apiece over the course of a day; and tinker

Junior Farrin, South Bristol

mackerel weren't much faster than herring. Ten or twenty shags could clean out the pocket in a day or two unless you stood there with a shotgun to keep them off.

And hauling the trap with that many fish in it was not going to be easy. We would need to cut them in half, or maybe just take a third, and we weren't sure how they were going to react to that kind of disruption. If we were able to give them enough space they could be fairly docile, but if they were crowded, they could sound and get very heavy. We had never handled one hundred thousand pounds of mackerel, even if they were tinkers.

That many herring would have been easy, the gentle sleepy herring pumping aboard a carrier, the sound of the cash register ringing. What a lovely way to make money. Hauling fifty tons of tinker mackerel by hand would be tricky and exhausting.

Junior broke the silence, which almost never happened. He said he needed time to think. Time to think and to make a few phone calls.

There was the possibility that a sardine cannery would take forty or fifty thousand to experiment with canning mackerel. And maybe there was a frozen market for tinkers as zoo food, you know seals, sea lions, penguins, killer whales and so forth, that he hadn't explored. So we went home.

We left the trap door open. With such a big body of fish, the shags seemed to be too scared to go into the trap. We didn't care if they did.

By late afternoon, Junior had explored all of our options and none had panned out. We decided to take a few thousand for bait and for the Boston market, and dump the rest.

Dumping wouldn't hurt them. They would live to swim another day.

Around four o'clock, we started hauling. We didn't bother closing the door since we were going to run them out anyway. We put heavy weights on the corks on the south side of the trap—two one-hundred-pound iron pigs on a bridle so they could be draped over the corks. We used them in stop-seining to run the herring into a pocket. Loosened up on the southern corners of the trap and put on enough pigs to put the corks under by about six or eight feet. Alva tended the weights from the skiff while we hauled through the trap and drove the tinkers over the corks. As they ran out, we could see the dark cloud of them roiling over and heading for deep water.

"I hope they don't run back in," Junior commented. Then he chuckled as something occurred to him.

"They could, you know."

"I've seen that happen before."

Then he paused and said, "I don't think I've ever seen this many, though."

When there were roughly a few thousand left, Junior signaled and Alva hauled up the weights and we dried as usual, rolled the two thousand into the dory. Took them to market.

It was a strange day.

THE HOUSE

THROUGHOUT THE '70s, MAINE was neck and neck with West Virginia for the title of poorest state in the nation and *our* combined annual income hovered between six and seven thousand dollars. But Joy and I figured out how to make enough money to get by every year, and we had no doubt that we could keep doing that if we wanted to. This was our life at the national poverty level.

At our tender ages, major life events happened fast; and many times we were unaware of the emotional charge, or valence, they actually carried. The fact is, we made a lot of decisions without thinking much. If it felt right, we did it.

Sitting in the kitchen of our Christmas Cove rental one spring night with my college friend, Lee, she asked us if we were married. Not a strange question among friends, but given the conservative culture of the Maine coastal village we lived in, it wasn't a question anyone in town had ever dared to ask us. I was devoted to Joy and, in my childlike heart, I felt that we would be together forever.

"No, we're not married.

But if Joy really wanted to get married I'd marry her," I replied.

"We've been together a long time and I don't expect that to change."

"You would? You'd get married?" Lee said turning to Joy.

There was a pause, and then Joy said, "Do you want to get married?"

I said, "Sure. Let's get married."

Not being a woman, I was utterly blind to the import of the conversation that had just transpired. I knew what I had said, and I meant every word. But to me, getting married was a foregone conclusion, a formality, not a moment that triggered a momentous series of events.

But a trigger of events it was to be.

As Lee and I watched, Joy rose from the table, took two steps to the phone behind her, lifted it and dialed long-distance to Wilmington, Delaware.

"Mama," she said, "Paul and I are going to get married."

In June we put up a big tent in front of our rental, and brought the many worlds around us crashing together: our college friends from Cambridge and Amherst, fishing buddies from Henry's and Junior's crews, Gladden and family, friends from winter carpenter crews, and both sets of parents (who had never met).

We stuffed ourselves on a gigantic clambake of lobsters, steamers, potatoes, and corn on the cob, all roasted in a deep bed of seaweed on a cooking iron made from a flattened 55-gallon drum, and the party floated from afternoon into a fog-filled night on a river of alcohol.

Near the end, Henry was roaring drunk and had fallen head over heels for my beautiful friend Annie from Charleston, South Carolina, and a crowd of us drove him home as a means to pull back the throttle. But Henry insisted that we make a refreshment stop at Roy Vose's trailer. Packed into Roy's tin house, all of us downed more whisky, and Henry enacted the evening's finale by grabbing a kitchen knife and offering to cut another of my friend's hair for him; he was a long-haired sculptor from Cambridge.

With a handful of hair in one hand and the knife in the other, Henry laughed and boomed out,

"You decide what I should do, boys. Trim his hair, or give him a shave."

Annie deftly and gently removed the kitchen knife from Henry's paw and kissed him on the cheek. The rest of us took this as the final cue to get Henry home. Two of us delivered him safely to his kitchen overlooking the drawbridge, and then stopped to hand Herb Kelsey a beer in the bridge house before heading back to Christmas Cove.

Party ended. Wedding over. Marriage begun.

A year later, Joy and I decided to buy a piece of land and build a house. But wait, we had very little money. No matter. The economics of poverty applied to those selling land as well as us.

At that point, we had been in Maine almost two years. I had saved a little money working in the winter as a carpenter and in the summer mackerel trapping with Junior, but the majority of our savings stemmed from Henry's big herring set in November.

Joy had long since left the diner and was working as an art teacher in Damariscotta. And though teaching was what she loved, she had five hundred-fifty students in seven different elementary schools and no classroom. She also had no storeroom for her supplies, so the storeroom was our car — a green 1965 Dodge Dart with a white fender I had replaced from a junkyard when Joy had gone off the road on ice. She told me one of her school principals had raked her over the coals because she didn't know all the names of her students.

Fed up, Joy quit teaching and landed a job doing paste-up and layout at the local Damariscotta newspaper. Looking at the ads she was about to place, she saw that George Woodman was selling land in South Bristol, so before the paper was even printed we went to see him. George said that he wanted seven thousand dollars for a plot next to his: 2.7 acres with a tiny bit of shore property on the Damariscotta River. When we asked him why he was selling, he said he was lonely.

George lived on this long stretch of road with no neighbors and he lived with his mom, who was getting on, and he wanted something going on in the neighborhood. The land had kind of a funny shape to it because it was squaring off another parcel, but he said that if we could get it surveyed, he would sell it to us. In the end, we went to the bank and borrowed a total of ten thousand dollars with a resulting payment of $138 a month. I planned to use the extra three thousand dollars to build a house.

That was a ridiculously small amount of money to build a house with a contractor and traditional materials, and most people would have just bought themselves a mobile home and called it good. But I had been on a carpenter crew that built two houses from start to finish, so I thought I could pull it off. Even so, I needed materials as cheap as I could get them. So that winter I decided to work with Junior in the woods cutting spruce for the pulp mills. Junior was cutting a big area on his land overlooking upper John's Bay where he eventually wanted to build a house. The stand was all softwood, a mix of white pine and spruce, and the plan was to sell the spruce to the paper mills for pulp, and keep the pine for lumber. We would cut the spruce into four-foot lengths; Junior would sell the pulp

The homemade house, South Bristol

wood for around twenty-seven dollars a cord and I agreed to take half of the pine logs in trade for doing the cutting.

We stacked the spruce in cords and skidded out all the pine logs with Junior's tractor over the frozen ground, hired a logging truck to pick them up, and took the logs to a small two-man sawmill in Round Pond, over on the Bristol peninsula, run by Dick Callahan. Dick agreed to cut for nine cents a board foot if I worked with him on the brow, or log ramp, rolling the logs up to the saw. It was hard for one man to roll the logs with a single peavey, so he appreciated the help. Two guys with two peaveys made all the difference with the big logs. Dick ran the saw himself, and hired a kid at a daily rate to throw the slabs — the waste wood — as it came off the saw and to stack the green lumber.

The other part of the deal was based on how many nails he hit. Most of the bigger saw mills wouldn't take logs that hadn't been x-rayed for nails and barbed wire and other stuff that had been nailed into the trees over the years, so Dick would be charging us for the teeth on the saw he had to replace if he hit nails.

Dick was very old school. The saw was stationary and about six feet in diameter, and because it was only a single blade, it could easily bend if you ran the carriage with the log on it too fast against the blade. A good sawyer would watch the path of the cut and the saw carefully and not push the log too fast. The result of being careless was boards or timbers that were "thick and thin" meaning they varied too much because the sawyer pushed the wood through the saw too fast. Since I was helping Dick on the brow, I got to stand there and watch him. After a while, I began to notice a strange behavior every ten minutes or so.

Dick would stop in between logs and would stare for a full minute, looking way off in the distance kind of like he was looking for something coming from far away. After two days of working with him, I finally asked him what he was doing. He turned to me and yelled over the drone of the diesel that was powering the mill.

"See that house up there on the top of the hill?" he said nodding toward a little white house about a mile away.

"I'm looking at it to straighten out my eye."

On the next log, he pointed to the spot where the saw blade was cutting through the log, as I watched over his shoulder and he pulled on the lever to push the log against the teeth of the spinning blade. Apparently, he would get very tired staring at that spot — which he had to do in order to make sure he wasn't driving the carriage too fast and bending the big blade — so he would take a break every once in a while and stare at the white house on the hill. Like he said, he needed to straighten out his eye.

In the evenings, I worked on building a model of the house on the kitchen table of our rental in Christmas Cove. I needed a model because it was kind of a different design: big shed roof, windows all across the front facing south, framed with 6×6 posts and 4×6 rafters, a post and beam design like a barn, vertical board and batten siding, but joining the timbers with big 12-inch bridge spikes to avoid having to waste time doing all the hand chisel work to make mortise-and-tenon joints. I built the model because I wanted to be sure of how it would actually look and how the pieces should be joined.

The lumber was all rough-cut. Dick didn't have a sizing or planing machine like the big mills, so the pine boards felt like they had sticky wet animal fur. The boards were a full inch thick instead of ¾ inch or ⅝ inch like you'd get from the lumberyard, and the 2×4s were an honest two inches by four inches and they were hairy, too.

I let the boards dry for a month under cover in Junior's barn, and then come April 1, 1974 I started building.

I hired my friend Craig to help me frame for two weeks and taught Joy how to use a power saw, which I'm sure scared the shit out of her but she did it, God bless her. We worked at a fever pace. By the time the black flies came out and started biting in mid-May, we had framed the house, had the siding up, and roughed out the windows. Then we bought the glass and set to making our own windows, and by June we moved in with one layer of siding on the house, the windows all in place and the electrical wiring done.

I remember marveling at how strange it was that mosquitoes and black flies wouldn't fly through the spaces between the pine siding — by June it had dried out so much there was as much as half an inch between most of the boards. Inside, it smelled absolutely wonderful. Pure pine vapor — and the newly sawn wood was as bright as a sunrise.

Being inside those walls touched us deeply, but that first winter was a little rough.

The house was not finished by any stretch of imagination, but we had already moved in and were trying to live in it and finish it at the same time. Though we had made good progress in the spring, summer put me back into mackerel trapping with Junior again, which meant up at three am back at seven am if we had no fish, or ten am or later if we had fish and needed to get them shipped to Boston, do a little work on the house, take a kink in the afternoon, wake up for supper, then go out looking for herring at the edge of dark until eight or nine pm and get to bed and do it again the next day.

By fall, I hadn't even started the exterior sheathing. I had taken a radical approach to insulation and had chosen to spray on polyurethane foam on the outside of the first layer of siding, but had not completed putting the last layer of siding on the outside of that. The house was all encased in this foamy stuff that had been sprayed on by a crew that looked like they were wearing space suits.

By October, we had a house heated by a used oil stove (bought from Ralph Gray for ten dollars) which also served as our cook stove. But we had no running water, no front steps, just a ramp made from a couple of planks nailed together with cleats to get into the house, and a set of back steps that led to the outhouse made from some big oak logs I had cut up with a chainsaw and stood on end so you could step down like you were walking on the Giant's Causeway in Ireland. They were a little tricky in the dark.

With winter coming on, the house had no sheathing on the outside, just bubbly yellow urethane that made it resemble a refrigerator with the metal skin ripped off.

We had no running water because we couldn't afford the money for a drilled well. Like many homes in the area, our new house sat on bedrock ledge. We tried hand digging a well but the soil was hardpan, a little softer than concrete, but not much. It took me half a day just to dig a hole with a pickax for the outhouse. Every day Joy drove to the town hall spigot and carried water back in red plastic five-gallon jerry jugs and we took baths in an old galvanized washtub on the kitchen floor.

No water. No flush. And ten dollar oil cook stove to keep us warm for the winter. We were living in a house that was a half-finished do-it-yourself project, and still as primitive as a shipping crate.

It was eighteen months before we scraped together enough money to drill a well, but the cost of blasting the ledge to bury an in-ground septic system remained totally beyond our means. For ten years we never replaced the outhouse with an indoor toilet.

Facing that winter was the first time I had a sense that we were up against forces we might not be able to shrug off, that our life was becoming less about love and more about struggle, that the darkness of despair and failure was tactile, or closer than I thought — maybe even visible in my peripheral vision.

HAKE *(Merluccius albidus)*

Part Two

MISS ANGEL

TAKING A RIDE

AFTER TWO SEASONS, LOCAL FISHING had radically changed. Stop-seining had all but disappeared around home. Henry kept looking, but Gladden moved on, focusing on his writing and playing softball in a fast pitch league up around Augusta. The boys on the other side of the Bristol peninsula had a few big sets in Muscongus Bay, but John's Bay and the Damariscotta River were barren.

Mackerel trapping wasn't much better. Junior with his open heart had taken me in like an orphan when I couldn't tie a single knot or tell north from south and I had stuck with it for nearly two seasons. But by mid-July, the oily and stupid pogies (also known as menhaden) had arrived. Along with them came the mauling and brawling bluefish who's only reason for living seemed to be biting pogies to bits. When this pair of uglies showed up, the mackerel went elsewhere.

By September, I hadn't made a dime in two months. After a lot of empty hauls, we started pulling a few of Herb Kelsey's lobster traps (with his blessing) and cooking short lobsters, sitting around the boat drifting with the engine turned off, while we cooked and chowed down on boiled lobsters. How depressing to be stuffing ourselves with luxurious lobsters when we had no money at all. This was the kindness of Junior to keep us all going — and we all loved Junior — but I had finally concluded that the mackerel drought was a permanent condition. So, I spoke to Junior and told him that I was going to look for something else.

The something else was gillnetting for ground fish (cod, haddock, pollock, hake) thirty to fifty miles offshore with Arthur Poland.

As I had done with Junior, taking a ride with someone was a good way to find a job on the water. You went along, helped out, and if everyone got along and you didn't make a complete fool out of yourself chances were good that you would get a berth on the boat.

I heard that Mad Dog was doing a short stint with Arthur on the *Miss Angel* to help him out, but Mad Dog didn't plan to stay on. Mad Dog had a face like a gargoyle — a knowing grin and eyes full of mischief. He was a very salty guy from Cape May, New Jersey, where he had run some big offshore boats going after fluke and had grown up on all manner of boats as a child. Flaming red beard, longish curly hair, smoked weed when he was ashore, but all agreed that he was a cool customer on deck — not easily rattled. I tracked Mad Dog down one night on the picnic bench behind his house and he seemed to think I could find a berth on *Miss Angel*.

So off I go. Taking a ride offshore with Mr. P.

From catching herring and mackerel in my back yard, to chasing ground fish offshore. Big changes if it worked out. But it was clearly going to be a hard charging, all or nothing situation.

Soon enough, Mr. P would become the master of risk and the champion of humor all rolled into one, and — outside of me — the most desperate man I knew. Mr. P was driven by the bank, while I was driven by the need for shelter. Either way, we were to become a matched pair. At least for a while.

INNER FALL

IN 1974, ARTHUR POLAND, WAS thirty-five years old. He was red-faced, and short, about five foot five, wore glasses and talked like a machine gun. He also had a roly-poly walk, not because he was all that overweight, but when he was in the Army he had developed a problem with his inner ear that affected his balance — made him walk on shore like he was balancing on a pitching deck. In other words, if you didn't know him he looked like a stumbling drunk.

Mr. P spent a few years with Albert Thorpe on the *Amy Jo*, a sixty-five-foot dragger, and made good money shrimping in the winter. Enough money to get him thinking he should run his own show, and enough to float a loan for thirty-four thousand dollars to build a forty-two-foot Bruno & Stillman, mass-production, fiberglass boat.

At that point, turnaround on construction of a new Bruno was three weeks start to finish. Built with double hulls, they were incredibly strong boats. Word was you could drop one fifty feet from a crane onto concrete without a whole lot of damage. I think they had a video at the factory showing that. It probably sold a lot of boats.

But tough or not, new boats are their own special kind of floating disaster. With everything new, they present a fresh glow and the illusion of coherence, but inside they are usually a moraine of unconnected systems, missing pieces, and a lot of stuff that doesn't work right.

Picture *Miss Angel* sitting at the South Bristol Fisherman's Coop float with her beautiful sea green gelcoat finish, her hull so shiny you can see a funhouse mirror reflection of yourself if you stand close to her. People drinking cheap bubbly from plastic cups were doing just that at her christening, standing on the float at the Coop, rubbing their hands on the new gelcoat and whistling under their breath.

Inside, *Miss Angel* was barely cured, still wafting solvent, and as bare bones a boat as you could get. No deck lights, no deck hose to wash down after fish, not even a bilge pump. Not much more than a yellow turbocharged Caterpillar diesel, a few hydraulic hoses, autopilot, radio, and a steering wheel. Now with seven years to pay off the loan, Arthur Poland had to get the *Miss Angel* making money as fast as he could.

Mr. P's plan was simple: put the cart before the horse. And do it immediately.

Second day back from the factory he and Mad Dog ran forty miles off-shore and dumped a new gang of fifty gillnets on a stretch of bottom called the Inner Fall. With the gear in the water, the clock was ticking.

The remainder of the day was slated for the construction of fish bins and a picking table, and the installation of a net hauler, remote steering, bilge pump and deck hose — all the basics required to haul the gear and handle the fish. But in a scant half-day, the combined talents of friends and family barely got the net hauler and remote steering station opera-tional and nothing else. Meanwhile, the monofilament gillnets sat on the bottom forty miles away filling up with codfish, hake, pollock, sharks, dog-fish, and monkfish, snagging anything that came near them.

The next morning, I joined a rekindled work crew on the Coop float in a race against the clock. Standing over a pile of lumber and power tools, Mr. P laid it out for us.

"Okay, boys, we need a picking table not a kitchen cabinet, so I don't give a shit what it looks like. All I know is, we gotta get this party offshore in a goddamned hurry."

The work was crude — plywood, spruce strapping, and two-by-fours — but a little after noon we had an unpainted, temporary picking table slapped together.

No time to waste, we heaved the power tools and trash ashore and cast off, friends and all. Fresh faced and bright with adventure, we were soon headed straight into a stiff southerly breeze at full throttle, watching the spray wash the sawdust and wood scraps off the afterdeck. Given the composition and experience of the people on board, we were closer to an extended boat-launch party than a professional crew. I think we had a loaf of bread, a jar of peanut butter and strawberry jam, and a case of Coke for lunch and dinner.

Mr. P still had major gaps in his operation, but with gillnets in the water he had no choice but to go; and with a three-hour steam ahead of us, we would be lucky to get the gear hauled by sundown. Among the list of missing items was a set of deck lights. In fact, the only lighting on deck consisted of a small round dome light on the overhead. The silly dome light put out something in the range of forty watts and would have been a better fit in somebody's shower stall than trying to illuminate the picking table of a gillnet boat. Worse yet, *Miss Angel* had no deck hose rigged to wash the blood and gurry off of the deck, and the bilge pump was yet to be connected. As standard factory issue, Bruno & Stillman had bolted a crude handpump to the deck, the kind with a metal rod attached to a big rubber diaphragm.

Unfortunately, the crew wasn't any less green than the boat. Outside of Mad Dog and Mr. P, no one else on board had ever picked a fish out of a monofilament gillnet or cut and cleaned anything more than a handful of ground fish.

Monofilament gillnets snagged everything a fish possessed, the hinge of the jaw, spines around the eyes or mouth, and the gill plates. The nets sat on the black ocean bottom, standing up like a fence but waving like a belly dancer with the current. Most fish were caught when they tried to go straight through. Since fish were built for muscling their way forward through the water, they were not very good at backing up. Or, as Mr. P put it "fish are known to have very poor reverse gears." Fish powered into gillnets, got hooked around the jaw or gill plate, drifted back a bit, powered ahead again, picked up another mesh around their head, and repeated that struggle over and over again until they died.

Cause of death was usually the inability to circulate water though their mouth and across their gills either because the gill plate was now squeezed tightly shut by the mesh around their head, or because their mouth was wired shut by the tangle around their jaw. With any significant catch, this series of death throes turned an otherwise orderly piece of fishing gear into a nasty tangle of fish and plastic mesh.

The fish picker's job was to sort this all out on the picking table, toss the fish into a bin on deck, and free the twine so it could be flaked into a big pile in the stern of the boat. That way, when the gang was completely hauled, it was immediately ready to be set out again. If you hit them well and you thought the fish were still there, that is exactly what you did.

Picking large ground fish like pollock, hake, cod, and haddock out of a gillnet turned out to be a combination of puzzle solving and intuition. But it was a skill that could only be learned by picking a lot of fish, and by developing a complete memory store of the ways fish could get themselves snarled up. The struggles of fish and the resulting tangles looked unsolvable at first, but there were finite variations, not infinite, and over time you began to see patterns emerge regardless of how horrifyingly complex the whole mess looked.

In some ways it was something like dealing with those annoying wire and ring puzzles your cousin gives you at Christmas. You're way better off fooling around intuitively until you learn how the pieces interact, instead of trying to logically think it through. Unfortunately, picking fish when you are in the process of learning can take a very long time, and the guy running the net hauler — who is usually the guy who owns the boat and is motivated by a big monthly payment — doesn't stop because you can't figure it all out.

Over time, as I built up a mental catalog of known gillnet puzzles, picking became less stressful. Once I reached a certain level of mastery, the fish seem to fall out of the tangled ball of fuzz with the right combination of flips and contortions. That said, the first time I saw a gillnet full of fish come around the net hauler, I could not escape the feeling of dread — and the accompanying belief that no human being could possibly get those large and sometimes slapping fish out of the rat's nest of catchy monofilament piling up in front of me.

The trip to the Inner Fall was pleasant enough, cloudy, light chop and wind out of the south. Even so, the weather radio was talking about the wind swinging over to the southeast in the late afternoon. This always meant rain and usually a heavy blow. Arthur had his stocking feet up on the shiny white cockpit dash and had the throttle "in the corner" with a chip of wood jammed on the inside of the lever to keep it there. At full throttle, *Miss Angel* kept the cockpit windows wet and showered the stern deck with spray as she rode and leaped like a wild creature.

"If she can't take it, we don't want her," he explained to me when I asked about the wooden wedge in the controls.

About ten miles below Monhegan Island, we steamed close to a boat with an unusual profile — too large for a typical coastal dragger, but too small for a commercial freighter. I remember noticing that the boat had a clipper bow that raked forward — definitely not an American fishing boat.

As we got closer and steamed past her stern and along her starboard side, the working side, we could see that she was fishing. She was the *Taiyo Maru #14*, registered in Tokyo, and was hauling longline gear. The boat was close to two hundred feet in length and had a crew of eight or ten men dressed in white oil clothes and white boots working on a brightly lit foredeck. They were hauling and landing the catch on the foredeck through a cutout portion of the gunwale. We saw one fish come on board that looked big enough to be a giant bluefin tuna, and we watched as four of the deck crew unhooked and began butchering the fish with large knives.

The scale and sophistication of the operation were unlike anything we had ever seen. No one had ever heard of longlining in the Gulf of Maine. The only longlining we had heard about was for swordfish on the Grand Banks and on Georges. Nobody longlined for bluefin tuna because the price was so pitiful — somewhere in the range of four or five cents per pound. That was a fishmeal price, meaning that the only outfit that would have bought bluefin at the time would have been the fish reduction plant in Rockland. There, a majestic twelve-foot, eight-hundred-pound giant bluefin would have been cooked down and dried to make chicken feed. Apart from the awful smell of the fishmeal plant, it was not a very attractive option. At the time, most Americans didn't eat bluefin tuna, now a staple on any sushi menu in America. The older fishermen in town called the bluefin "horse mackerel" and occasionally harpooned them for sport. In 1973, the domestic U.S. market for bluefin was nonexistent. But all that was about to change.

Someone in Japan had seen fit to run a fishing experiment in the Gulf of Maine. With dimwitted Americans harpooning bluefin tuna for sport, why not send a boat to the Gulf of Maine, catch the fish and ship them back to Japan. The price of bluefin in the domestic Japanese market was significantly higher than our four or five cents per pound. More like five dollars a pound, and that was wholesale. In late August, with the fish having spent the entire summer gorging on mackerel and squid, their fat content was at its highest, particularly around the belly. The belly cut of the fish, the toro, fetched the highest price. Bluefin tuna fishing methods, and the market, were well developed, since the Japanese had been catching bluefin in the Japan and China seas for centuries. But the worldwide range of the giant bluefin tuna was a mystery at that time. It was clear to us though, and clear to the Japanese fishermen, that giant bluefin tuna liked to spend the summer swimming in the Gulf of Maine.

We spent a little time watching the *Taiyo* crew haul, but we had another hour to reach our gear, so we pushed on to the Inner Fall. Once there, our memories of the efficient Japanese crew would be held in sharp contrast to the bedlam that ensued aboard the *Miss Angel*.

By the time we reached our gang of nets and started to haul, it was after four pm. The wind was still out of the south but a dark lowering sky presaged the coming rain. With no fish pens, the fish would go in a loose pile on the deck, and the nets flaked in the stern. But nothing could have prepared us for the sight that came over the rail.

Mr. P had done his job well. The previous day, he and Mad Dog had set the gang of nets on a heavy concentration of cod and pollock, so heavy that now all we could see were fish coming over the roller.

The big fish had been feeding on adult sea herring. When a large school of herring sat near the bottom, they showed as black clouds, even on simple sounding machines like depth finders. When they were near the bottom, herring became a sure-fire draw for foraging ground fish. Mr. P and Mad Dog had seen the concentration of feed and dumped the string of gear right on top of the herring. Most of the ground fish had distended bellies from their last meal — some regurgitating half-digested herring, which smelled oddly like freshly cut onions.

Despite the load of fish coming over the side, Mad Dog was the only one on deck who really knew what he was looking at. He promptly upped our level of understanding by whooping and shouting, "There's one in every window, boys, one in every...fucking...window," meaning that the fish were thick enough to imagine one fish for every available open mesh in the net. It was an exaggeration, but it was a shitload of fish. Had Mad Dog not been there, we probably would have believed that this was the way gillnets always looked.

It might as well have been 'one in every window' when it came to the combined crew's pitiful picking skills. And not only was the crew as green to gillnetting as it was to say, shearing sheep, but the high concentration of fish struggling overnight in the net created tangles that were even more complex than usual. Struggling fish that are that close together get snarled up and hooked up with other struggling fish. We had no way of knowing that, and it wouldn't have made any difference anyway, but it certainly contributed to the nightmare. On they came, around the capstan of the net hauler, mounding up in a mass of fish and monofilament on the poor excuse for a picking table we had haphazardly nailed together that morning.

Everyone, except the two guys attempting to flake nets in the stern, turned to picking and piling fish on the deck. Time passed by without awareness as we unraveled the puzzles in front of us. We had been at it for hours, all of us heads-down, concentrating on finding our own personal solutions to the fish-plus-monofilament puzzle, before I gave myself the chance to lift my head and really look at the total situation. In five hours, we had picked a pile of fish big enough to make it difficult to move around on deck — in the range of ten thousand pounds — but we still had a long way to go. The catch was mostly big pollock with some cod mixed in. The pollock averaged three and half to four feet in length, and were stiff as a board if they were dead. Some pollock came up alive and kicked powerfully, unlike the cod who just lay there, or at the most squirmed around a little.

The two guys in the stern flaking twine were just as inexperienced as the pickers. Their job was to unravel the snarls and separate the corkline and leadline so the nets could be set again. The long gang of gillnets was weighted at each end with a large stone, but the combination of strong current and the large mass of fish had flipped the stones at each end and caused the gang to twist and wind up like the rubber band attached to the propeller on a model airplane. Numerous times, Mr. P yelled at the net crew to give up trying to untangle the twists and just move on to get the nets out of the way.

The other thing I noticed, when I looked up, was the weather. The wind had not swung to the southeast. Instead, it had stayed due south and was starting to blow hard and kick up a nasty chop. The low ceiling of dark clouds was spitting rain. All of this combined to make our picking efficiency even more pitiful as we began to get tossed around by the chop, and the darkness came early.

Those of us picking, huddled under the little forty-watt dome light to see what we were doing. The guys flaking twine in the stern were just trying to stay upright and out of the twine. At times, we made a comical picture, each of us yanking the tangled fish this way and that to get enough light to see what we were doing.

Soon it was pitch black and blowing with a stiff breeze and I remember looking to windward as we lay side-to the chop still hauling, still deep in the nightmare, and seeing the white of the whitecaps and hearing them hiss as they broke just beyond the dim light of the deck.

Finally, hours later, Mr. P muttered something to Mad Dog who then passed along the command in a loud voice to stop picking and lend a hand roping the fish and twine altogether, piling the mess on top of the fish on deck. There wasn't much of the gang left to haul, only part of a fifty-fathom section, so it came aboard quickly, but it made for an ugly pile.

Given the fact that the *Miss Angel* was now heavily laden with no bilge pump save the crude diaphragm deck pump, the weather was turning sour, and we could not see well enough in the stern to avoid a bad tangle setting out, Mr. P let it be known that we were heading for the barn, and would not set back again that night. I know it pained him because the fish were probably still there, or at least findable, but we had a lot to deal with yet. Normally, the gang of nets would be set back right away, and would fish overnight, hauled the next day, and set again. This was the gillnet tread-mill. This was how you made money. But we were in too much of a mess to pull that off.

We were exhausted, and given the fact that no butchering could be safely done in the dim light on deck, most of us stripped off our oil clothes and went below to the bare bones forecastle and tiny galley. As we got underway and the pitch of the Caterpillar's turbocharger whine ascended to its maximum, I looked at my watch. It was eleven pm. We turned off the galley light and tried to sleep. With the bunks full, Mad Dog did his best to stay put sleeping on the galley table, but slid off numerous times only to have his boot hit the oil-fired galley stove and smell up the place when the *Miss Angel* took an extreme roll.

We arrived home at three am and put the boat on the mooring so we could sleep for a few hours and avoid the early morning lobster catcher traffic at the Coop float. By ten am the next morning we had the fish butchered, boxed and iced, and they were on their way to Boston. All told, the trip was over fifteen thousand pounds, a good start for the *Miss Angel*.

OFFSHORE

AS FALL TURNED INTO WINTER, working offshore radically shifted our view of the world. In the two years I'd fished inshore, I had never been out of sight of land. Offshore, everything was big and we were small.

If the NOAA weather forecast called for twenty-five knots, it blew a steady thirty-five knots offshore. And when it blew a gale at fifty knots out of the south or southeast, we found ourselves climbing the backs of twenty foot seas for days after the wind had let go.

It wasn't really a case of whether the boat could take it or not, but the crew was another matter. Speed had its cost; deafness and wear and tear among them. *Miss Angel* jumped around like a wild animal in sea action like no other boat I had ever seen. In rough weather, she threw us around like ragdolls — more so than a wooden boat of comparable size would have done. Over time, I was very glad to be a nimble five foot eight instead of a lumbering six four on this maniacal plastic boat.

"She may be a fucking Clorox bottle, but she's *our* fucking Clorox bottle," Mr. P would say.

More importantly, I felt as though I was in the midst of an irreversible transition. Though I was committed to making money to finish the house, my desperate plunge offshore had completely hijacked my priorities and become all-consuming. So much so, that life on land began to feel foreign, and the crudeness of our half-baked house had shifted from a state of crisis to nonsensical or trivial by comparison. How could carrying five-gallon jugs of water or taking baths in a washtub be all that bad? Hell, I was just glad to be home where I wasn't bracing for an acrobatic roll every thirty seconds. And I was definitely not powered by the love of fishing anymore, not with the winter upon us.

View from Rutherford's Island across drawbridge to mainland

"I've made an appointment with a lawyer," Joy said one night over supper.

"How come?"

"You need a will, is how come."

"Oh."

"Well, yes. Oh, is right."

"Do you really think that's necessary?"

"It is, if you keep charging around in that little boat offshore with Arthur Poland. You just might not come home, you know. And then what do I do? I end up fighting with the state of Maine for this house. That's what I do."

"All right, all right, I get it."

Mortality was definitely part of the picture now. For the first time in my life, I felt the ague of no longer being eighteen.

Thirty years later, I still pay attention to weather patterns and wind direction, forces invisible to all of my friends. When I tell my friends that the Boston weather forecasters are completely wrong in predicting that a winter storm will deliver snow instead of rain, they find it amusing. And when I explain that the wind is currently out of the southeast and that unless it changes to the northeast we will get rain not snow, because in my experience I have never seen snow arrive on wind out of the southeast, and that the only precipitation that comes from the east or southeast is rain, always rain, they smile politely.

I am sure they are asking themselves why I care and why they need to know this information. It's habit, that's all, an inculcated awareness of the weather after two winters with Mr. P, watching and waiting for small windows of moderate wind conditions within which we could dash offshore forty to fifty miles at sixteen knots, haul our gillnets, and get home without getting hammered by a substantial winter blow.

Traveling offshore that fall also provided a window to the world outside of the tiny village of South Bristol. The day we unloaded the *Miss Angel*'s first trip, we heard the news that the *Taiyo Maru #14* and its crew had been seized and impounded in Portland, Maine. Though it was 1974, a few years prior to establishing a two-hundred-mile fishing limit, the U.S. did have a twelve-mile limit in effect and the Japanese longliner had been caught inside the line.

But the most interesting item — included in almost every news story — was the fact that the captain of the boat had denied any ownership of the longline gear currently in the water. By all accounts, the *Taiyo Maru #14* had set its gear as far as Matinicus Rock, and we could certainly confirm at least one data point, having seen the boat hauling back ten miles south-southeast of Monhegan Island. And rumors were flying in the fishing chatter on the FM marine radio that her starting point was off of Portland, a distance of over fifty miles.

Regardless of where they started, we knew where the gear was and the next day the *Miss Angel* steamed by it at roughly two pm. We were on the way out to set again on the Inner Fall and there it was, lighted buoys flashing in the low light of a heavy overcast cloud cover. The captain of the *Taiyo Maru #14* had left his gear. This time we stopped briefly to take one of the lighted buoys on board and have a good look.

Since none of us had been swordfishing, we didn't really have anything to compare it with, but it looked heavily rigged and well built. The lighted float was rigged with a tarred nylon twine mesh around a hard plastic ball and the light was on a photosensitive switch so it wouldn't waste the battery. We also spotted a radio buoy, and judging from the fact that it was not on the end of the gear, we concluded that it was only one of many which were snapped on at some interval in the set as well. By anyone's measure, this was relatively sophisticated gear for the time. Maybe the radio chatter was right and she had dropped fifty miles worth of gear. Either way, the *Taiyo Maru #14* had left a lot of money floating in the water.

For the offshore fishing community, though, the most important fact was the boat's public denial of ownership. In our minds, when the *Taiyo Maru's* captain claimed that it was not his equipment, he gave every fisherman the right to salvage the drifting gear in its entirety. So it was off to the races from Portland to Matinicus rock with as many knives as could get out there and find the gear, slicing and dicing until it was gone. Had we not been on a mission to get Mr. P's gillnets in the water again and start paying the bills, we would have taken our share.

But the biggest impact of the impoundment of the *Taiyo Maru #14* was on the price of giant bluefin tuna. Probably realizing that it was easier to buy the fish locally instead of sending a two-hundred-foot boat all the way from Japan only to be seized by the U.S. Coast Guard, Japanese fishing companies raised the going price of bluefin from pennies per pound to over three dollars per pound literally overnight, changing forever the way Maine fisherman viewed the fish. This radical change in price meant that handlining or harpooning a single eight-hundred-pound fish could bring in twenty-four hundred dollars. Later the price went even higher.

HACKED TOGETHER

AFTER GILLNETTING WELL INTO the winter, Mr. P decided to rig over to dragging shrimp, hoping to make some easy money in our back yard, John's Bay. We quickly hacked together a set of dragging gear — an old winch nobody wanted and a castoff shrimp net from Albert Thorpe. Arthur did buy a new set of doors and have a new set of steel dragging gantries made — but everything else was ramshackle stuff that barely worked. A friend of Mr. P's welded a scrounged hydraulic pump to an undersized free winch. Unfortunately, the whole rig bent itself into a pretzel on several occasions hauling back, and we were forced to free-spool out all of our towing cable and leave our dragging gear sitting on the bottom with buoys tied to mark it. After we patched up our Rube Goldberg winch design, we'd go back out and haul the net and heavy doors back off the bottom and try it again. God, we were pitiful.

All the while we struggled with the gear, I had a sore throat that wouldn't go away. It had persisted for six or eight weeks and finally I went to see a doctor in Damariscotta. He was a good guy. After I described our half-built house and the hopeless progress of my winter shrimping adventure, he said,

"You're not sleeping."

"What do you mean?"

"You're just pretending to sleep, but you're not getting rested."

"Okay, so what do you think I should do about it?"

"I want to give you something to sleep."

"Wait a minute. You have no idea what my day is like."

"Don't worry, if the boat catches fire you'll be the first one out of your bunk."

Miss Angel rigged for dragging

I relented. He prescribed Diazepam. Turns out Diazepam was just a generic version of Valium, the *I-don't-care-what-happens, everything-is-cool, nothing-could-possibly-hurt-me* drug. Sure enough, after two nights of taking the stuff, my sore throat went away and I felt like a million bucks. I slept like a stone. Thing is, it lasted longer than just lights out, and there was this crazy patched-together winch I had to run every time we set out the dragging gear at four am.

When Arthur had worked on the sixty-five-foot *Amy Jo*, she had sported separate winches for each towing cable, port and starboard. All the two deckhands had to do was lower each of the twelve-hundred-pound doors barely into the water on both sides, ease off each winch brake a little

79

bit, and then Albert would put the old girl in the corner and the doors and the net would pull the cable off the winches smooth as butter. Albert could look out the aft window of the wheelhouse and watch for the markers on the towing cable. When the markers showed up, he would just back her off to towing speed and the winches would stop spooling cable. The two deckhands would tighten up each brake on the winch, and she was towing nice and easy for as long as you wanted to tow.

The *Miss Angel* didn't work that way. She was a wild and crazy bucking bronco with a lot of horsepower and a hull that was so light she jumped ahead every time you put the boat in gear with the engine idling.

So there I am standing at the brakes of this old-time winch out of some junk yard, with a head full of Diazepam and Mr. P yells, "let her go" so I ease off the brakes and the drums on the winch start turning, the heavy doors are plunging into the dark water and out of the deck lights and they are starting to pull against the water but Mr. P goes ahead and gooses the wild horse under harness, the six-cylinder diesel turbocharger singing the high note, he puts her in the corner like his old skipper did on the *Amy Jo* and she leaps ahead and the cables start snapping and popping and they are going out much too fast for my liking, and I'm trying to slow down the spooling on the winch by tightening down a little on the brakes, and the smoke is starting to come off the brake shoes they are getting so hot, and I can smell that asbestos brake shoe lining going up my nose.

And then I look aft at where the cables go through this set of big sheaves that are through-bolted to the fiberglass-coated plywood deck, and I see that the strain on the deck sheaves are making the whole aft deck flex up and down a good two or three inches like a trampoline, the whole aft deck is breathing up and down from the tension on the winch and on the cable and from Arthur putting the *Miss Angel* in the corner.

But I don't care. I am completely calm. In fact, I am watching myself — as though I am three feet above and behind my head — in a tranquil, satori state.

There I am with my hands on the winch brakes and I am thinking to myself, this is not good. It is not a good thing that you are not scared, that you are not reacting at all to what is happening here. This is not a good situation at all. You should be turning around and screaming at Mr. P something like, "slow the fuck down asshole, you are going to rip the aft deck right out of this stinking plastic boat if you do not back the fuck off!"

But that was not what I did. Instead, I stood there and watched it all happening and smelled the smoke from the brake shoes. And the marks on the cable came up and I snubbed the brakes and the *Miss Angel* settled her ass down in the water and dug in and started towing and Arthur slowed the wild horse down — when he was ready. And then I stopped taking Diazepam. Except, of course, for recreational purposes as long as it lasted. God, that was good stuff.

At the end of March, Arthur finally decided to give up dragging for shrimp and rig back for gillnetting. Defeated and exhausted, I had hit a new low. It was the poorest money making winter I ever had in Maine. From December to April I cleared a grand total of six hundred dollars working six or seven days a week but I had no choice but to stick with it and I prayed for spring fish and no wind.

April was still early in the season for gillnetting, so we planned to go three-handed because the fish were likely to be thin. That way we could make more money with fewer people to share up. The boat took seventy percent, and the rest was shared up between the three of us, including the skipper and boat owner, Mr. P. The third man was to be Mr. P's nephew, son of his wife's sister, Jerry Gamage. But then Jerry got in a mess one night at the end of March.

Jerry was nineteen, and had been with us throughout the fall. He was indestructible on deck, when he had slept the night before, and we were looking forward to having an experienced hand for spring fishing who knew the *Miss Angel* and how everything worked. But Jerry and two of his friends had been out drinking and horsing around one moonless night on the Damariscotta River. They were trying out a new skiff with a big outboard engine — probably too big for the skiff — and they flipped the boat out in the blackness of the river in the wee hours, out of sight and sound.

The water is very cold in March, as cold as it gets all winter, and all three died, two drowned and one died of hypothermia and was found draped over the upturned skiff at daylight.

Though Jerry was P's nephew and was known by everyone in town, nobody talked about the incident much. It was too big and too painful.

I can't remember ever talking to Mr. P, or to Jerry's father, Arnie Gamage, after it happened, except to say that it was an awful thing and that I was sorry. The subject of Jerry never came up again, not because we didn't love him or didn't miss him. We did.

There was just nothing to say. He was gone.

SPRING HADDOCK SURPRISE

GOING OFFSHORE FORTY or fifty miles in a small boat like the *Miss Angel* was eerie sometimes. Often in midsummer, and sometimes in the spring, when we got to our gillnet gear at daylight, the water would be as flat and as still as a millpond, not a breath of air. You couldn't see land in any direction, but the horizon would have a purple glow at sunrise — like a mist that was very far off but that circled the boat three hundred and sixty degrees. You definitely felt small. But at the same time, you felt strangely powerful standing there in the middle of nowhere; kind of like you were the only people on the earth.

Then it was time to haul. The boat was out of gear and just idling, laying there blowing and burbling diesel breath and water through the wet exhaust out the stern. At some point after drinking his coffee, Mr. P would take to the deck with a white, five-gallon bucket of seawater to take his morning dump. He was old school and didn't like using the flush with the handpump. It all ended up in the same place anyway. Probably the only hard and fast rule on the boat was not to bother him while he was in process.

After that ritual was complete, we would tromp on deck making booming sounds through the fiberglass-covered plywood deck that echoed like a drum, turn on the deck radio, break open a new box of gloves, pull on a fresh pair slapping our hands together and jamming between the fingers to get them on tight, do windmills with our arms and shadow box to limber up like we were getting ready to go into a football game. It was eerie because we mostly got the shit beat out of us on a regular basis that far off shore — particularly in the winter. Even in the spring, it would often blow quite hard and we had a long way to get home, so there were many days when we regretted choosing to go fishing and wished we were working in a hardware store. That is why it was so strange when it was flat calm — it didn't seem like it could actually be the same place where you occasionally thought you were going to die in January or February, and it made you wonder when something was going to happen.

Some people were immune to the fear, though. Anyone over thirty had enough experience to know better. We were on a favorite spot of Mr. P's — a little forty-three-fathom spot just above Toothaker Ridge, forty-two miles south by east from Pemaquid Point in April, when we met some fearless young characters. It was a very quiet morning and we were catching a few haddock, one of the prettiest of the ground fish in the Gulf of Maine — silver with a single horizontal black medial line from head to tail, with a big eye that seemed to express more innocence than most fish, and a delicate set of pinkish lips. They were a spring fish, full of big sacs of pink spawn when you dressed them. Plus, they were the only fish moving in the spring, so we were happy to see them coming over the rail because the price was high and they were nice to look at. Catching haddock was kind of like seeing the first crocuses come up. You knew it was spring.

Far on the horizon we could see a boat coming at us as we hauled along and soon enough a boat that was even smaller than ours came alongside and spoke us. She was a wooden "Novi" boat, built in Nova Scotia where boats were cheap and built to last only six or seven years. She couldn't have been more than thirty-six feet and she had the classic Novi swayback with a high bow and a high stern but quite low in the middle. Easy to work out of and a fairly good sea boat if you didn't take a big wave amidships.

On board was the youngest crew I had ever seen. The skipper was the oldest at fifteen or sixteen, three or four years younger than Jerry Gamage had been when he drowned, and the crew of four were all in their early teens. They told us that they were going tub trawling, an old way to fish with a longline that lay on the bottom with periodic hooks with bait hanging off on shorter lines called gangens or snoods. Tub trawling had been popular back when Gloucester schooners were putting men off in dories, but it was still a low-cost way to go, since you could rig pretty cheaply. As the young skipper talked, we could see the tubs stacked on deck and some of the crew working on baiting hooks and coiling line into the tubs. They were from Portland and headed to Cashes Ledge, he said. Apart from being way the hell off course as a result of a poorly compensated compass — they were off by about thirty degrees from where they should have been and we told them so — there were none of us on the bright new *Miss Angel* who would have wanted to go all the way to Cashes in that old Novi.

No matter to the kids, though, they were probably going to lay on their gear and spend the night because it was quite a distance — probably a six-hour steam in the Novi. As they told us their story, we all looked at each other on the *Miss Angel* with blank faces that we hoped kept our fear hidden for the children in that old boat. We wished them luck and Godspeed, waved our wet gloves at them, and watched the teenage skipper point her to the south on the new heading brimming with the courage of youth.

I'm sure they survived just fine, but it was a memorable meeting and on that particular day we were especially glad to not be them.

After Jerry Gamage was lost everyone in town knew we needed another deckhand, and Mitchell Kelsey showed up one day on the wharf saying he wanted to go because he was bored of lobster catching. Born and bred in South Bristol, Mitchell had a long history of being the black sheep of the Kelsey clan, but it was hard not to like him. Heavily in debt, he was divorced after a very short marriage, had bought himself a black Corvette, wore long hair and an outrageous handlebar mustache, smoked dope and had loud parties with all welcome. He also had one of the strongest Maine accents of anyone in town. This was not uncommon among the younger crowd, who seemed to compete for the most outlandish Maine twang they could muster and practice exaggerated accents over the radio to each other. Unlike Mr. P and myself — both of us were short — Mitchell was tall and lanky. This was somewhat unusual offshore since you got thrown around so much, and most guys who lasted it out tended to be shorter. In the end, Mitchell turned out to be one of the best guys I ever worked with on deck. Though he only went with us for four months, I was sad to see him go back to lobstering in July. Though it was a boring job and involved almost constant bickering over territory, lobstering was money in the bank, so we couldn't blame him. He had the boat and the traps, so he had to go.

Fishing on Toothaker Ridge was good business that April as the haddock kept coming and we had the place pretty much to ourselves, but one late morning we had a nasty surprise. Gillnets were very catchy gear and would often pick up bits of bottom growth like sponges and other stuff that looked like testicles on long spindly stems. Even though gillnets just sat on the bottom like a fence, the process of hauling the gear would often sweep the gillnet across the bottom as the boat above was pushed by the tide or wind, and a long string would pick up the odd thing. We had a lot of nets in the string — close to sixty — but the fish were scattered so I was back in the stern with Mitchell hauling the twine and flaking it into a pile instead of standing at the picking table where I would normally be. We were enjoying the day. The sun was flicking off the wave tops with enough breeze on the water to make waves and the water droplets coming off the plastic monofilament gillnets sparkled like diamonds, Mitchell hauling and flaking the leadline and I was stacking the corks, basking in the sun in the stern.

Mr. P had a deck station with built-in controls set up next to the net hauler so he could stand at the rail and run the hauler and control the boat at the same time. Often, a fish might be loosely caught in the monofilament and about to fall out so they needed to be gaffed aboard, or they could be heavy — like a thirty or forty pound whale cod — and have to be hefted over the net roller we had mounted on the rail.

So Mr. P was bent over like. We couldn't even see his head he was bent over so much, just his ass sticking up as he hung over the rail and then he is yelling at us,

"Get up here, you assholes!"

Still leaning way over the rail, one foot on the deck, "give me some help, Goddamnit!"

"Whaaaat now," I said annoyed.

Mr. P shouts back, "It's a fucking bomb for Christ's sake."

Mitchell and I run up to the hauling station and there is this bomb hanging off the twine just bobbing its head out of the water and Mr. P is now standing back up at the control station and going back and forth on the reverse gear and turning the boat, the rudder hard over, to get some slack because the tide is racing, and he is getting all red in the face and huffing and puffing.

But it isn't much of a bomb. Just about a foot or sixteen inches with fins on it, like something out of a cartoon or what you would see dropping off the wing of a World War II airplane in a war movie, not too rusted up though, which seemed surprising. But how much of a bomb does it have to be? In other words, we're thinking, shit this thing could still go off.

Then, Mitchell and I both run back to the stern and started yelling back at Mr. P.

"You take the fucking bomb out, asshole, we're not going to get blown up."

Then Mr. P back at us, "Fuck the both of you guys, you stupid pussies. You're sure as shit going to get blown up just as much back there as you are up here. Now, get your asses up here and help me take this fucking thing out of the twine, for Christ's sake."

We look at each other. We can't argue with the logic, so back up to the rail, and Mitchell and I stretch over the rail and carefully slack up the twine on either side of the bomb while Mr. P takes off his gloves and picks off the monofilament from the bomb fins, and his fingers are getting this red-brown rust crud on them from the bomb, and then he cradles the bomb like a baby and tosses it as gently as he can over the twine and away from the boat, since he doesn't want it to go down and get caught again on the sloping net reaching all the way to the bottom.

Then we all duck down under the rail.

And nothing happens.

Just kerplop.

VISITORS

PEOPLE JUST SHOWED UP MOST OF THE TIME. We all had telephones, but almost no one would call before they came over to visit. I don't really know why that was. But that's what people did and what was expected. In a town of five hundred people, everyone knew who you were and where you lived. When they visited, you offered them something to eat, a coffee, or a beer, or some rum or whiskey if you had it. In the winter, there were times when not a lot was going on, and people would visit to just pass the time and tell stories and gossip about the news in town. When we first moved in, strangers would show up bearing a pail of crabs or shrimp and beer, but after living in town for a few years and becoming part of the fishing community, an established circle of friends would drop by on a regular basis.

Even so, the occasional outlier would show up and present a puzzle. One such puzzle was Andy Lambert. Andy was a young guy in his twenties who had been adopted by a family in the center of town after years of bouncing around foster homes in Maine. I didn't really know him except through watching the sun set with a buzz on at the beer stop. I'd join them once in a while, packed into a smoky pair of cars winter and summer, and had run into him there.

One afternoon in April, Joy's parents had come by the house on their way up to Tenant's Harbor for the summer. They were retired and so much treasured their life in Maine that April, still considered winter by anyone's measure, was none too soon to open up their house. In Tenant's Harbor, they lived in a small uninsulated cape with a big black cook stove in the kitchen to heat the whole house. Joy's father, a chemical engineer who had worked on the Manhattan project with Robert Oppenheimer, and then ran a lab for DuPont for nearly forty years, loved the routine of maintaining the woodpile and feeding the stove. And when he wasn't repainting the woodwork to glossy perfection, he had the unique ability to turn any ordinary chore into a science project. I loved them both, but they were from the era of cocktail parties and genteel Yankee etiquette that was nigh impossible for me to understand.

Years had passed since our first meeting in Delaware in 1969 when Joy and I had shocked Tuckie and Francis over dinner with the news that we were living together. Now that we were married and living in their favorite state of Maine, the uncertainty of our future was somewhat eased. But like most mothers who want the best for their daughters, Tuckie had wept when she first saw our house the year before.

Now, they had come for lunch. Our floors were still unfinished and were a mixture of painted particle board in the kitchen and rough pine partially covered with construction paper everywhere else, the front porch was nonexistent, save for the bare creosote treated cantilevered timbers, our front steps consisted of dual planks held together with wooden cleats, and our previous oil stove had been replaced with a wood stove made from the welded inner-tanks of two salvaged water heaters. For us, lunch was a stretch, but we were managing and were cheerfully clearing away the dishes from our tiny card table when Andy showed up.

He was drunk.

Drunk is okay, but Andy was a mean drunk. With his hands cupped on either side of his face, he peered through the big windows of our front doors at the fragile luncheon coming to a close in our crude house.

Anyone in our circle of friends would have looked at the scene, poked their head in the door to say hello, and begged forgiveness for intruding. But Andy was coming in to stay. I invited him in and made the huge mistake of offering him a glass of wine.

"I'll take a beer, if you don't mind," he said.

Beer in hand, he commenced to apologize for the "inner-ruption" with heavy emphasis on the "ruption" half of the word and projected a hostile tone that meant he was looking for someone to object to his being there.

Tuckie and Francis quickly prepared to flee like a determined pair of geese headed north with hurried kisses and hugs. Andy looked on and hoisted his beer in a salute to their leaving. As the door closed, Andy continued repeating his "inner-ruption" apologies while Joy and I set about cleaning up the dishes and food.

I had dealt with Andy's visits before. Over time, I had learned that it was best to ignore him without antagonizing him, if at all possible. As we picked up and cleaned, he rattled on about how he wanted to get to know us because we were from somewhere else and he always wanted to learn new things, but Joy and I didn't give him a lot to work with. We gave him calm assurances that it was good to see him, that Joy's folks had been preparing to leave anyway, and that he should sit down and relax and tell us what was on his mind.

Finishing his beer, he let loose an enormous belch and then started in with a whole lot of nothing — most of it designed to start a fight.

"I dunno why I came over here. I just did it, that's all. Just did it.

"An now I'm here and I doan know why I oughta explain anyway.

"Do you wan me to explain?"

Joy and I responded passively, no we don't want an explanation, and so forth.

Finally, Andy concluded that it was too hot in our house (he was sitting near the stove and had never taken off his heavy jacket). Wheeling to the door, he told us that he needed to cool off, flung the door wide, stumbled down the front ramp, stopped to piss on our wood pile and tore off in his pickup, gravel flying.

Two days later, Joy was at work at the newspaper in Damariscotta and I was home when Andy appeared again. Flush with drink, his face blotchy, eyes glassy, he was fueled and brimming with greetings and veiled hostility.

"Where's the wifey?"

When I explained she was working, he said,

"Well, aren't you the lucky man."

The two of us stood in the front room. I wasn't going to sit down or offer him anything.

"I'm real sorry I busted in on you guys on the weekend and all. Joy's people looked like good people."

"Yeah, they are good people. They're summer people."

"I could see that. Nothing wrong with summer people. I got nothing against 'em."

"Look, Andy, I've got to get down to Henry's. He wants me to help him shore up some pilings under his wharf and I've got to see Junior about cutting some of his oak for that, so I've got to go."

"Okay, okay. No reason to get all huffy."

"I'm not getting huffy, I just gotta go is all."

"You know, you and me, we got a lot to talk about. You know that?"

"Andy, I really don't know what you're talking about, but maybe let's have coffee at Ralph Gray's or something."

"I don't want no coffee at Ralph Gray's."

"Well, I'm going, Andy. I told Henry I'd be there."

"Awright, awright."

I threw on my coat. Opened the door for him.

"I don't need you for nothin anyways," he said over his shoulder going down the ramp.

Coming home from Henry's later in the day, I saw Andy's pickup parked about a quarter mile away on the long stretch of road in front of our lane. It was parked at the entrance to an old section of the road that had been abandoned when they straightened out the curve at the foot of the big hill. I didn't think anything of it. A lot of people parked there to walk down to the shore for clamming or to go hunting.

Two days went by and I went to grab a coffee at Ralph Gray's store, a combination lunch counter, coffee shop, and hardware store at the drawbridge in the center of South Bristol. Ralph was in his mid-eighties, but worked seven days a week for something to do. He wore the same uniform every day — khaki work shirt and pants, a large pocket protector for his reading glasses, and a too-small straw hat with a brim that curled upwards all around and perched on top of his head like a birthday party hat.

Ralph was a quintessential grump with a very soft heart. Most requests — whether for a cup of coffee or a galvanized lag-bolt with washers — elicited the same outward expression of annoyance. "What do you want that for? I don't have that kind of stuff here for Christ's sake. If you can find it somewhere in those bins, I'll sell it to you. But for God's sake, stop asking questions. I'm trying to have a conversation here." He was also a terrific tease when he had an audience of coffee drinkers at the counter, especially if you asked a naïve question. But when you got him alone, he was generous and kind. He once sold me a refrigerator for thirty-two dollars.

Ralph Gray in his store

"Did you hear about Andy?" Ralph asked. His face, normally half-smirking in preparation for a joke, was intent and serious. Reacting in slowed time from some formal part of my brain, I answered with a voice that I wasn't sure was my own.

"No, I didn't, Ralph."

"He blew his head off down the street from your house."

Silence. Herb Kelsey and others at the counter stared straight ahead, not daring to look at me as Ralph continued.

"He did it with a shotgun. Found him yesterday afternoon lying there about 200 yards from his pickup."

I stood there for a long moment. And then I began recounting that I had seen him two days ago — a mechanical litany of what had happened, how he was lit and was spoiling for a fight, how I hardly knew him, didn't know why he had come by at all. Then about how I had seen his pickup parked there at the foot of the hill for a couple of days.

Ralph was shaking his head. He was impassive on the surface, but deeply shaken as he went on.

"He left his dog in the truck. After a couple of days someone saw the dog in the truck and stopped to see what was going on. He was lying there with his shoe off and his bare foot next to the shotgun. You know, to shoot it."

I sat down at the counter on one of the swivel stools as Ralph poured coffee into an indestructible sea green mug in front of me.

"I guess maybe I was the last person to see him."

"I think you were."

I pushed it down and down and down, the thought that I could have listened, just listened as long as it took. This, I pushed down to a place with a door with a lock where I hoped I would never go again. But it was not possible. Instead, more thoughts continue to pour in, how I could have called Mr. P, my friend and captain, or Mitchell Kelsey, maybe asked them both to come over, strength in numbers, and many other improbable stories.

I felt a weakness all over. I drank my coffee and listened to Ralph and Herb Kelsey talk about it while I drifted off to a darker place and pictured the car at the foot of the hill and Andy's bare foot. But I didn't picture Andy and his visits. They were gone. They had been erased. They were exhaled. Part of the air.

The State Police came by the house the next day. South Bristol had no police force, just a civilian constable appointed in town and the State Police drove through town on an irregular schedule, or when called. They had spoken to Ralph Gray about my being the last person to see Andy. I told them what I knew. It wasn't much, but they were satisfied and they didn't press me for more.

I didn't know what it meant that Andy had shot himself, or what anything meant. April was a hard month. It was supposed to be spring, but it was still so much winter, and that was the month that people did it, when people killed themselves.

It was April five years before when our neighbor had shot himself in the shed next to the yellow house on Rutherford Island where Joy and I were living. And it was in April two years prior when an eighty-five-year-old man (not a half mile down the road from that same house) had locked himself in his car and run a vacuum cleaner hose from the exhaust pipe in through the window.

I told myself that it was a desperate time of year in Maine. Or as Tom Eliot put it, "April is the cruelest month." But I also realized that I was now part of the story.

KIPPIE

NOT EVERYONE INTERPRETED LIFE in South Bristol as such a desperate struggle. Some were impervious to the difficulties of scraping by. That was certainly true of one of my shipmates on the *Miss Angel*. After Mitchell Kelsey went back to lobster catching, we took on his cousin, Kippie Kelsey, son of bridge tender Herb Kelsey.

Kippie turned out to be one of the strangest, happiest and most innocent guys I ever shipped with. Nothing ever bothered him. Even when Mr. P and I screamed at him red-faced like drill instructors over something he'd forgotten or couldn't do right, he never got angry, and he slept like a log both on board and at home. Unfortunately, this also meant that Kippie was rarely on time. After a month of shipping with him I had learned that I needed to walk over to Kippie's rental, which he called the ghetto, and pull him out of bed.

Kippie called his house the ghetto because it was not fit for human habitation. The ghetto was nothing more than a made-over fish house sitting out on a wharf. The owner usually rented out the ghetto for the summer, but Kippie was trying to winter over with his wife and three-month-old baby boy. Unfortunately, their tiny bungalow was completely exposed to the north, and because the wharf stood on homemade oak pilings out over the water, the wind actually blew under the house as well as over it. To keep the wind from blowing up through the cracks between the floorboards, Kippie and his wife, Darlene, had stapled plastic sheeting to the floor. They had also stuffed the open studs of the ghetto's interior walls with pink insulation. When they were done, the wallpaper in their bedroom consisted of the silver foil backing of the insulation with Corning printed on it in diagonal red letters every two feet. Kippie had also stapled sea-foam green carpet scraps over the plastic sheeting on the floors, donated by the carpet man, a bachelor drinking buddy of Kippie's. Lately, Darlene had sacrificed light for comfort by stapling two old throw rugs over the northern windows because they leaked so badly.

Like many small Maine houses, the ghetto was heated with an oil stove that burned range oil, a slightly more refined and less smelly version of kerosene. They put out a lot of heat but the rate of flow of oil was the only way to adjust the temperature, so it was not very exact. Most of the older people I knew with oil stoves kept the temperature absolutely roasting, but in Kippie and Darlene's case they had no choice. Despite the pink fiberglass and the plastic sheeting, on most days you needed to wear insulated boots and long underwear bottoms around the house because the floor was so cold. At the same time, your face felt so hot you thought you might have a sunburn.

At 2:20 am when I opened the door to the ghetto, I breathed in hot air carrying the sweet smell of baby. Kippie was dead to the world, lying on his back snoring with his shoulder length blond hair tangled in his mustache from tossing and turning. The only way to get him up without disturbing Darlene was to touch him. I hated that. I wasn't afraid that he would exhibit some kind of reflex self-defense reaction and grab me, I just didn't like getting that personal. Even so, it was the only way to get him awake.

Kippie slept so soundly that shouting didn't really work. The only one who woke up from the shouting was Darlene and that sometimes also woke the baby. Only then would Kippie wake — but only because Darlene practically pushed him out of bed. The best thing for all concerned was for me to shake him by the shoulder, but I still didn't like it. I was usually pissed off and resentful that I had to go up there to begin with. Getting that close to the intimate scene in the roasting ghetto was not what I wanted, and it was probably not high on Darlene's list either. Once Kippie was upright and on the edge of the bed, I usually said, "See you in ten minutes, right, Kippie?" To which he usually replied with a sarcastic military salute, a cigarette already hanging from his mouth and said, "Okay boss, I'm on it."

One morning in February, Kippie didn't make it and we had to leave without him. We had no choice. Our navigation system, Loran, was down. Without it we were likely to miss our end buoy and could end up wasting a lot of time steaming around searching, particularly if there was significant sea action. At that time, the class of radar in use on small fishing boats could not distinguish the twelve-foot pole of an end buoy amongst the clutter of wave tops — even though the buoy pole had an aluminum radar reflector on top that looked like an origami Christmas tree ornament in the shape of a snowball.

Albert Thorpe, taking a break from the monotony of dragging, had mounted a net hauler on the *Amy Jo* and turned to gillnetting. With a gang of gillnets a mile to the east of our set, he had offered to put us on our gear. The gear had been in the water for three days and though the water on the bottom had cooled significantly by February, we were at the limit of the time fish would keep. Any longer and we would be picking rotting fish that stank and were the consistency of soft cheese out of the nets. The plan was to follow the *Amy Jo* since we didn't have a working Loran.

Mr. P didn't like the weather forecast. The radio predicted thirty-five knot winds out of the north, but we both knew that the winds would be much stiffer offshore. With sixty-five feet of boat under him, Albert was rarely shy of the weather and was going anyway. The most the *Amy Jo* could do underway was eight knots versus the *Miss Angel's* sixteen, but the heavily buttressed *Amy Jo* was a kinder ride. *Miss Angel* was fast, but as Mr. P put it, she bounced around like a bathtub toy. Mr. P could either wait another day, hoping we could get the Loran repaired, or take a chance on the weather. He chose to follow Albert to the gear. Unfortunately, Albert waited for no one. Mr. P knew that all too well.

When he was fishing you could set your watch by Albert. At 2:30 am he emerged from his pickup, walked fifty feet to the end of the wharf and stepped aboard the *Amy Jo*. The engine would be running, the mercury vapor lights throwing white light from the boom overhead, the deckhand watching Albert and breathing steam in the light out on deck like a horse ready to pull in winter. Albert would dance quickly around the wheelhouse turning on all the electronics, autopilot, radar, loran, plotter, sonar scanner, depth recorder, fish scope, CB radio, two FM radios, single side band radio, and FM radio scanner, open the aft door, lean out and make a slight motion with his hand to cast off the stern line, put the boat in gear to take a strain on the spring line, nosing the *Amy Jo* in against the wharf as he put the rudder hard to port and powered her stern away from the pilings, also swinging the *Amy Jo* away from a ledge that lay directly off her stern, then cast off the bow as he backed out into the harbor with enough angle to stop sharply and turn only once for the channel at full throttle — always full throttle. Unfortunately, I had arrived at the wharf the same time as

Albert and didn't have enough time to get to the ghetto and back. As expected, Kippie was nowhere to be found. At least, not onboard the *Miss Angel*. We had no choice but to go two-handed, just Mr. P and me.

The trip out was uneventful save for the boredom of running at half speed to keep pace with Albert — the two-hour steam took us four hours. We found our end buoy but it was already blowing thirty knots. The fish were scarce, maybe twelve hundred pounds in four miles of net. I alternated picking fish with stepping aft to flake nets. With so few fish, the gang was fairly straight and the snarls were infrequent so flaking single-handed was not that bad. I mainly hauled the corkline and let the leadline and monofilament twine pile up at my feet. Every four or five fathoms, I would reach down and grab the accumulated pile of monofilament and leadline and sweep it to my right. The rhythm was haul, haul, haul, haul, haul, sweep right with the twine and leads, then again haul, haul, haul, haul, haul, sweep — for four-and-a-half miles.

The gang was set northeast-southwest, and with a strong northerly wind, Mr. P had no choice but to jog the *Miss Angel* straight up into the wind and fall off the wind so the gear would be clear of the boat. Since the starboard side was only partially closed with plywood panels, Mr. P was constantly facing directly into the wind in order to watch the gear and gaff the occasional fish that started to either squirm or float free. The wind had been steadily increasing, and by the time we were halfway through the gang, the wind was blowing well over fifty.

I hadn't been out in that kind of wind before and I noticed how differently the surface of the water acted. The chop was now running at ten feet and the tops of the waves were blowing off and creating a kind of foaming layer that would run down the back of the waves. Sometimes the foam would fly through the air as scud, but I remember being more fascinated by the streaky foam that was now coating the backside of every wave. The front side of the waves had also taken on a wrinkled corrugated appearance, the way a small cat's-paw gusts over the surface of a lake and makes the water wrinkle under it. With the wind out of the north and only thirty miles of water between us and the land, we weren't likely to see a long swell develop in that short a distance, even if it continued to blow this hard for some length of time. But it was clear that the chop was going to be very steep and close together and that it would be right in our face all the way home.

Facing into the wind for the two hours that it took to haul the gang, Mr. P's face was well beyond red when we were finished. It had a darker purple shade to it and his lips were turning blue. He stepped into the cockpit and closed the door as I tied down the end buoys. With this catch we would not be setting back and we didn't have the latitude to steam any distance in this breeze. When I stepped inside and closed the hook-and-eye latch on the plywood door, Mr. P had gotten himself a cup of coffee and was jogging the *Miss Angel* slowly ahead. Even jogging slowly, we were hitting the backside of each wave with a thump, a lift upwards, and a small pound down on the other side. Mr. P was on the radio talking to Albert. Albert had an anemometer on the *Amy Jo* and was reporting gusts of sixty-three and sixty-five knots. He had finished earlier but was waiting for us to wrap up before he got underway.

As we headed for home, the best we could do was roughly five knots so the first twenty miles took us a painful six hours. Moderate throttle up then slack on a big wave with a fair amount of green water over the bow. In most weather conditions the *Miss Angel* threw a lot of spray, but green water was the actual wave washing over the bow. If it struck square on the windows, it could break them.

Most boats that worked consistently offshore, and took a lot of green water over the bow because they were heavy in the nose, kept a set of plywood panels to bolt over the forward windows. An aluminum or steel channel was welded to either side of the forward windows that allowed the plywood panels to be easily slid down and locked into place. Usually, *Miss Angel* had the opposite problem. She was so light in the bow that she bounced and pounded—half the boat's length coming out of water and landing with a crash. This was the only time I had seen enough green water over the bow to make me wish we had rigged for plywood panels.

Albert, meanwhile, kept the *Amy Jo* at nearly full throttle. While she was still in view, we watched the *Amy Jo* blast her way through the steep chop sending spray as high as her mast the whole length of the boat. In two hours she was almost out of sight.

No matter how heavily built we thought the *Miss Angel* was, she had numerous crash landings over the next five hours that made us wonder if all the parts put together by workers stoned on fiberglass resin were truly where they were supposed to be. Jumps that took us off our feet at the top were followed by crashes that were so jarring we couldn't stand up without bending our knees when she planted. I remember looking back at the pile of gillnets in the stern and seeing it thrown a foot into the air when the *Miss Angel* landed.

In the beginning we whooped like cowboys and roller coaster riders. But after two hours we fell silent watching each other out of the corner of our eyes wondering if the other was feeling the same things. I have to admit that I considered something happening that would cause me to die. I had no idea what form that would take, but I knew that it would happen very quickly. And I definitely remember regretting that I had chosen this life, moreover that deciding to go fishing was one of the stupidest decisions I had ever made.

I kept saying this is stupid, stupid, stupid.

In the midst of all this Mr. P got a call on the radio from his mother. P's mother was legendary in the amount of time she spent on the radio. She spent most of her time talking on the CB (Citizen's Band) radio, but she had recently acquired an FM radio so she could reach P and hear him clearly offshore. The wind was howling on shore as well as here, and she was calling to see that he was all right.

Apart from their utility in sharing the logistics of arrival, radios were the ultimate public gossip channel. Since they broadcast the contents of every call to everyone tuned into a particular channel, most people edited their conversations accordingly. If they had good news about their catch they lied, sometimes with prearranged codes for various conditions. "Didn't do much," or "About the same as yesterday," could mean you killed them and needed to order more ice for the truck to Boston. Personal conversations, particularly family conversations, were usually kept short or edited to sound businesslike, sticking to estimated time of arrival, what the weather is doing.

But Mr. P and his Mom were completely uninhibited and used the radio like it was a private communications channel, as though no one else was listening. On a regular basis, Mr. P would unabashedly tell his wife Tricia how much he loved her, or what he wanted her to buy at the store, or what he wanted for dinner that night, everything short of sex talk. But that afternoon, Mr. P's mother even succeeded in embarrassing him. In her strong drawn out Maine accent, she voiced her concerns for all to hear.

"Are you all right, honey? It's blowing something terrible in here. Are you going to be all right in that boat of yours?"

That did it. After hours of merciless pounding into a steady fifty-knot gale, Mr. P finally lost it.

"Jesus Christ, Ma," he screamed at the microphone.

"What do you think I'm driving here, a goddamned punt?"

"Of course I'm fine. We're just taking a little longer to get home that's all. Now call Tricia and tell her to turn on the radio at four o'clock so I can talk to her, okay?"

"Okay, honey. I was just worried it was blowing so hard. You know I worry about you in that little boat way out there."

"Jesus Ma, everything is fine. Just call Tricia will you?"

"I love you, dear."

"I love you too, Ma."

As I was listening to Mr. P talk with his mother, I noticed that the sheet metal weather cap on the top length of stovepipe had been blow off by the wind or knocked off by the green water. The lower part of the stovepipe itself was still standing — braced by four small cables bolted into the fore-deck — so we had little risk of taking water through the stove hole in the foredeck. At that point I thought that if losing that little piece of galvanized sheet metal was the worse that happened I'd be happy.

With five hours of crashing and banging behind us, we were finally abreast of Monhegan, roughly twelve miles from Pemaquid Point. The wind was still holding above fifty-five knots according to Albert's wind gauge, but with only a twelve-mile run over water the wind had considerably less chance to make substantial chop, Arthur throttled up and put Miss Angel in the corner.

With less than an hour to the dock, and only the occasional leap and crash to contend with, I started to dress the fish. All of them were frozen hard, the pollock straight as cordwood and most of the codfish permanently curled. In both cases, butchering now required prying open their frozen bellies to rip the entrails. The wind had swung to the northwest and the sky overhead had cleared out pale blue from horizon to horizon. As we reached within one or two miles of land, the temperature dropped as we ran into colder air coming off of the land. Even in February, the water offshore was still roughly forty degrees Fahrenheit and had a considerable warming effect on the air as it made a long trip over water. As a result, the air was typically ten to fifteen degrees warmer offshore. Coming off of the snow-covered shore it felt like the air from an open freezer door on my face, and I could suddenly see my breath again.

By the time we were tied up at Henry's, Mr. P had connected with Tricia and ordered up drinks. Tricia arrived with a bottle of rum and a big jug of Coke and sent them down in the fish basket. We drank rum and Cokes as we unloaded the frozen logs of fish. Kippie showed up and we threw slimy gloves at him and called him an asshole but then we gave him a rum and Coke in a dirty coffee mug and he and I overhauled the gang of gillnets. It was impossible to be mad at Kippie for any length of time.

BUTCHERY

I AM CUTTING POLLOCK — some of the biggest fish we have caught in a long while. They average two and a half to three feet long, twenty-five pounds apiece, and we don't need to rip the gills out because the weather is still cool. I am cutting and Kippie is hauling guts. The mound of guts on the table is a mix of pale and greenish intestines and the contents of stomachs — handfuls of pink half-digested tiny shrimp — krill.

Mixed in with the offal of the big females are pink sacks of spawn the size of your forearm. The males are full of masses of purple and white milt that look like the ruffles on a high school prom tuxedo shirt. Kippie is saving the spawns in five-gallon buckets. If they are not too ripe, we can get thirty-five cents a pound for them. Periodically Kippie gives the mound of guts a shove, or *Miss Angel* takes a roll, and they slide out the chute and overboard and the big black-back herring gulls dive on them screaming and bickering with each other in the water. It is a late haul in a window of calm between winter blows, close to midnight, but the gulls never sleep when it comes to food.

On a one-day set many of the fish are alive. I hold them belly up on the table with my thumb on the underside of their jaws and my forefinger in their eye sockets and I slice through the narrow isthmus of throat between the gills and white belly. As the knife plunges, I am cutting straight through their hearts and often a stream of blood arcs up at me and onto the bib of my oil pants. After a few minutes there are glossy red sheets of blood on my yellow oil pants and on the gray deck. The pollock hearts fall out like pebbles — about the size of cut stone on a driveway — so there is a mound of red sticky pebbles at my feet, some of them still pulsing. Even though they are cut in half they are still beating.

Pollock are a low-priced fish with darkish meat that some people don't prefer, but to me they are beautiful and majestic. Kippie says they look like ministers. Probably because of the dark gray of their skin — maybe that looks like the cassock that ministers wear, or maybe because they are stiff and resolute. All muscle, they don't snake around on the table like a cod or lay there docile and beautiful like a haddock, the pollock beat hard on the picking table if they come over the rail alive.

By the time we are done unloading and cleaned up, it is close on two am. Kippie asks me if I want a drink at the ghetto.

I am polite and walk over with him. We pick up cans of half-frozen soda on the porch and go in. The wind is blowing hard out of the northwest and whistling under the planking of the little shack. The stove is cranked up so hot the doorknob is warm to the touch on the outside. Inside the radio is playing softly. Our sounds are much louder, boots shuffling, male voices trying to be quiet. We sit down and pour white rum and slushy cola and smoke a joint. We watch puffs of dust shoot up through gaps in the flooring as we smoke and feel the northwest wind push on the walls.

"Going to screech all night," I say.

Kippie snorts, "Yeah, let it blow. We're not going anywhere."

I nod, "No more fun and games. No more chasing and butchering and ripping the guts out of anything more today."

We listen to his wife snore and breathe through her dry lips in the next room, the oil stove fluttering with the wind blowing down the stovepipe.

We are dog tired, dragging-ass-fall-down tired.

"I don't know about you, Kippie, but it'd be okay with me if somebody went down aboard tonight and drilled a hole in that plastic bitch and sent her right to the bottom."

"Then we probably wouldn't have to go again until April, right?"

Kippie was grinning under his droopy mustache and bobbing his head as he sucked on the joint.

I get interested in his teeth. We are, both of us, pretty well squashed.

"What's with your front tooth, anyway?"

"This one? It isn't mine," pointing to an off color tooth in the front.

"My old man knocked it out."

"What for?"

"I came home drunk."

"So?"

"I was sixteen. He broke it right off at the gum.

"Then he bought me a car because he felt so bad.

"He bought John Rilleau's '58 Ford, green and white, with white interior, but the front seat was kind of ripped up. John always carried tools in his pockets and ripped up the front seat.

"I got my tooth fixed and I tried like hell to learn how to drive it, but it was a standard and I couldn't get the clutch right, which made the old man even more pissed off."

"But you drive now, don't you?"

"I learned on an automatic up to school."

Darlene groans in the other room. Time to go.

"Hope I don't see you for a week."

"Likewise."

On the porch, breathing in the cold air feels like inhaling menthol.

WATER FIRING

GLADDEN'S WIFE, JAN, CALLS. The family dog has nearly killed their new kitten. I guess the kitten got too close to the dog bowl and the dog grabbed it and shook it by the scruff. Probably broke its neck. Jan is pretty upset and she says both the kids are crying and Gladden isn't home. Says, the kitten is lying on the floor twitching. It isn't dead, but probably isn't going to make it. Jan wants me to help somehow — maybe figure out how to take care of the kitten. She isn't being too clear because she is crying, too. It's dark, about eight at night. I've been asleep since seven so I can make the boat at 2:30 am.

"Jesus, Jan, I'm not sure what I can do."

"Well, I don't know either...but we need to do something." I'm groggy and she's tense.

"I only have the shotgun and that wouldn't be good. Maybe Herb next door has a pistol. I could get that, I suppose."

"Well maybe we can figure something out together...I just need some kind of help, right now. Can you please come down?"

I drive over there not knowing what to do, but when I get there I can see that I do need to do something — anything really — because everyone is crying and they won't touch the kitten who is still lying on the floor next to the dog's bowl. He is breathing a little, but he is out cold and pretty messed up with bits of blood on his neck and a gob of shit hanging onto the matted fur of his hind leg.

The only thing I can think of is to take him down to the town float and put him out of his misery. I ask Jan for a feed sack to put him in but all she has is a paper shopping bag.

"What are you going to do?"

"I'm going to the town float. It's the only thing I can think of, Jan."

She nods. I put him in the bag.

Down at the float, it is very dark, no moon. I kneel down at the water and tear some holes in the paper bag so the water can get in. Push it down in the cold water like I am punching the air out of a blowup toy. But that isn't working.

The bag is floating around because it's dry and it is not sinking, so I open it up and take the kitten in my hand.

The water is firing — tiny sea creatures in the water are lighting up as they are disturbed — and my tearing apart the bag is making sweeping swirls of phosphorescence in the black water. I take the kitten in my hand, free of the paper bag. He seems still, but I know he had been breathing before.

Instead of being inside a feed sack with a stone headed to the bottom as I'd hoped, he is in my hand now. I put him under the water. He starts to struggle. He doesn't struggle strongly at first, but then the cold salt water hits his lungs, I guess, and he begins to thrash and with the water firing, light swirls in the black water where his feet are kicking and I am not sure what to do because he would be half drowned if I pulled him out now and I would have to revive him and he has a head wound and probably a broken neck because he was totally limp when I picked him up to put him in the bag so he is essentially dead, isn't he?

But now he is fighting and I am holding him underwater and I am drowning him. I don't have much time if I am going to do something, change my mind. Whatever it is I have to do it quickly, but then I think maybe this is just a death throe and it is all over anyway, so I hold him with the water firing all around him. And then I feel his chest heave twice or three times as he breathes in the water — and then he is quiet. It is too late, now. There is no way he is coming back after that.

I take him out and lay him on the float. I retrieve a floating piece of the brown shopping bag and wrap him in it and then I take him back to Jan's house.

I knock on the door and hand the dripping package of the brown shopping bag and the wet kitten to Jan when she comes to the door. And then I leave. I know the kids will want to bury him.

I wish I hadn't helped. I still wish that.

SLIME EELS

WEATHER — OR IMPENDING WEATHER — sometimes caused strange behavior on the *Miss Angel*. In my second year with Mr. P, 1976, one night in January, he called me at home around six. We had already made a trip that same day for about thirty-five hundred pounds at a place we called the Outer Harris Ground, but Mr. P was very worried about the weather and wanted to go out again that night and pick up our gear. It was roughly thirty miles steering south by west from Pemaquid Point, a little less than a two-hour steam. I suppressed a groan over the phone as he rattled through the logic.

Earlier that day, we had returned sometime after two pm, tied up, cleaned up with the hose and brushes and all gone home to nap, then get up and have a drink before dinner. We'd been home now for four hours. But after two whiskey and ginger ales, Mr. P had been sitting in front of his TV watching the weatherman and was freaked out by the satellite pictures from the south.

It wasn't that big of a storm, but it was clear that we wouldn't be able to get to our gear for two days or more. The storm was offshore and was going to brush the coast causing a long swell and dish out forty knots directly out of the south. Unlike a northwesterly blow that came off the land and flattened things out, southerly blows caused long heavy seas and tended to be followed by a full day of strong westerly winds. The first day of a southerly blow was unworkable and the second day when it swung westerly was usually just as bad, with nasty cross chop out of the west on top of a long southerly heave. Two sets of wave patterns on top of the other: short waves from the west on top of long waves from the south. Very unpleasant.

To make matters worse, the tide bored very hard through Outer Harris and the gear was set in deep water — averaging sixty fathoms. All the while you were hauling, the tide was sweeping like a river and pressing against the gear that was on its way up. In sixty fathoms of water, you were probably getting tide pressure on ninety fathoms of gear because it bowed out so much on its way up. This made for a godawful strain hauling, breaking the plastic corks as they came over the roller and driving Mr. P crazy. Mostly because he hated to see something else he paid good money for that would need to be fixed later and also because it made him very jumpy.

The plastic corks were football shaped and about six inches long, and the strain either broke open a hole, which eliminated their flotation, or they would sort of explode. Not like a bomb, but with a loud pop and with pieces of black plastic flying around. P would be standing next to the gear coming over the rail, gaffing fish with his right hand, steering the boat with his electric steering handle and remote throttle and gear shift with his left hand, all the while looking down into the water at the gang coming up, like he was peering down into some dark dream. When the strain got that bad, the polypropylene head line was crackling and talking to him like popping corn, and then bang, one of those corks would go off. He said it felt like he was standing next to a firecracker or a dangerous animal.

Arthur Poland, Ed Gastaldo, Bob "Mel" Ryan hauling gillnets

Mr. P mostly overreacted to the whole thing, but it did make him tense. P was tense anyway. But when he was trashing his gear and getting hit in the face with plastic shards from the corks, he was practically hyperventilating.

Sometimes he would say, "I've got to get me a pill. This is too much." And he'd stop hauling and step into the cockpit and take something—I think they were Valium.

Anyway, trying to haul on Outer Harris's even when it was flat calm was a pain in the ass because the tide always ran like a river in springtime, but trying to haul in a long swell turned it into a nightmare. As you rode on a ten or fifteen-foot swell, the pressure on the gear was slacked on the way down to the trough, but amplified on the up swell. Up and down on an unrelenting elevator you couldn't control.

Even so, not getting to our gear for two days was not usually a problem in January because the fish kept pretty well in the cold water. But not on Outer Harris's. For whatever reason, the Harris Ground had become the home of the slime eel. Any more than a one-day set on Harris's and you were likely to lose better than half of your catch to slime eels.

The sea produces some things of beauty, like the scales of a herring with their multicolored shimmering backing, a paste you could smear on your fingers that looks like silver eye shadow. Or the beautiful green and blue striped coat of a mackerel, the proud and powerful swimmer with a desperate silver face and wild black eyes. But slime eels were the most disgusting sea creatures I have ever encountered.

Also called hagfish, slime eels are about as big around as your finger and have skin the color of human Caucasian skin when it comes out of a hot shower—a bright pink. This pink color is not something you would expect in a sea creature and is part of the eerie quality of the slime eel. They don't appear to have eyes, at least we could never find them, but the books say the eyes are there and that hagfish have a good sense of sight and smell. They obviously have a wonderful sense of smell judging from their efficiency at finding fish trapped in gillnets. Slime eels bored through the side of the fish and ate them from the inside out, leaving the skeleton and the skin intact. Flesh gone, they looked like a fancy paper kite made to look like a fish.

That night, going back out again all stemmed from the fact that Mr. P could not stand the thought of coming back in two days and having to pick six or seven thousand pounds of racks and fish kites out of four miles of net. "It'll bring tears to me eyes," was the line he liked to use.

Back out on Outer Harris, we hauled the end line up at 8:30 pm and the first net broke water, the jeweled droplets on the green monofilament in the floodlight. The fish were almost entirely pollock, but nearly every other fish had two or three eels slither out of their gill covers.

Kippie stood in the dark of the stern flaking twine while I picked. The fishing was not very heavy and the fish hadn't had the time to suffer and snarl themselves up so they were easily unsnagged. Kippie went forward and got an old oil coat which he threw in the down-side scupper. This plugged the water running off of the deck and the slime eels backed up against the oil coat as they slithered off of the picking table. Soon we had hundreds of pink slime eels blindly snaking on deck, trying to make their way back to the water, lifting their heads over each other, rubbing each other, not seeing each other, glistening in the light of the bare bulb deck lights.

We let them freeze there and then shoveled them overboard with the slush when we were sure that they were dead. It had begun to snow out of the northeast and the breeze made for a wet ride home, but we were tied up in South Bristol at half past midnight. We covered the fish in the bins to unload in the morning and headed home.

WHEN THINGS HAPPEN

GILLNETTING WITH MR. P, I discovered an aspect of my behavior that many people have in them but never get a chance to see. It was not something that could be learned, and it was not something that was easy to identify when sizing up a potential deckhand. It was a reflex reaction that some people talk about experiencing in trauma situations — something I considered a gift and was grateful for.

Working on the water entails dealing with unusual events and experiences, all of which usually happen very quickly. I expect it's similar to firefighting. If something makes a hole in the hull of a boat, water rushes in extremely fast. Something catches on fire, the fire spreads extremely fast. Nylon lines under a heavy load part and whip past your face extremely fast. All of these unanticipated events cause most sailors and fisherman to be in an altered state of alertness usually characterized as sleeping with one eye open. It's not a bad description.

Fishing brought the frequency of those experiences to a new level. On the one hand, statistically, spending significant time on the water meant that you were almost guaranteed to experience a crisis of one kind or another on a regular basis. But the awkward nature of the fishing process itself was the main contributor.

Fishing usually involves going some distance in a boat too lightly loaded for its overall design, putting complex and heavy equipment into the ocean under a variety of sea conditions, the process of which significantly disables the maneuverability of the boat, loading that heavy fishing equipment up with unpredictable amounts of heavier fish, sometimes also loading up your fishing gear with unexpected foreign objects like rocks or unexploded ordinance, sometimes snagging your gear on underwater immovable objects like wrecks, then retrieving the fishing gear plus fish, loading the boat with gear and fish, and then steaming home in a boat that is often too heavily loaded for its design.

To make matters worse, during the time that I went, commercial fishing was completely unregulated from an equipment point of view. No one ever went on board your boat and inspected the equipment you had assembled to determine whether it would kill you when it flew apart or whether it would likely drown you when it locked up and rolled your boat over. In the 1970s, you could design a piece of equipment for your boat that would sink it the first time you used it or crushed your hand when you threw the big lever, and no government agency or inspector would ever stop you from leaving the dock. In that environment bad things happened all the time.

Instinctively dealing with bad things is a gift. I learned early on that I often had an involuntary reflex reaction to life-threatening situations. They caused me to go into another zone of operation. In that zone, I would find myself on autopilot calmly doing the right thing — sometimes while other people were screaming at each other, or were frozen by the knowledge that we were all in a really bad fix. It was nothing I could control, but something I was grateful for. Kind of like being able to suddenly play the piano beautifully for five minutes, even though you have never touched one. But then it was gone and I was back to normal.

Sometimes the bad things started small and barely exhibited the signs that they would turn into a bigger mess. Those situations were the worst because they looked so innocent. And there were deckhands like Kippie who were — themselves — so innocent that they were simply unaware anything bad could happen. In other words, Kippie had no sense of danger and not a care in the world. He wasn't fearless. He was oblivious.

In my second year on the *Miss Angel*, we were fishing a place called Toothaker Ridge. I always loved the name, though I have no idea of the origin. Toothaker was a small hump forty-two miles to the southwest — a long trip — but we were catching a fair number of haddock there at the end of March so we kept going back. It was small enough that we had to double back several times with a long gang of nets just to fit them on top of the ridge. Early spring could be hard because groundfish activity was just barely coming alive and if one spot heated up sooner than others, you were better off sticking with it than scouting around. The water was very cold, in the range of the mid to upper 30s, having chilled down all winter with very little relief. At those temperatures, you had roughly fifteen minutes of consciousness if you went overboard, probably less before you reached irreversible hypothermia.

Spring fishing was usually very light, so the crew was just Mr. P, me, and Kippie. We had hauled and picked seventy-five nets of fifty fathoms each for around 2,500 pounds of cod and haddock and were setting back again. Kippie was tending the leadlines and I was tending the corks. Like most gillnet boats, we set the nets over a set of steel goal posts mounted on the stern to avoid snarls and to keep the nets from catching and tearing on other parts of the boat or snagging crewmembers as they ran out over the stern. But occasionally a single, football shaped plastic cork from deep in the pile would get picked up by a mesh on top of the pile and start to pull the whole stack of nets over the stern in a lump, or a kink in the leadline would do the same thing. That possibility caused Kippie and me to stand on either side of the pile so we could remedy the situation quickly.

Better than halfway through the set, I looked over and saw Kippie leaning way back and bracing his foot against the transom. He looked over at me but didn't say a word. When I looked at his foot, I could see that a bight of leadline had taken a turn around the toe of his rubber boot and was about to shoot him overboard like an arrow from a longbow.

The gang of nets was on its way to the bottom some forty-five fathoms down and I pictured Kippie, his boot still caught and now his snaps and buttons snarled up in the monofilament, on his way down with them. He was likely wearing two pairs of clothes and a long pair of boots, over which he wore oil pants and oil jacket. At these temperatures, the shock of the cold water sometimes caused an involuntary gasp, which made you inhale some water, but the multiple layers he had on might prevent the cold water from shocking him quickly and might even give him some initial buoyancy. Even so, the probability was not high that Kippie would be able to successfully fight his way out of the monofilament while he tried to kick off his long hip boots from under oil pants. The only way to get him out of the net would be to aggressively back down the *Miss Angel* without sucking him and the gang of nets into the propeller (what we called the wheel). Once we had enough slack in the descending gang of nets, we could quickly pass the net up to the net hauler and haul Kippie back up like a fish. But he would likely be dead at that point since he couldn't breathe like a fish.

I yelled at Mr. P, who always kept the aft window open in the wheelhouse. He threw the boat into reverse and started to back the *Miss Angel* down. As she backed down, I lay down across the pile of monofilament to take the bight of leadline off the toe of Kippie's boot. Kippie couldn't lean over and do it himself because the strain was too great on his foot. He needed to lean back with the heel of his boot hooked under the gunwale so he wouldn't get slingshotted over the stern.

While we waited a few seconds for the *Miss Angel* to back down enough to take the strain off of the leadline, he finally said something. But what he did say told me that he really did not understand his predicament. He said calmly, "It's okay, my toes aren't in there."

By this, Kippie meant that even though the bight had strangled the tip of his boot, his toes had not been pushed all the way to the end of his boot, and the noose was not tightening down on his big toe. This fact caused Kippie to believe that the world was in complete harmony. He had no sense of how close he had come to becoming a pasty white dead person. I freed his boot and we went back to setting.

REMINDERS

IN THE HEART OF MAKING GOOD MONEY, June and July, the weeks passed quickly and we slept like the dead and rose reluctantly in the quiet hours to commute offshore. Certainly, the farthest thing from our minds was how we were dealing out death and destruction to sea life on a daily basis. But occasionally, we did catch creatures that made us feel bad, and they would live long in our memories and color these moments of good fortune.

Once a year we would find a blunt-nosed harbor porpoise wound up in the gear and have to cut him out of the twine. We were in deep water forty miles offshore, and had no idea what caused a harbor porpoise to dive to the bottom in seventy fathoms (420 feet) of water, but it happened. And like a message, or a reminder of what we were doing, the porpoise was always dead. Unable to get to the surface for a breath he had drowned, and the only way to get him out of the twist was to cut his tail off so the snarl would fall apart. Each time I cut their tails off I marveled at how much their skin was like hard black rubber, like a wet suit made out of recycled rubber tires.

That July, when I'd finished cutting the drowned porpoise out of his corkscrew snarl, and we could all see his red flesh that looked so much like our own, Mr. P told me in a low voice, "Some people say it tastes good, like beef. But I've never tried it."

Then Kippie and I cradled him against our chests and horsed him over to the rail, tipped him like a dead sailor sewn into his hammock to let him slide out of our arms, and then watched as he dove soundlessly into the water without a splash.

Kippie said, "He may be a little fella...but see how heavy he is, how he dives down so fast."

Still transfixed at the rail and staring deep into the water, he added, "Ain't that somethin."

"Yeah, headed for the bottom and the corruption and reduction of the sea."

Kippie looked at me crooked-like and said, "That's some real philosophy, man. Where'd you come up with that shit?"

"I think they used to say stuff like that when they did a burial at sea. Like in the Napoleonic wars. I guess I must've read it somewhere."

"The what wars?"

"You know, in the days of sail when they had all those cannons on double-deckers and were blasting away at each other."

"Oh yeah, in the olden days."

"Yeah, the olden days."

Later when we were done shacking and sorting the fish and were scrubbing up and washing down with the deck hose, Kippie wanted to talk more — like the porpoise had stirred up something we couldn't get away from, some stuff we needed to talk about that we didn't know was there before.

"How come you don't have kids?" he asked.

"I got enough problems without having to worry about kids."

"Yeah, but don't you think there are kids of yours sitting out there just waiting to be born?"

"What are you talking about? What kids?"

"Don't you think they're like waiting out there to come on stage?"

"What, like actors waiting in the wings of the theater to come on and do stuff?"

"Yeah, like that. Just waiting to come on stage and into your life."

"My life is fucked up enough as it is, Kippie."

"Aw come on, that's no way to live, is it?"

"It's the only way I know how, at the moment. And besides, didn't you feel bad with your wife and your new baby living in that little fish shack out on the wharf all winter long, freezing your asses off?"

"Naw, he didn't mind. And it weren't so bad there, really. Was practically free anyway. We just paid for the oil and the insulation I put up. And besides, it got better. Was just cold for a little while."

"Well, I wish I had your optimism, Kippie, I really do. Right now, I'm just working on this floating slaughterhouse so I can afford to finish building my house, that's all I know."

"Yeah, but you're good at what you do. You're good with that knife, and you won't always be doin' this."

"I won't?"

"No, you won't."

"Yeah, well you're probably right about that, Kippie. But I'm not bringing no kids into this mess, that's for goddamned sure."

"All right, but I know they're out there waiting for you."

"If that's what you want to believe, you're welcome to it."

"Maybe there's things you can't see. Ever thought of that?"

"Yeah, maybe there's things I can't see. I'll give you that much."

I brushed it all off, all the stuff that he'd managed to dredge up about my reluctance to have children. In reality, I believed that I would be a horrible father — driven, unkind, never there — probably a drunk with a temper. And I had to admit it that Kippie seemed fundamentally happier than me, maybe even happier than I was ever going to be. Maybe that's why I yelled at him and berated him for no good reason.

"Jesus, mother, Mary and Joseph, will you get that pool of blood over there in the corner with the deck hose. I need a coffee and you're holding up the works."

"Sure thing, chief."

See, I thought, no problem. Nothing bothers him. Nothing at all. And he beats me at cribbage, hell he beats everyone in South Bristol at cribbage. No matter how smart I think I am, he's happy and I'm turning into a miserable sonofabitch.

WATCHING TV

LOYD CUSHMAN WAS THIS strange guy out of Portland. He ran the
Miss Julie, and lately he was becoming a regular pain in the ass for
anyone else fishing south of Monhegan Island. Every other boat we fished
with set their gillnet gear northeast-southwest, or north-south. Most of
the hard bottom ridges ran northeast-southwest, so you could set along
a ridge, up and down the hard bottom and just touch the mud where the
slime eels seemed to live.

Lloyd was different. He would set across everything and everybody,
east-west, in a straight line. Worse yet, he had these big honking six-foot
grappling hooks for anchors at either end of the string. The grapples must
have been a hundred and fifty pounds or more because there was no way
you could haul his gear up at all. We tried a few times, got it close to the
surface, but Lloyd's gang of nets was as taut as a bowstring and we were
tearing up our own gear in the process. The strain was ripping our string
out of the cast iron teeth of the old net hauler as we tried to bring the
snarl up.

When other guys set across our gear, most of the time the anchors
or bags of rocks at the end of the string would be light enough, or small
enough, to drag. That way we could get the whole mess up to the surface
to work with. Once we had it up, we could untie our nets at a fifty-fathom
break, or just cut and retie. That was the protocol. But Lloyd's gear was
impossible.

Mr. P had talked enough with Lloyd on the radio—everyone had.
When we were hauling, Mr. P was running the hauler and driving the boat
from the deck station, and he always ran the radio through the deck speakers,
so we could all hear. A lot of news was passed over the radio, and a lot of
lies. We always heard Lloyd talking while he was hauling—a slow talker

with long pauses as he held the transmit button down while he took a big breath or sighed. Very theatrical.

And then when he was tired of talking to someone, he'd say something like, "Well, I've got one coming," as in "I've got a fish coming over the rail and I need to deal with it," which was a lie because he never left the wheelhouse.

Mr. P decided to go aboard the *Miss Julie* one day to see what Lloyd was all about. Lloyd was very friendly over the radio, said, sure, sure. Come aboard, boys, look the operation over. See what you think of it.

It was a calm day so Mr. P put the *Miss Angel* gently alongside and he and I hopped on board the *Miss Julie*.

What a scene. We'd heard that Lloyd was kind of a slipper skipper, and hired anybody he could find off the streets of Portland, but jeeze what a hard looking crew they were. Honestly, they looked like street people. There were six of them. Their oil clothes were all ripped up and they had long scraggly hair and beards and they didn't say anything to us at all when we came aboard. It was like we weren't even there. They just kept picking fish from an absolute rat's nest of a pile in front of them.

Lloyd had been in the business forever and was famous for making a business of doing nothing but gillnetting. He rigged all his own nets instead of buying them rigged, and set tremendous quantities of gear. He also used incredibly small mesh — it looked like three and a half or four inch — so he caught everything that moved and there was a lot of picking. The rumor was that he had a crew of grunts off the streets of Portland and paid them a salary — no shares — and when they would quit, he'd just hire some more. No experience required.

That day Lloyd was into a pile of dogfish. There is nothing worse. When you're catching dogfish in a gillnet you just want to commit suicide instead of haul anymore. You can't sell them, they smell bad, kinda musky like old socks, they squirm around on the picking table and roll themselves over like snakes and try to stab you with the spine on their tail, and when you throw them overboard a lot of them swim back into the net immediately and get caught again. The deck of the *Miss Julie* was littered with dogfish livers and blood and these really disgusting broken yellow egg sacks that were attached to the unborn baby dogfish. I guess one of the guys had been gutting them before they threw them overboard.

Lloyd didn't even stop the hauler when we came on board. The hauler kept right on turning round and round and the twine kept piling up on the table. One of his guys was standing at the roller with a hammer where the twine came up over the rail, and was knocking every dog on the head as it came over the steel roller so it wouldn't snake around so much.

In the wheelhouse, Lloyd was watching The Today Show on TV. He had sneakers on and wasn't wearing oil clothes. He clutched the *Miss Julie* in gear every once in a while and spun this big destroyer steering wheel around to keep her stern-to-the-tide. He said, "What do you think? Nice operation, right?"

You couldn't even see the guys on deck from the wheelhouse. All you could see was the half of the hauling head that protruded through the wheelhouse bulkhead and the twine going round it full of dogfish and every once in a while a pollock or a codfish.

I said, "Jesus Christ, Lloyd, that's a lot of dogfish isn't it?"

He said, "Dogfish? Naw, this ain't bad. This ain't bad at all. When they're head-to-toe and three abreast for three or four miles, that's a lot of dogfish."

P and I just looked at each other and then Lloyd kicked the *Miss Julie* ahead again and said, "Stick around, Gene Shalit is coming on with the movie reviews in a minute."

Mr. P said, "Hey Lloyd, is there any way I can get you to set a little different like? Most of the guys out here set no'theast-sou'west. You know, up and down the hard bottom. Right now, you're setting right across everybody and your gear is so heavy we can't even get it up to get clear."

"Naw, that's just the way I've always done it. The tide runs out of the east so hard out here, it's just easier to set east-west. Over hill and dale. Up over the mountain and then down in the mud. Then I can just haul to the west with the tide, you know? Go with the flow, right?"

He continued, "I am sorry about getting over on top of people. And I use those Christly big anchors cause my nets get so loaded up with fish that they get all balled up if I don't, you know what I mean?"

"Okay, Lloyd. Just thought I'd ask."

We paused while Jane Pauley talked about a young mother who had thrown her baby out the window to save it from a fire.

Then Mr. P broke the awkward silence and said, "All right, all right, Lloyd, we gotta get going."

"Wait a minute, c'mon guys, don't you want to watch Gene Shalit? The guy's a riot. That big fucking mustache, he looks like he has a Halloween mask on for Christ's sake."

"Nah, we gotta go. We'll catch you on the radio, Lloyd."

"Okay guys, don't get hurt going over the side. We'll see you around."

A lot of my friends who were lobster catchers said they would rather work in a factory than go gillnetting like we were doing, but I thought we had it pretty good after visiting with Lloyd and his guys. Going aboard the *Miss Julie* was kind of like small town meets big city. Except it was on the water.

EARLY PARTY

I HAD BEEN WITH MR. P FOR MORE than a year, when my friend Robert Rothstein came to visit one February morning from Monhegan. He called me on the radio while we were steaming home from some ridge southwest of the island. With a three am start and only a few fish — two thousand cod and pollock — I figured to be walking in the door of my house sometime in the late morning. Robert was steaming to South Bristol to sell his lobsters and to fix a leaking gas tank on his boat. I offered that he should come by for lunch and spend the night on our couch.

The weather was crappy all the way home, blowing thirty-five knots out of the west, making a nasty cross chop on top of a long southerly swell. We could hardly stand up cutting the fish because the *Miss Angel* was jumping around so much, throwing her ass up into the air and coming down with an awful shudder every once in a while, so we knocked off and sat on the hatch coaming until we got in the lee of Damariscove and Outer Heron islands.

By the time we had weighed and boxed the fish and scrubbed the blood off the bins, I was home by eleven am — and there was Robert sitting with Joy over a cup of coffee. Robert was from away, like Joy and me. His father had been a doctor on Long Island and owned a house on Monhegan, so Robert had summered on the island all through his childhood. Unlike the mainland, being from away was almost the norm on Monhegan. It was a tough place to live, twelve miles offshore, no electricity unless you installed your own diesel generator, and the lobster season started in January and ended in June. Fishing on Monhegan meant living on Monhegan, so almost anyone willing to put up with the isolation and the hassle was welcome to it.

In the winter, Monhegan was the bleakest place I'd ever seen. As an island, it is small — only a mile long and a half mile across — and it has a harbor that is a nightmare by anyone's measure.

In fact, calling it a harbor is a generous use of the term. Monhegan's harbor is formed by the proximity of another small island, Manana, so it is not closed like a cove. Manana Island is really just a rock with a Coast Guard station on it, and lays a scant 250 yards from Monhegan itself, so the wishful harbor that is created between the two islands is more like a gut or a channel. So much so, that an already strong east-to-west offshore current gets squeezed between the two islands of Monhegan and Manana — like the wind between the skyscrapers of Manhattan — producing an even stronger current that can run through the harbor like a river.

Weather protection is not much better. The harbor is partially protected from the northeast by a large rock known as Smuttynose, but lays completely open to the southwest. As a result, winter storms tend to roar through the harbor with a vengeance.

Robert sat there drinking coffee with Joy, but it had already been a long day for both of us and we hardly saw each other during the winter so we decided to start drinking rum and coke. Noon was our five o'clock as far as we were concerned. As we got a buzz on, Robert told us the story of his leaking gas tank.

Robert had this little red boat. At twenty-six feet, it was easily the smallest lobster boat on the island and I don't think she even had a name. He had bought the boat the winter before for three thousand dollars and she was powered by a small four-cylinder gasoline engine.

He sat there telling us the story at the table, big Fu Manchu moustache, three day growth of beard, a great mop of curly auburn hair like a French courtier, old gray sweatshirt cutoff at the forearms to keep them clear of the bait juice. Joy was smoking cigarettes and I decided to light up a joint as the story began to unfold.

"You know my little red boat is always easy for me to spot in the harbor. It's the only red boat. Everybody else's is white. So we had this terrible blow last winter. I mean it blew close to 120 knots out of the west and it was very cold and I had never been through a big blow out there, so I talked to one of the old-timers the day before and I asked him what's going to happen if it really blows hard like they say during the night, and he just said, we'll see what's left in the morning. There may not be anything left.

Or something like that. You know, I was kind of shocked, right? That was all he said.

"So I got up in the morning and a bunch of us were down on the fish beach and I couldn't see my boat, you know the red hull standing out against all the white boats, and the tears are streaming down my cheeks. But then after a little while I realize that all the boats are covered in ice because the wind has made such a lot of spray during the night, you know by taking the tops right off the chop, and it's frozen on everybody's boats because it's so cold and I see that my boat is still there but I can't see the red because the hull is all coated with ice. That was a bad moment, you know?

"So anyway, I get this leak in my gas tank yesterday. It's an old copper tank, under the stern deck, right, and I've heard all these stories about guys getting the gasoline in their bilge and then they go to start their engine the next morning and it explodes and blows them right out of the boat. So I'm really scared to start my boat even to come in here to get it fixed in South Bristol. So my neighbor tells me the thing to do is to pour like a quart of ammonia in the bilge and the ammonia fumes somehow lay down on top of the gasoline fumes and it doesn't blow up even if there's a spark. So I go ahead and pour in the ammonia, and I get into my skiff alongside. You've gotta laugh, right. There I am at my little boat on the mooring, right, standing in my skiff in case it blows up and reaching in over the wash rail to the starter key to start it up. Pretty funny stuff."

Then, as Robert and I are sucking on the last bit of the roach and laughing and coughing hysterically about this story, we hear this *clomp clomp clomp*, on the front steps. Our house is all windows across the front to get the sun in the winter and it's all one big room anyway, really just a big cabin. And there we are stoned and drunk and we see that it's my neighbor from way down at the end of our lane, a retired insurance guy from New York, a fit man with short cropped white hair who moved to Maine three years ago and he's knocking on the door. The house reeks of marijuana and we have a bottle of rum on the table and we're having a big laugh and guffaw and there is my neighbor come to tell us that he is closing up his house to go away to Mexico for late winter and spring. Of course we open the door and invite him in and offer him a drink and do our best to explain that we've been up since the wee hours and all that. He's come to ask us to look in on the house now and then. He doesn't seem to mind, but God knows what he is really thinking.

NICKEL HAKE

AUGUST OF 1976, NEARLY TWO YEARS with Mr. P. We were on a run of very poor fishing, burning hot and flat calm every day, and hake were all we could catch. No codfish, no pollock. We didn't know why. The good fish had just gone to some place we didn't know about. Morning at 2:30, thumping onto the deck of the *Miss Angel*, making sandwiches for lunch, getting coffee on, the bilge smell and fiberglass resin, oil leaks baking on warm diesel, squatting in the pitifully small engine compartment, head just out of the round hatch, bubbling yellow paint peeling for the rust beneath, checking oil on the dipstick, headphones on against the clattering, running Caterpillar, paper towel coal black with the oil, smells of sulfur, rub it on my fingertips, feel the grit.

Make breakfast and coffee, the hull vibrating from the engine idling, the wet exhaust spitting seawater through the transom. My head full of voices, why are we still doing this, look at all the damn things that can go wrong, you must be a damned fool.

The week before the fuel tank vent under the gunwale where the fish bin was full of slimy hake had started sucking seawater and blood and fish flesh juice back into the fuel tank. We were pouring water from the deck hose, cold seawater to keep the fish cooled down and fresh. But the water was getting sucked down through the vent into the fuel tank and then the diesel would just spontaneously shut down thirty miles offshore. The filtration system circulating all the diesel fuel was plugged with seawater and gluey clear slime and the slippery clots of blood from the pink hake bin. It was not a pretty picture.

Hake are a soft fish with a disagreeable pinkish skin and an ungraceful swimming motion like an eel. You can't even make a good chowder with them because they fall apart so, and their flavor is little better than a watery gruel. A poor man's fish, in the best of times, they were selling for ten cents a pound. Since it cost us five cents to truck them to Boston, we cleared a nickel a pound. At one point the price dropped to seven and a half cents and Mr. P threw in the towel and refused to go. But at the end of the month, the price shot up as high as eleven cents and he decided we should go back at it again.

The worst part of catching seven thousand or ten thousand pounds of hake was the shacking. Every hake had to be gutted and headed and the heads had to be kept and sold for lobster bait. Hacking off and then handling the heads was that much more grunt work for next to nothing. At six cents a pound for the fish, and six dollars a bushel for the heads, it was hardly worth it.

In the last week of August, we set off for the Outer Fall with a full crew. It was fifty miles, a three-and-a-half-hour steam. And since we had no gear in the water and were setting for the first time in weeks, we couldn't very well steam back and out again—an extra hundred miles—so we shut down the engine and spent the night laying on the end buoy of our gear. I was miserable and ready to quit.

We never spent the night on the *Miss Angel*. She was a wonderfully fast day boat, but not much for camping out. Unlike a wooden boat, she bounced around like a cork and transmitted every lap of water that hit the hull.

South Bristol harbor

Amid the farting and snoring of four other bunkmates, I barely slept at all and spent most of the night wondering why I was still doing this to myself.

In the morning, we barely had three thousand pounds of fish, so we put the nets in the stern and set off prospecting. Cleaned up, I made my way onto the foredeck and sat there on an upturned bucket with my hand on the forestay — the one quiet spot on a fiberglass boat. The sky was very hazy and not a breath of air stirred the water, so hazy that it was hard to pick out the horizon. The combination gave me the eerie feeling of sitting in a large room full of water. I used to enjoy standing in the wheelhouse watching the sound machine and talking to Mr. P about his intentions and thoughts of where the fish might be, but I had lost interest.

Next to me was a coil of line and a harpoon. We always kept a harpoon on the foredeck in case we came across bluefin tuna finning on the surface and could put the iron to them. At the new price of $3.00 a pound, it was well worth the effort. Besides, we were just coming back from a broker trip and didn't have enough fish to pay for the fuel we burned. After half an hour, I began to see a few fins in the distance. It was mirror-like so I could see them a long way off. I rapped on the cockpit window and shouted at Mr. P through the open vent and into the clatter of the wheelhouse, "Fins about four or five miles." He nodded and I unfastened the harpoon from the forestay.

I'd seen tuna finning before, but these were different. These fins were huge. And they were moving slowly. If they were tuna, they were awfully big. Plus, they were everywhere. By the time we got up on them, there were black fins as far as you could see in almost every direction. Each fin was about 200 yards apart, almost evenly spaced. It was also strange that the fish weren't jumping or sounding. The fins just soaked along slowly, and they were all moving in the same direction — roughly southwest.

By now, Mr. P had throttled back and had pushed open the cockpit window so we could talk. As we came up on the first fin, he yelled, "Give it to him, go on give him the iron." But I wasn't about to throw it. We had slowed down and were barely moving so I got a good look at the fish. Its broad back was brown and speckled with white spots like the hide of a fawn and it had a huge mouth that gaped open like a bushel basket and showed pale pink inside. "It's a fucking huge basking shark," I called back.

Mr. P threw the boat out of gear and ran out on deck to gawk over side with the rest of the crew. The fish was as big as the *Miss Angel*, at least forty feet long, nose to tail. Curious to see if they were all that big, Mr. P pointed the boat to the southwest and came alongside another one. It too, was as long as the boat, just lazing along and obviously unconcerned that we were there. They showed no acceleration of flight, though I am sure they could see the shadow and shape of the boat, and feel the vibration of the engine. At one point as we were alongside a third shark, its big boney tail swept gently against the *Miss Angel* and gave her a little roll.

"Hunh," Mr. P commented, "I guess we won't be throwing any iron into those old things. That's for goddamned sure."

What caused that many basking sharks to be there some thirty-five miles south of Monhegan, all headed to the southwest as far as you could see at the end of August, 1976 was beyond me. Something good to eat, I'm sure, but they were headed as though they all had a compass and a plan, and we seemed as inconsequential to them as anything could possibly be.

WHO ARE YOU

AT THIS POINT, I HAD PRETTY much decided that this was my last trip with Arthur. My time was over. Cutting my way through a mountain of cheap hake was more like the numbing boredom of a regular job than fishing. I was ready to move on.

I really didn't know what I was moving on to, but I was leaving the *Miss Angel* and I told him so. As I was down in the forecastle collecting my gear, Mr. P came aboard to see me off. He waited until I was done packing my small duffel with the change of clothes and sleeping bag I kept in my bunk. He stood in the companionway, blocking my exit from the galley, looking down at me gathering my belongings. As I faced him, about to mount the ladder with everything in hand, Mr. P surprised me.

Here was a man I had spent almost two years with, taking risks I never thought I would take, someone I would realize later I had gotten to know at a level of mutual fear and commitment that was rare in this world, someone with whom I had endured deckhands who either couldn't get up in the morning or couldn't stop the previous night's party, and he stood there and asked me a simple question.

"Who are you, really?" he said.

I was speechless for some time, and just stood there, so he rephrased the question.

"I mean, what are you really doing here? Are you writing a book or something, or are you running away from the law?" he continued.

I couldn't believe what I was hearing, but the honesty of Mr. P's question was unmistakable.

I could tell from his face that Mr. P was clearly genuine in wondering whether I must have some ulterior motive for pounding around in the Gulf of Maine. And it wasn't the length of time we had been together that made his question so startling. It was the fact that he had never brought it up, or given any indication that he was curious about my past or where I had come from, especially given the intensity of the emotions we had been through together — crushing levels of disappointment, exhaustion, and fear.

We had taken winter trips when the two of us honestly wondered whether we would make it home alive but were afraid to admit that to each other. We had been through an entire winter and shrimp season where we didn't catch enough to eat — a winter when I took home a total of $600 for four months of work — because our dragging gear was so messed up. We had made it through high-volume gluts of fish that dropped the price to six cents per pound, senseless work that brought us to a level of exhaustion I would never have believed a person could actually remain awake through, let alone function in. We had endured broker trips in February, running fifty miles offshore to haul two miles of gillnets for two fish. Did he think that I had stuck it out this long for something other than making enough money to survive? How could this be, I wondered?

It was ironic, as well. Writing a book, indeed. Though I had intended to work seasonally and write in the offseason, my plan had failed and I had thoroughly given up on writing. Isolated in a town of five hundred, with no connections to other writers, I was totally blocked.

Instead of continuing with the tortured life of non-writing, I had turned to a new religion, fishing. I wanted life to be as simple as possible. Work on the water, hopefully making some big money in a short period of time without getting killed, and live in the pure beauty of the Maine coast. These simple goals were about the only clarity I could get to at the time, but it was also clear — given P's question — that I was still a mystery to him. The harshness of our experiences in those two years was certainly not on a par with sharing a foxhole in combat, but they revealed the raw places in our characters and exposed the limits of our tolerances and our fears in ways that could never be repeated. Even so, I felt that I would always remain an outsider, no matter what.

There were many things I wouldn't miss about the *Miss Angel* — the incessant whistle of her turbocharger which I was sure was making me deafer every day, and the mad unnatural jumping of her buoyant plastic hull. I wouldn't miss these things, but I knew that being on this boat had changed me forever in ways that I couldn't explain.

I had handled things that I didn't know I could handle. I had learned to judge whom I could trust to do the right thing in bad situations and whom I could not. And I also knew that Mr. P had succeeded in getting to know me at a depth that would probably not occur again. We had seen involuntary reactions and raw parts of each other that neither of us had ever seen before and we both knew that counted for something.

Yet I couldn't answer his question. The voices in my head had been interrogating me along the same lines, but they were more like harsh critics yelling at me. No, the honest curiosity of Mr. P had stunned me and left me speechless. Arthur Poland had no other agenda than understanding who I was, but his questions had exposed the fact I had no clear idea of where I was headed.

"Look Arthur, I'm just a guy. That's all," was the best I could muster.

He obviously didn't believe this line of bullshit, but he was kind enough to keep it to himself and step out of the companionway to let me pass.

ADULT ATLANTIC HERRING *(Clupea harengus)*

Part Three

NORMIE & CANDY B

SMOKERMAN

AFTER NEARLY TWO YEARS butchering ground fish on the *Miss Angel*, I took a long stretch of time off. I slept as long as I liked and worked on the house, winter arrived, I read books and lounged around like a bum.

Over time, I realized that I actually felt good about Arthur. I had asked for the berth and I had earned it. He hadn't cheated me, the work was what I asked for and the money had been good — enough to pay for someone else to finish the siding on my house and build a porch and steps, even enough to buy a decent woodstove.

But I wasn't done with fishing. Like many who worked on the water, I wasn't sure that I could bear to do anything else. I had tasted the delicious shift in priorities away from the world of regular jobs, and had become a permanent misfit when it came to keeping to a schedule. I think every fisherman goes through that transformation. You work for a share in the business. When you catch fish, you make money. When you don't catch fish, you work on the gear and the boat, or regroup and push on to the next species. It is that simple. Moreover, I relished the fact that it was work on demand, not on a schedule. I didn't care what day of the week it was, but when I made a commitment to go I suited up and went.

In March, 1977, after six months of vacation, I went back to chasing herring and signed on with purse-seiner Normie Brackett. At forty-six years old, Normie was a seasoned veteran and proven producer. Unfortunately, he had already lived through three minor heart attacks. Just how minor I had no idea, but they were probably related to the fact that he smoked five packs of unfiltered cigarettes a day. Regardless, Normie was one of best shoal herring seiners around. I knew of another named Bobby Warren out of Carver's Harbor on Vinalhaven Island. But Normie fished out of New

Candy B, New Harbor

Harbor, a thirty-minute drive, and I didn't want to move to Vinalhaven, so I signed on with Normie.

As I soon found out, saying that you were fishing out of nearby New Harbor was merely nominal and did not translate into spending more time at home. Purse-seining for herring meant lots of travel. You went where the fish were, and Normie was gone all the time. But that was the only way to make money.

Herring can be notoriously hard to catch consistently, and have driven many a sane man out of the business. It is an all or nothing game. But at a coarse-grained level, the inshore stock have a predictable summer-to-winter migration which causes the fleet to travel with them. In summer herring go north — into the Gulf of Maine. And in winter they move south — Isles of Shoals, Cape Ann, Boston Bay and then through the Cape Cod Canal and points southward.

With that much travel we lived on the boat and drove home on the weekends. It also meant long hours steaming to find the fish. As a result, we all did our share of smoking and coffee drinking to pass the time and dampen the frustration, but Normie had us all beat with his five packs a day.

To understand how someone could smoke that many cigarettes in a single day, you really need to consider the whole twenty-four hour period. Even Normie couldn't suck down that many smokes without making use of the full twenty-four hours. If you do the math, five packs at twenty cigarettes per pack makes a hundred cigarettes. Smoking a hundred cigarettes in a normal waking day (which for most people is roughly sixteen hours) means smoking a little more than six cigarettes per hour. That's almost impossible.

But if you smoke through the night you can get that number down to around four cigarettes per hour. That gives you fifteen minutes per cigarette, five minutes to smoke it and seven minutes to recover and want more. Otherwise, six per hour was practically chain-smoking, bordering on binge behavior. Normie was addicted, not obsessive. And he was consistent.

Normie kept one of those old-time ashtrays I had last seen at my grandfather's house. The ashtray had a cloth pouch attached to the bottom filled with sand, or at least it felt like sand, so you could set it down on an irregular surface like the rounded arm of an overstuffed chair and it wouldn't fall off. In Normie's case, the irregular surface was his stomach. The ashtray with the sand-pouch anchor would sit on his stomach when he was lying in his bunk at night, allowing him to smoke a cigarette lying down and put it out without getting up.

It was also important that the cigarettes be unfiltered. Normie believed that unfiltered cigarettes had their own built-in fire alarm. When the cigarette burned down and he was dozing off, the heat from the end would eventually start to burn his lips, and he would wake up. He could then decide to either stub out the cigarette in the sandbag ashtray or light another one.

Filtered cigarettes were much too dangerous. They could burn down without periodically waking the smoker. This naïve lack of planning would ultimately lead to the smoker drifting into deep sleep, dropping the cigarette, and turning the forecastle into a flaming coffin. As it was, Normie's crew probably lost a good five years of healthy living, breathing his smoke all night long, but that was really just background noise in our average risk environment. Besides, we were all in our twenties and thus invulnerable.

Normie also liked unfiltered cigarettes because he could recycle them. He saved his butts, and after a few weeks of smoking would pull out a tin where he stored them. Then he would grab his pipe, squeeze and roll the butts between his thumb and forefinger to sprinkle the remaining tobacco into the pipe, and smoke the rich mixture of tar-soaked tobacco, inhaling deeply and blowing the smoke out his nose like a dragon. I remember this having a much more satisfying and calming effect on Normie, compared to his usual condition when smoking cigarettes, which was somewhere between agitated and frantic.

This is what probably made Normie such a productive seiner. He never gave up. Normie was somehow able to maintain a heightened level of alertness long after the average deckhand had crawled into their bunks and curled up in a state of complete exhaustion. Sustaining that intensity was not without its cost, however. That March the bulk of the herring had moved on but he was getting reports of the Gloucester boats still making some big sets off of Cape Ann. When I came on board, he had decided to put away his double-ended seine boat and small seine and rig the big hydraulic power block on his main boat so he could set his bigger twenty-fathom seine from the *Candy B*. Carrying the bigger seine made it impossible to load fish on the *Candy B*, so he had secured a deal with a separate carrier to freight the fish to market. Stinson Canning in Bath said they would take the fish if he caught them and made the *Joyce Marie* available off Cape Ann.

Next morning we steamed from New Harbor to Cape Ann, a good fourteen hours. We didn't get away from the dock until a little after nine am, so we weren't off the Isles of Shoals until after eleven pm. Normie had taken a few kinks as we took turns at the wheel, but for the most part he remained awake in the wheelhouse talking on the radio to get the news. The weather was good, so we looked around Isles of Shoals for an hour or more, saw nothing, and struck off for Cape Ann. By the time we hit the green buoy off of the Dry Salvages, it was around 2:30 am. As we were snooping inshore around Pigeon Cove to the north of Rockport Harbor, Normie began to complain of a pain in his stomach.

He was in the middle of telling me this story about how he had taken the advice of a friend a few years ago about drinking grapefruit juice, gallons and gallons of the stuff, when he got a very pale look on his face and I could see that he was breaking out in a sweat on his forehead. He was in his chair at the wheel, and we were very close to shore, so he wouldn't give up the helm to anyone. He said that he had to get to a sandy spot in Pigeon Cove because it was a place he had set before, a small place that was likely to have some fish. But now he was hunched over quite badly as he leaned on the wheel in obvious pain.

"It's just indigestion. Too much coffee, I guess. I'll be okay."

"Yeah, but Normie, you don't look very good. C'mon look at you, you're sweating."

"I know. I think it's my stomach."

"You sure? This sweating thing, that's not good. Don't you think it might be your heart or something?"

"Naw, naw, I'll be okay. I just ate something bad. Thinking about all that grapefruit juice made me feel bad." He lit up another smoke.

Normie looked ashen at this point, but there was nobody going to take the wheel away from him. One of his old hands, Ronnie Crenshaw, started harping at him, too, but he wasn't in the mood. Normie just kept focused on the sonar scanner and the sound machine while he swept around the cove.

By then it was 3:30 and light would be showing in the sky around 4:30 am. That was our last shot. If the herring were going to show at all before they headed for the bottom, it would be at first light. And clearly, Normie was going for the full twenty-four hours.

Another hour went by. Nothing in and around Rockport and the color began to come back into his face; he began to straighten up. Maybe we were seeing things. With light in the sky, he looked much better. But I was convinced we had witnessed another heart attack. No matter. It was past the high water slack. Nothing was showing and nothing was going to show.

Normie pointed the *Candy B* for the Annisquam Canal. In an hour, we tied up just shy of the Blynman Bridge on a float at the Cape Ann Marina and turned in.

Long day, no fish and a probable heart attack. All in a day's work. Time to light up another and hit the bunk.

To say we were off to a slow start was an understatement. After two more nights searching Boston Bay all the way to Provincetown, Normie was convinced the herring had broken up and gone through the Cape Cod Canal to Buzzard's Bay. The season was over. But not before I had experienced the essence of Normie Brackett's catch-fish-or-die-trying hunt for herring.

COASTIES

SPRING PROVIDED A NATURAL break to repair and paint up until the herring reappeared northward. Normie took extraordinary care of his gear — all boats were hauled on his private railway, hulls were sanded with orbital sanders using two levels of grit, paint was thinned to the consistency of milk and applied in two coats, and the decks were painted with an old-time pine tar and linseed oil mix. Including repairs to seines, winches, and engines, the whole process took two months. But being around home with Joy was fine with me, since I knew we would be a traveling crew for the next ten months.

By June the operation was ready for the season, but there weren't any herring to speak of around Monhegan, so Normie decided to go seining for mackerel in southern Maine and to base his operation out of Portsmouth, New Hampshire. Normie had a friend who owned a restaurant on the Piscataqua River, so we would fish for mackerel in the daytime and tie up at night in front of the restaurant and drink ourselves into a stupor on rum and coke at the bar. We looked for mackerel from Cape Ann off of Gloucester, around the Isles of Shoals, then on to Cape Neddick, Wells Beach, and as far as Cape Porpoise. Naturally, we passed by Boon Island quite often.

Boon Island looks like the bald head of a man (albeit, a giant man) rising from the sea. But the giant has a 133-foot granite tower sticking out of the top of his head — the Boon Island lighthouse. Not entirely smooth, the island is littered with giant boulders, as is the sea bottom around it, and with granite slag from the construction of the tower. Though it is tiny and with little elevation, the island is surrounded by a treacherous collection of ledges. And because it is located seven miles from Cape Neddick, it seems to pop out of the ocean in the middle of nowhere. Hence the reason for the light.

Normie Brackett was obsessed with Boon Island and the eponymous book by Kenneth Roberts, an account of the famous incident of cannibalism among the survivors of an 18th century shipwreck on the island, and had read the book three times or more.

One flat calm day with no mackerel showing, Normie's curiosity got the better of him as we were passing Boon Island for the tenth time, and he declared that we should go ashore and see the island firsthand.

The lighthouse was still manned at the time and we thought it would be interesting to give the Coasties a little human contact, so we anchored up the *Candy B*, piled into the skiff, and motored ashore. We had taken our time getting the anchor rigged with a buoy on one of the flukes so we could easily pull it should it get fouled among the boulders, so the Coasties had plenty of time to notice that we were coming ashore. Even so, when we landed on the little wooden dock and tied up the skiff, there was no one to be found. Given the solitude of the place, I expected the keepers would be running down waving their hands and shouting hallooo at us, but no such number.

The lighthouse had a cinder block house attached as the living quarters for the keepers and when we were about halfway up to the house, we saw one of the Coasties come out the door. He was dressed in a tee shirt and gym shorts, had a week's growth of black beard and longish hair. He looked like he had just rolled out of bed. He came towards us for a bit, but then veered off as though he hadn't seen us. He seemed to be acting as though we weren't there. As we got closer, he stopped and stood there staring out to the west.

"How's it going," Normie offered.

Pause. Without looking at us, then "Okay, I guess."

Normie, attempting to recover, "Kinda quiet here."

No answer.

Then Normie taking another tack, "Okay if we climb the tower?"

The Coastie still not looking at Normie and staring westward, "Sure go ahead, what's-his-name is in the kitchen."

"Okay thanks."

When we got to the door, we knocked and went in. The door opened on a kitchen where another equally disheveled Coastie greeted us and introduced himself. His name was Peter and as we peppered him with questions he brightened up, and soon was talking incessantly.

"Yeah, we're here for six weeks at a time. That's way too long if you ask me, but nobody asks me, know what I mean? The helicopter comes out for the crew change." Pointing out the window, "See the helipad out there?"

"Doesn't anybody come ashore to visit?"

"Yeah, well the lobsterman give us a mess of lobsters every now and then."

"Do you ever go fishing?" Normie asked.

"Fishing! Yeah, we go fishing."

Peter practically leaped across the kitchen. He jumped like a coiled spring and nearly knocked Normie to the ground. He threw open the freezer door to the refrigerator and pulled out a huge striped bass, easily thirty pounds, and frozen solid.

"There now, look at this!" he shouted as he held the frozen bass up over his head like a barbell. We all laughed hysterically and I fell down holding my stomach, as Peter paraded around the kitchen with the frosty fish overhead.

"Jesus Christ, you boys don't have a lot going on out here, do you," Normie commented while we continued laughing.

"What's it like in the winter?" Normie went on.

"Oh shit, this winter was a bad one. Last December we had this rock. I mean this boulder, really. It was like the size of a Volkswagen. This is no shit. I'm telling you, it come through the wall here," pointing to a new section of wall.

"It come right through the fucking wall, man, and we had to take to the tower, you know, we had to drag our mattresses up to the second landing and sleep up there. We stayed up there for two weeks before they got some guys out here to get that fucking rock outa here and rebuild the wall."

"Like, the ocean was just washing through there for a while and then we stuffed some spare mattresses and blankets in there so'se we could warm it up, you know. It was not good, man. Not good at all."

Peter turned to making a fresh pot of coffee for us, so we took our leave and set about climbing the tower. At the top, we had a breathtaking view standing next to the great rotating lens and looking down — the island looking even more like a scrap of rock and the *Candy B* like a toy.

Back in the kitchen drinking coffee, Peter talked more about catching stripers. Then, as we were leaving he said, "You guys watch out for Ray out there. He's getting weird. Everybody gets a little weird out here after six weeks." We nodded and headed for the door.

"Oh, wait! Shit, I almost forgot. You gotta see the ships, the sailing ships. C'mon, I'll show you. You gotta see this," and he led us out to the helicopter landing pad.

Just north of the crew's quarters, the Coast Guard had poured a concrete helipad, a level spot on the rounded hump of granite ledge. I'm sure the pad had been built to some mandatory size specified by the regulations.

But there on the smooth face of the ledge surrounding the helipad were the chiseled carvings of ships — schooners, brigs, square-riggers with sails set complete with rigging and pennants flying. The masons who had built the lighthouse tower in 1855 had left their stone chisel handiwork all over the peach colored granite of the baldheaded Boon Island. Most had also signed their names with the dates.

Most striking was the fact that the concrete pad partially covered some of the ships and names, so it had clearly been poured over many more of the carvings than we could see. Nevertheless, the tall tower had stood for more than a 120 years and a few of the carved ships remained with their sails drawing wind to memorialize the masons.

We said goodbye to Peter, wished him luck with his loony crewmate, and carried on looking for the dark ripples of schooling mackerel. In the end, we landed a few small trips, but had little to show for the month of June other than our sunburns (nobody used sunscreen in 1977).

But all that changed in an instant one fine boring day off Cape Porpoise. A private radio message from Bobby Warren sent us packing in a great hurry — north to Vinalhaven — and back to chasing herring in the black of night.

SEAL ISLAND

PEOPLE SAID IT WAS LIKE NOTHING they had ever seen before. In July of 1977, an enormous body of herring had amassed between Vinalhaven Island and Seal Island covering many square miles. And they came night after night.

Herring tend to bunch at the surface around the edge of dark and then again at first light. Throughout the night they usually disperse and spread out. Sometimes they become uncatchable with a seine because they thin out so much, and you need to wait until first light around three am to get another crack at them. But this mass of fish was nearly solid all through the night. You could steam over them and see the black smudge of fish on the depth recorder for miles. During the day, the fish would take to the bottom. Then at the edge of dark, they rose up again. As far as the eye could see.

Bobby's call put us on the fish well before the Gloucester fleet. The word was: if you had a market there were plenty of fish to go around. Bobby had already stopped off a cove on the northern side of Seal Island with thirty to forty thousand bushels. He had so many fish shut off in the cove, he didn't even bother to make a pocket to hold them. Bobby and crew just left the running twine in place, shore-to-shore, and set their ten-fathom purse-seine inside the running twine whenever they wanted to load a carrier.

At one point, a humpback whale had torn straight through Bobby's running twine and they had to let the end go from the shore and chase the whale out. But it made no difference to the fish. The herring were equally heavy outside the running twine as they were inside it, so Bobby pulled the stop-seine back through them and tied it back on shore. He said he couldn't see that they had lost any fish at all.

Candy B bailing herring

The herring were adult fish and they were spawning. Some boats reported that the fish were releasing spawn and milt, essentially mating in the fish holds. It looked like they were covered with yellow corn meal mixed with milk.

Normie had secured a contract with a packing house in Boothbay. They would take a boatload every day if we could deliver. Unfortunately, we had no carrier and had to freight the fish ourselves, so we loaded the shoal seine into Normie's forty-foot double-ended seine boat and set the seine from there. Then we bailed the fish aboard the *Candy B* with a big bull net on a hoist and used her as the carrier.

Most nights we had a hold-full and a deck-load, when we struck off for Boothbay with the seine boat in tow. If we completed loading by midnight, we could be at the factory when it opened at eight am. In Boothbay, we unloaded for three hours, cleaned up, provisioned at the store, and turned around for Seal Island again by noon, or one pm at the latest. That put us back on the fish by the edge of dark, which was seven pm. Then fish and load again, freight to Boothbay, unload and turn around. It was a brutal schedule. With a crew of five, we were doing two hours on and four off on the steam back and forth to Boothbay, round the clock for weeks on end. Toward the end of three weeks, we were praying that the herring would go away.

The *Candy B* would carry close to forty-five thousand pounds with a hold-full and deck-load, but she was very down by the stern and barely did six knots. Most nights, we had a scant six inches of freeboard at the transom. The weather was calm but it was a very slow trip and it was hard to get around on deck. The fish were a good two-feet deep on deck, so you had to put on your hip boots just to take a leak over the side. Worse yet, the small lazarette compartment that housed the rudderpost in the stern was the only floatation aft of the hold full of fish. If the lazarette flooded, we all knew the *Candy B* would go down like a stone.

Normie got the idea that we could counterbalance the boat with some weight on the bow, so he bought a waterbed in Boothbay and we filled it with seawater from the deck hose and lashed it to the foredeck. It worked for a while until we got a fresh breeze on the run from Matinicus to Monhegan. As the boat began to react to the chop and roll, the waterbed sloshed itself over the side like a giant jellyfish and set the *Candy B* back on her haunches, digging a hole in the ocean all the way to Boothbay.

With such a density of fish, the humpback whales were a constant presence gorging on the big herring. One night as we came up on Seal Island we saw an incredible sight. We had been through a solid week of fog and it had finally burned off. The sun was a red ball setting in heavy haze over a barely visible Matinicus to the west of us and the water was glassy calm. Normie had the boat out of gear and we were just laying there taking our time getting ready, pissing over the side, hauling the seine boat alongside, pulling on oil clothes, everything covered in herring scales.

Normie sang out from the wheelhouse for fish showing off the starboard bow, pointing to a disturbed area in the water about the size of a house. Then, we heard a hissing sound, *shooosssshhh*, as the area filled with the silver bodies of herring leaping, almost dancing on the water and flapping, driven right into the air. And in the next instant four or five humpbacks burst straight up through them, with such force and speed that the whales were half their length in the air, shoulder to shoulder in a group, their mouths agape and filled with herring, fish spilling out the corners of their huge mouths, then the whales falling over each other like children playing a schoolyard game. The whales plunged down and back into the water chaotically splashing as they swallowed their meals, then as a pack they regrouped and blew and breathed, rolled up a few times, showed flukes and sounded, leaving the water to settle back to a glassy millpond. Two or

Normie Brackett on Candy B with hold-full and deck-load

three minutes of calm passed and we saw the fish beginning to show almost in the same spot, and then another ball of fish chased out of the water, and the sound, *shhhhhhooosshhhh,* the low silver cloud of fish defying gravity, and up they came again, the five whales and the spilling river of fish from their mouths, falling down and regrouping. Over and over and over again. We stood there transfixed and watched them for half an hour.

It was impossible to see this and not perceive their intelligence, how the humpbacks herded and drove the herring right up to the surface, coordinating their jump together. As we boarded the seine boat for the night's fishing, I think we all understood that it was unlikely we would ever see anything like this again as long as we lived. Stocking caps pulled tight, it was cold at Seal Island, even though it was July.

Some nights the fish did thin out and go deeper, but the water was firing especially well at Seal Island. In fact, the phosphorescent plankton was so thick and so deep in the water column, we could easily see the herring as they disturbed the soup of bioluminescent creatures in the water.

When we dropped into the seine boat, Normie steered from a station just forward of the seine boat's mast. I stood in the bow and shouted back to him on the density of the fish based on the way the water was firing. All

I had to do was thump my heel on the deck. Not hard, just a gentle thump, and the fish would stir enough as we steamed over them to make the water glow. As I thumped I called out a single word: light, or heavy, or deep, or shoal. Normie watched the sound machine as he steered, and was picking up the fish too, but he couldn't really tell if they were dense enough to set on. After doing this for a few nights, we got very good at filling the *Candy B* in one or two sets. The second night in, I saw a great glowing orb cut across the bow at an angle as I stood there and thumped the deck. I continued to see it for quite a distance as it pulled quickly away. Then I heard the humpback blow nearby and then I could smell the strong odor of herring on his breath as we steamed on.

But sometimes amazing sights got in the way. Light was the enemy when you were trying to purse-seine herring. Herring are very light-sensitive, so any form of light makes them behave erratically. The moon was a problem. It was always important to anticipate moonrise and moonset because with anything beyond a first quarter phase, herring could become spooky and unworkable, especially once the moon has fully risen. But northern lights were even worse. Maine did not have enough northern latitude to show the colors you might see in the Arctic, but the lights could be quite bright at times.

About two weeks into our grueling session at Seal Island, the northern lights put on a spectacular show. I had seen them before, but never on such a grand scale as that night. A large part of the sky would just light up — for one or two seconds — and then disappear and go black in an instant. No fade or gradual glow. Just light, then black, the northern lights flashing on as though someone was throwing a switch. To the herring, it must have been like someone setting off a massive photographic flash.

We could see the fish on the depth recorder, but they were so spooked and reactive we couldn't catch more than four or five bushels to a set. We must have set more than ten times and were taking a smoke break when my friend, Joe Upton, came by in his boat, the *Amaretto*. I had met Joe in South Bristol, as he was resurrecting an old sardine carrier called the *Muriel*. He renamed her the *Amaretto* and had laid up at Junior's wharf all spring while he put in a new GM 671 diesel, lifted off the old wheelhouse at the Gamage shipyard, and then built a new one by himself. Joe was from Seattle and had fished in Alaska. He was a great photographer and had already published a book based on his many seasons of running a salmon tender through the inside passage of Alaska.

As we stood there watching the northern lights display and praying to ourselves that Normie would not torture us all with another futile set, Joe slid in close and leaned out of the *Amaretto*'s wheelhouse. He shouted, "Great show, isn't it?" pointing to the sky as he sailed by us.

Normie, was furious. He wanted to catch fish and make his commitment to supply the factory in Boothbay. He didn't get it. He turned to me and snarled, "What the fuck is wrong with that guy. Can't he see that we can't catch a fish? Jesus." Shortly after that, we threw in the towel and put into Carver's Harbor on Vinalhaven for the night.

I realized that I was becoming inured to these events, becoming as callous as Normie was to the inescapable beauty that appeared in front of me. These were events that I would never see again, maybe events that would never happen again in anyone's lifetime. They would be irretrievably lost to all of us. And I was worried about what? Getting some sleep. Thank you, northern lights.

We continued to haul fish to Boothbay for nearly the whole month of July. In the end, the turnaround watches got the better of me. It all came to a head in a nasty shouting match with Freddy Curtis over something very stupid like eating the last hardboiled egg. He grabbed me by the scruff and threatened to beat me senseless. I knew I would get my share of what we had delivered and didn't relish the thought of the coming ten-set nights as the fish thinned out, so I called it quits.

That fall, I took some time again to work on the house. As autumn turned to winter I took a job as a finish carpenter, warm and inside I made a decision. In the spring, I would go on my own, mackerel trapping. Keep the overhead low, take a break from the traveling herring show (live hand to mouth if it came to that) and put my life with Joy back together again.

ROY'S TRAILER

SEPTEMBER. Early dusk, warm wind out of the southeast and spitting rain. Dark woods backed with fading light in the sky. Roy Vose's trailer borders the graveyard and Mr. P's driveway. He has a small wooden sign nailed to a tree — Boot Hill. The trailer looks down on P's house. Joy is away and I want to hear someone talk.

I can hear him coughing through the closed door so no need to knock. Open the metal door but the trailer is dark. Roy sitting there at the table cigarette glowing. The outside light over P's garage streaming in the window of the trailer's kitchen.

"What we got here, Nappa?" he says. "We got us a visitor. Yes, now we can have other drinks, Nappa, other drinks. We always likes that. Other drinks with other drinkers."

Nappa the black lab lying next to the heater grate gets up slowly on hobbled hind quarters then nubs his nose in my crotch.

"Goosin he is. He likes a goose, Nappa, don't he. He's a funny fella. He likes a goose." Monologue all the while he is fetching the whiskey.

"You like the ginger ale?"

"Whatever you've got, Roy. I'm not fussy."

"Ho, ho, Nappa, he not fussy. No, no. Not fussy. Not with my whiskey, he not fussy."

Roy was Henry's pilot for many years. He is part Indian, Passamaquoddy, I think and his accent is part Maine and part something else — old style up country. He doesn't talk much in a crowd. I see him almost every day aboard Henry's boat for coffee and he hardly says a word. He and Nappa go down to visit Henry at four am every day. He smokes and drinks coffee and then his day is pretty much done. Walks the dog home to his trailer.

The milkman, Robert Sproul, comes by on his route and they have a pop. Mr. P looks out for him and takes him where he needs to go.

Juice glasses clinking. More coughing. "Yes, he a funny fella, Nappa. Funny fella. But we always like the visitors. Sitting here in the dark." Canadian Club and ginger ale is fizzing in front of me.

"That a slippery go easy fella, ain't he Nappa. Slippery go easy. That who he is, slippery go easy."

Roy had named me when I first went herring fishing with Henry on the Outer Heron Island set. On that adventure Roy had named me and it had stuck with everybody. It was kind of a joke, but I hadn't objected to it strongly enough, and it had stuck to me like glue. I suppose if I had gotten angry or threatened someone when they used it or knocked them down it might have stopped. Truth is I was too new and too scared to do anything like that. I was just a kid and from another planet. The planet of Massachusetts and the planet of college. And now I was known as Slip in the strange family that was anyone who fished out of Henry's wharf— Arthur, Albert, Gladden, Gordon, Roy. I didn't like the nickname, but I never liked my given name, Paul, either. Everyone had called me something else most of my life, PC, Paulie, Ely, anything but my real name, so Slip had stuck like a spiny little burr to an old sweater.

Roy sat at the table. "We had actions night before last, we did. Actions. Mr. P had lots of actions. Was a long night at the table here. Long night. Actions in the night."

"So what happened?"

"I couldn't sleep much and I leave the window open here to get the fresh air cause this heater is going so strong, see. And I always like the entertaining that come through that window, too. That is good entertaining coming from Mr. P and Mrs. P down there. And I see they are having this party on at P's and Mr. P and his brother-in-law Jimmy Dolan was over and they was lit up. Oh and carrying on and lit up. They was lit up, Nappa, wasn't they? Out on the porch listening to music with the sliding door open. All of 'em lit up and music going.

"But Jimmy doesn't like it. He don't like how the hi-fi is working. I don't know what it is. But he gets in a fight with Mr. P about it and Jimmy is taking off the records and he starts smashing the records. They's all going flying across the porch and they was these old kind a records and were smashing on the floor and on the porch railing.

"So P tells Jimmy to take it easy. Take it easy, boy. Take it easy big fella. And then Jimmy decides to tell Mr. P that he's a cocksucking sonofabitch, so P tells him to step outside. And there is a commotion, big commotion. And Jimmy's son holding him away from the fight and then P goes back in and things calm down a little bit.

"Then Jimmy comes on up here to trailer, bangin on the door. And then Jimmy, he's acting like a funny fella and he is huggin and kissin me, and then he is crying and he tells us that he wants a gun so he can kill himself. He's made a big fool of himself, he says, and he wants to kill himself. But nobody going to kill himself. Nobody going to do that here. And then Mr. P comes knocking, too, and we get some coffee going cause it's almost time to go down to Henry's anyway. It must be three thirty and light is coming in the sky, so everybody is going easier now and Jimmy is telling Mr. P that he loves him and blubbering some more and the two of them huggin. That was a night. That was a big night."

Roy paused, then turned to his dog and said, "See, we had actions here, didn't we Nappa old boy. Actions."

We sat there quiet for a while. The whiskey and ginger was a good buzz and then Roy made us another one.

"Did I tell you what I been doing with the little fellas, the little stripey fellas?"

"No."

"I been looking for the home of the stripey fellas. Yes, looking for the home."

Coughing and laughing to himself, "Did you ever hear how to do that?"

"No, I never did. Jesus Christ, Roy, I don't know what you're talking about."

"Like the old fella says, they likes the sweets, the little stripey fellas. So you give them the sweets. A plate of sugar water or a bowl like that. You put that dish out there and the little stripey fellas come. All kind a little stripey fellas come then." He's laughing more at the look on my face and that makes him go into coughing again.

"They take a little drink from the dish and then we watch the little stripey fellas fly home. And we watch which way they fly."

"Yeah, so?"

"Well then, see, we got to see how far away is the home so we get us a little dob of this white glue, see, and we put a little dob on one of the stripey fellas, so we can tell who he is when he comes back, and we see how long it takes him to come back. If it takes too long, then the home is too far away like and we don't want to have to go hunt too far for the home, right?"

"Yeah, but what are you trying to do?"

"We are trying to get to the honey, that's what we are trying to do. Get to the honey."

He's laughing and coughing now that he's got me going.

"Okay, so then what?"

"Then we move the dish. We move the dish on the little fellas, in the direction they've been flying in, see? And they come back to the dish and the fella with the white mark on him comes back and it gets shorter and shorter."

"How long did it take? You know, to find the hive and everything?"

"Couple of days. Ha, ha, but then it was too high up in a tree to get at it and I didn't want to drag no ladder out there and make a big commotion. It was worth it just to find it. Just a little fun with the stripey fellas. Just a little fun."

HOMEMADE

THE IDEA WAS TO GO SMALL — scale down and see if I could make some money in my backyard. I had made a fair bit of money with Normie and had seen him wrap a purse-seine around herring when others had given up and gone home, but the traveling life was close quarters and long nights, like living on a Greyhound bus all the time with twenty-five tons of herring crammed in the back and everyone smoking and living on coffee when they weren't asleep and snoring like a den full of bears. I felt like I could do it again if I had to, but I wanted to try running my own show and do it close to home.

No more crashing offshore, like I had done with Mr. P, going deaf standing on top of a shrieking diesel turbocharger, shacking slimy nickel hake, tearing open the stomachs of shivering creatures with mounds of pink half-digested krill and herring meat, letting the man in the wheel-house make all the decisions, no more steaming to the edge of the earth, no more trying to knock the sea on the head, running, running, running, grinding, churning it up like the raw wake roiling under the transom bubbles and dross, whacked up sheets of blood covering all of us, and for how long can we bear up under this and what is the point?

And why does it have to be the game of the one who wins is the one who can stand the worst weather, the longest hours, and stomach the highest level of the threatening force shaping its cold hands around our hearts, all the while pretending immunity to the darkest unspoken fear? Why such a life of thrusting unyielding power, a life separate and distinct and having nothing to do with our lives on the calm magnetic and immovable land, why must it have such a ragged edge that gashes so deep, that we push this fear down and grip it in cold iron cages, and invite the fiercest weather to pummel us in mid-winter, feel the internal tearing required to live this way? Why in the name of breathing and sleeping close to the hot and soft skins of our wives do we have to live this way, and why can we not find a sustaining way that is not wearing down, chafing, crushing, soul hollowing, faces of pale exhaustion, way of making money, another way of feeding the world with creatures with the pure wonder and desperate strength and purity of survival that we can only conjure as ancient dreams, why not make it simpler and less numbing, and recoverable and livable? That is what I am after.

I would scrounge and repair a few small boats, anchors, and build a mackerel trap. If I could put it all together for next to nothing, a half-dozen good trips of mackerel to the Boston market could give me a decent season. I could live my life and not die so significantly every day. I could live with the peace of the winters and stop fighting the wind that roars down the river and overhead through the ledge-clutching spruces around my house no matter what I do. Let it blow. Throw another chunk of wood in the stove, and live to do it again the next year and the next and the next.

The plan was simple. Take what I had learned from Junior Farrin, build as little new as possible, take some castoff boats that no one wanted, bring them back to life, put them in the water, and make a sustainable living. For boats, I could get away with a skiff and outboard, a single dory, and an open workboat. I knew the seine-maker in Warren could build the trap. Then, I only needed four heavy anchors, some lines for the frame and I was in a different kind of business.

I started with a skiff. I found one for twenty-five dollars that leaked badly, needed a whole new bottom, and had a transom that was too weak to hold an outboard. An easy project.

The real problem was the dory. Most of the wooden dories were already in use holding stop-seines and marking coves. Worse yet, they were too old and were hanging by a thread. I needed something that could carry a lot of fish, and I couldn't afford fiberglass.

That is how I met Sam Jones.

I heard about Sam at Frank Farrin's store. Frank told me that Sam had just set up shop as a wooden boat builder and was renting a house with a small barn attached.

I drove over and found Sam and his wife, Sage, in their kitchen. We drank tea and smoked hand-rolled cigarettes, lighting them with cedar sticks from the fire in the cook stove. The two of them were like kids at a lemonade stand, filled with wonder that anyone had come by and wanted to have something built. Sam had only mentioned to Frank Farrin two weeks prior that he intended to build small boats.

I told Sam that I needed a dory, one that could carry six thousand pounds of mackerel. I thought twenty-five feet would be enough. I asked Sam if he had ever built a dory and he told me that he hadn't. He said that he had built several small rowing craft, but that he wanted to build something substantial.

Sage chimed in, "Yeah, something substantial, right Sam?"

I told him my story — low-tech, low-budget — and he got very excited, almost agitated. He stormed out of the kitchen and then stormed right back in flipping through the pages of Howard Chapelle's *Boatbuilding*. Breathless, he showed me designs and measurements of Grand Banks dories, talking as though he had just discovered a gem in an old trunk.

He showed me plans for a one-man Banks dory.

"It's too small," I said.

"I can make it bigger," he said as he spread his arms and knocked a mug of tea over on the counter.

"Hey, Sam, take it easy," Sage said laughing.

"No, I can. I can stretch it out."

"These Banks dories were usually eighteen feet, but I can scale one up to twenty-five feet with no problem."

I left Sam and Sage thinking that scaling up boat designs was tricky, even with small boats. I doubted that the dory would come out right and thought that I might drop the whole idea.

Sam had grown up in Edwardsville, Pennsylvania, a mining town across the river from Wilkes-Barre. His parents were of Welsh descent as was much of the town. Many Edwardsville grandparents had been Welsh miners come to Pennsylvania to hack at another face of shiny, hard, anthracite coal — the same kind of coal face they had grown up with in Wales. The church Sam attended as a child had still conducted services in Welsh.

Sam had worked in a mine for a week after high school until his mother found out, and ordered him to quit because she did not want him trapped by that life. She had misunderstood his reason for going down in the mines. "I almost had it," he told me. "I almost got there; so I could really see what it was like. I was so close," he said making a grasping motion in the air, "but my mother would not hear of it." He had only wanted to experience briefly what life in the mines was all about. So many of his family had worked in coal mines, how could he be Welsh and not know what it was, what it felt like to be down there?

Sam told me that he had not seen the ocean until he was fifteen years old. Then, he stood on the Jersey shore looking at the gray winter waves churning the sand and might as well have been standing on the surface of Jupiter for the strangeness he felt. But that strangeness was life-altering. The landscape Sam knew best would have been just as alien to most people — kids in his neighborhood played on hundred-foot piles of slag in their backyards. Sometimes, people's basements would disappear, drop away, because a mine shaft had collapsed eight hundred feet below. In Edwardsville the mine had come too close to the Susquehanna River at a depth of sixteen hundred feet and the pumps could not keep up with the water — they were flooded forever, taken back by the river. Next door in Wilkes-Barre another mine had caught fire and had been burning underground for years, causing sulphurous emissions to bubble up out of the ground in unpredictable locations. For Sam, the ocean — when compared to the unnatural acts required by coal mining and its toxic by-products — represented a natural order on a vast, almost incomprehensible scale.

The idea of becoming a boat builder came to him when he saw the detailed drawing of a square-rigger with all its lines labeled with their proper names. He was awed that something so low-tech and complex could actually work, and needed to know how. He wanted to see if a life driven by nature, or coexisting with it, could work, too.

He heard from a friend about a boat project in Rockland, Maine, a place he had never been, and was hired on the day that he visited the shop. But that project was a strange combination of natural and unnatural — a large sailing yacht being built with a system of glued strips of wood, layered upon each other with epoxy resin. Sam had worked on the boat for a year, but so much toxin had built up in his liver in that time, he began to feel feverish and nauseated at work. Finally, his skin began to break out in large blotchy hives whenever he was near the epoxy. Forced to quit, but taken with the love of seeing a vessel take shape, he decided to learn about working in wood and signed up for a wooden boatbuilding apprenticeship at the Bath Marine Museum. He would come away from the apprenticeship knowing that he must build things.

The day after my visit to his kitchen, Sam clomped up the steps to my house holding a wooden half-model of a dory in his huge hands and wearing a toothy grin that made me laugh out loud. He had made a model based on his extended design and was eager to go ahead. He wanted to use native white cedar for the planking, which would make for a very light boat. He also wanted to put significant rocker in the bottom of the dory. This meant that the bottom of the dory was lifted — or curled up — at either end by six inches. He said that it would make the dory tow very straight when she was heavily loaded, but would make her tow very easily when she was light, since only about six feet of her bottom was touching the water.

Sam held his double-sized hands apart in midair shaping an imaginary object and speaking with a passion that could have been used to conjure as well as mold the real material.

He said, "Paul, I know that I must build things. This is why I am here. I know this."

Then almost hissing and looking directly into my eyes, he said, "I know that this is what I must do."

I almost laughed again at how strongly he was expressing what he knew, how extreme was his projection. I was so surprised that I said, "Sure, let's do it."

He and Sage had the bottom of the dory laid out the next day.

The workboat was another matter. I needed an open boat with power enough to tow the loaded dory and a pot hauler or a small winch to handle the anchors. Like most shoestring operations, my ragged dream was moved forward with a gift. Ralph Gray offered to sell me his old Cape Island Novi boat for $150.

Ralph's Cape Islander was a twenty-six-foot open workboat powered with a 1957 Chrysler Crown flathead six-cylinder engine. Flatheads had been reliable and quiet engines common in the '50s but in 1977, the Crown in this boat was already an official antique. I had no idea whether it would run at all. The engine also had an unusual updraft carburetor that would be impossible to find parts for. Most carburetors at the time were downdraft, but an updraft was thought to be more resistant to the moisture of marine environments. The engine was definitely a weak link. But if it worked, it would save me buying a replacement that would cost more than the boat.

The boat itself had one big problem. Like most "Novi" boats, she was built with materials available in Nova Scotia, hence the name. Some of the local woods like tamarack were long-lasting, but others like yellow birch had notoriously short lives. White oak, which would normally be used in Maine for the deadwood — the keel, stem, and transom — were nowhere to be found in Nova Scotia. Instead, Novi boat builders substituted yellow birch. If you have ever cut a birch tree for firewood — white, black, or yellow birch — and didn't split it for a single summer, you know how fast birch wood can rot. When it sits around un-split, birch turns "dozey" in a matter of months. It takes on the consistency of balsa wood, a wooden sponge of rot that can be compressed with your fingers. Yellow birch, milled and placed in salt water as deadwood in a boat can be made to last a long time, but if exposed to fresh water it easily develops rot. In fact, it was a wonder that Ralph's Cape Island boat had lasted as long as she had — presumably twenty years at this point if the engine had been put in new. But the stem of the boat had succumbed.

Ralph was straight-up about the rotten stem, so I went in with my eyes open. But replacing a stem was a daunting prospect. Besides, I wasn't a boat carpenter. Working a few winters on a carpentry crew and building my own house was one thing, but boats were like furniture. Worse yet, deadwood was the backbone of the boat and had lots of curved sections fitting together in puzzle fashion.

Rot on a boat is a good deal like rust on a car. What you see on the surface is probably less than half of the real problem. As I poked around, I could see that the rot extended three-quarters of the length of the stem. At the top, I could stick a jackknife in all the way up to the hilt, but the stem hardened up to the knife tip near the waterline. The question was whether the rot had extended beyond the foot of the stem and into the keel. If the keel was rotten, I was out of luck and needed to find another boat.

Like the transom at the stern, the stem is the corresponding critical piece at the bow to which all the planking is fastened. It needed to be replaced, but with most of my money slated for the construction of the trap, anchors, lines, and a new dory, I would need to do all of the work myself.

Sam seemed unfazed when I told him the story.

"Just pull out the rotten stem, make a pattern from the old piece, and put in a nice piece of white oak. Here, use this," he said standing up a 6-foot slab of 4"× 8" white oak with the bark still on it from out of his woodpile, "I'm using white oak for the dory frames anyway." His wife, Sage, was showing great delight at my bewildered reaction. She had a hand-rolled cigarette that looked like a joint hanging out of the corner of her mouth and nearly dropped it from the struggle to contain her amusement. "You can use the big bandsaw over there to cut it, Paulie," she said cheerfully when she regained her composure.

In March, I quit my day job as a carpenter and started working on the Cape Islander. Since she was hauled out and sitting in a cradle, I put up a small tent of plastic so the sun would give me some warmth to work in and commenced removing the rotten stem. I backed the iron screws out all the way down to the foot of the stem and began pulling the planks carefully away from it. When I was three-quarters of the way through, the stem practically fell on my head as the rotted center let go. I got the rest of the stem out in three pieces, threw them in the back of my pickup, and tore off for Sam's shop to get instructions on the next step.

For some reason, I thought I needed to get the stem back into the boat as soon as possible. I think I felt that if I left the boat with a great gaping hole in it for too long it might become a permanent wreck, a tangible symbol of my failure. The Cape Islander sat by the side of the road in a small makeshift boatyard — anyone could see it as they drove by. And once I had the tent off, they would see the boat with its nose rotted off. All was visible in South Bristol, especially when it came to fishing.

Most of the houses within two hundred yards of the harbor faced it. All eyes looked at the comings and goings of boats on both sides of the drawbridge. With the town so literally centered on the harbor, it was difficult for current events to focus on anything else. Inactivity was as much news as activity.

"Bobby hasn't been out in days," they might say. "Not very ambitious, I guess. I don't know how you can be anything but ambitious with a new truck and big mortgage like the one he and Marjory pay every month. You better believe she's going to have something to say next month if those lobster checks don't cover anything beyond range oil and the light bill."

"Gorry, that fellow-from-away, you know the one who went with Arthur? He ripped the stem out of that old Novi boat of Ralph Gray's and that was the end of her. They say Harvey Gamage himself couldn't put her back together. She was as rotten as a pear."

The wood was crumbling and spongy chunks were falling off as I carried the artifacts into Sam's shop.

"Put them down over there," Sam pointed to the bench.

"Not bad," he commented once I had laid out all the pieces.

"What do you mean, not bad? The thing practically fell on me when I let all the planks go."

"Relax, all you need is the shape. We're not rebuilding the *Bluenose*, for Christ's sake, we're patching up a Cape Island boat on her way out. It'll be good enough."

The foot of the stem was intact and rot-free where it notched into the keel and all the rotted and missing pieces were on the inside against the rabbit, so we had enough solid pieces to derive the correct length and the proper sweep to make a new stem. Sam hefted the white oak slab he had picked out onto the bench and laid the assembled pieces on top of it, leaving spaces for the missing chunks. Tracing the entire outline of the stem he said, "Just cut this on the bandsaw and then take it from there. The rest of it is just shaping the nose down to size with a spoke shave and a plane, and then you cut the rabbit in with a chisel. No big deal."

"What about the hood-ends of the planks? They're punky, too," I asked.

"Cut them back an inch and spray them with some fungicide. We'll shorten up the stem at the foot where it fits into the keel to compensate. Ralph's boat will just have to be an inch shorter, is all. And the stem will probably be a bit more plumb than it was, but I'm sure it'll look okay."

I spent the next few days working there with Sam and Sage — me on the stem and them on the dory. The barn smelled of cedar shavings, linseed oil and pine tar. They burned the scraps and shavings in a small sheet metal stove to take the edge off the cold. I was always afraid that they would set the place on fire because Sam loved to hear it roar.

Sage and Sam had running banter all day long because Sam liked to tell us how strong he was. He would say, "I've been doing pushups all winter and now I'm up to a hundred. It feels good. I am so strong." And then Sage would pipe in, interrupting, and say, "How strong, Sam? Show me how strong. Tell me how strong."

Author on rebuilt Cape Islander

Then Sam would make a fist and say almost shouting, "I am getting so strong that I just don't know what I'm going to do. I am getting so strong."

Then again, she would say, "How strong? Show me how strong."

They went at it most of the day like that, all the while Sam saying how strong he was and all the while Sage laughing about it. Then it would be Sage coming back at Sam and telling Sam how strong she was getting by planing new planks. And then Sage would be showing him how well she could fair them and whistling a dry whistle as she looked at how nicely the cedar strakes fit against one another.

When I was done hacking on the new white oak stem and it looked good to the eye, Sam and I took it down to my tent on the shore; we slobbered the rabbit with plenty of bedding compound and fitted it. I fastened the hood-ends of the planks, and painted it up. That was it.

Two days later, I pulled the drain plug on the gas tank and flushed out any gunk in the bottom, clamped a tractor muffler onto the exhaust pipe, and fired up the Crown with the boat still sitting in the cradle. It ran smoothly enough to convince me that we could have a launching.

Somewhere in the process of putting all of the pieces together, Sam decided he would go trapping with me. I was not surprised. We were of one mind about the concept of going minimal, and had become fast friends over the course of building the dory.

On May 29, 1978 we set the trap on the eastern shore of John's Bay about a mile from Pemaquid Point.

Our first few hauls were a mixture of mackerel, herring, small pollock, squid, smelts, and pogies, all small amounts in the range of a bushel of each. But I was shocked to see pogies (also known as menhaden), a prolific, oily, and inedible warm water fish, so early in the season. Valued only for their oil, pogies were sent to reduction plants. More importantly for us, they were chased by lunatic schools of bluefish. Not a good sign. If the pogies were here in May, they would arrive in greater numbers as the water warmed. And wherever the pogies went, bluefish followed. For mackerel trappers, bluefish were a season-ending scourge. When bluefish showed up, mackerel usually disappeared until the bluefish returned southward.

Despite the early influx of pogies, we landed close to thirty-six thousand pounds of big mackerel for the months of June and July, but by mid-August chomping schools of bluefish dominated the scene and the mackerel skedaddled. For weeks, we hauled day after day for next to nothing. Finally, we took up the trap and waited for the weather to cool, hoping the bluefish would leave and allow the mackerel to school in peace.

Never have I encountered a more crazed and vicious fish than the bluefish — the only fish I have ever seen that regurgitates a previous meal in order to eat more. Sam and I knew this to be true because we would regularly find large pieces of half-digested mackerel alongside chunks of still-bloody, fresh mackerel in the bottom of our trap. The bluefish would enter the trap, puke up pieces of their last meal, feast on the fresh fish in our trap, and then escape.

On August 12, we took up all our gear and called it quits. It was only our first season and we had shipped a fair number of mackerel, but we had been defeated by the bluefish and the pogy invasion. We could have kept going well into October, but I couldn't risk making no money at all and

Sorting through the mackerel trap catch

getting further discouraged. We hauled the anchors, coiled all the rigging, stripped off the long sea grass and the mussels which had grown to be half an inch long, stacked up the big styrofoam corner buoys, and stored the trap in an old trailer made out of the bed of a 1947 Ford pickup. Then we threw in several boxes of mothballs and spread them all through the black twine to keep the mice from chewing holes over the winter.

Several times during that summer, I had a wonderful recurring dream of being underwater inside the trap. Sitting motionless and peaceful, I watched fluid and luminous schools of mackerel stream past me as they followed along the dark meshed walls of the trap. But my daily reality had been quite different. Even so, I felt strongly that I could make trapping work and wanted to try again next year.

To do that, I needed to live to fight another day — make enough money to fund another season. And I was willing to go back working for some guy in the wheelhouse, some guy that knew how to catch fish and make money, so I could afford to go trapping again.

Sam, for his part, had orders for several large skiffs to build, but I was already thinking about going back with Normie Brackett. The herring season was still in full swing and would run well into late winter — and if I could stand the life, I could salvage the year.

OFF BLACK HEAD

SEVEN WEEKS LATER, in October of 1978, I signed on again with Normie. It had been more than a year since my last stint with him. We landed a few trips using the small seine, but in November Normie put the deep seine directly on the deck of the *Candy B* and shifted to using a factory-supplied carrier to freight the fish to market. He had a deal with a packing plant in Boothbay Harbor selling big herring to zoos and aquariums. The herring were starting their migration south, but there were still a lot of fish around Monhegan Island.

First night out with the deep seine, we were under the high cliffs of Black Head on the southern side of Monhegan. The wind was blowing close to a gale, forty knots out of the northwest, but in the lee of the massive cliffs we hardly felt the air at all. Normie had picked up a very big bunch on the side-scanner and told us to suit up and get ready to set.

It was pitch black with no moon, and out on deck the wind was roaring like a demon overhead. I remember the eerie feeling of looking up at the stars as we waited for Normie to get the *Candy B* lined up on the fish. With the wind blowing so hard up above, somehow I thought the wind would make the stars look blurry but they just stared back at me bright and peaceful. Against that blanket of starlight I could see the ominous black silhouette of the Monhegan cliffs shielding us from the wind, but I knew that if we drifted any significant distance away from the cliffs we would be in for a rough night.

Normie was on fish, and with New Harbor only twelve miles away, we thought we might have a shot at spending the night with our wives and sleeping in our own beds, maybe even pumping herring as early as eight or nine o'clock. It was looking pretty sweet.

The only problem was our lack of a bug boat — a small but powerful boat used to start the end of the seine off of the main boat. Normie was still old school on the matter of bug boats and didn't think they were necessary. All the bigger seiners fishing deep nets of forty or fifty fathoms had bug boats.

With our twenty-fathom seine, getting it started was easy. A heavy buoy with a red light heaved off the stern worked well enough to get it started. Normie was right; we didn't need a bug boat for that.

But bug boats were also used to tow the seiner out of the center of the seine while the seine was being hauled back. In that situation, the seiner was surrounded by the billowing twine in the water (hopefully full of fish) and was essentially disabled since it could not risk getting its propeller snarled in the seine itself.

When the seine is pursed, the main boat is inevitably drawn into the center circle of the seine. This happens because the rings and leads on the bottom of the seine are very heavy — and the boat is as much winching itself through the water as it is closing the bottom of the seine — so the circle initially made by the boat and the seine becomes distorted by the act of pursing.

In the end, the seine becomes a rounded heart shape with the boat at the cleft. This distortion happens naturally, but it also serves a purpose. With the seiner at the cleft of the rounded heart, the two halves of the heart sit on either side of the seiner. These are called the "arms" and they function much like the arms of a weir or a mackerel trap. The arms are important because the herring actually have a chance to escape during the pursing process, and it is the shape of the arms that trick them into taking another path.

Directly under the seiner where the two ends of the seine come together a gap exists, sometimes as wide as six or eight feet. Even so, the herring can't figure that out. Instead, they behave as a collective school, and run the twine along the contiguous wall of the seine always following the fish in front. As a result, a school of herring always follows the shape of the seine. They swim up into the arms of the seine, following the curved wall, and shoot right back into the center of the seine. Almost immediately, the school of herring is swimming in a continuously flowing figure eight pattern, completely missing the six-foot gap in the seine directly under the main boat. This behavior invariably continues until the seine is completely pursed, the rings are brought aboard the boat, and the gap between the two ends is closed.

By then, the bug boat has already put a line on the seiner and is standing off a hundred fathoms or more to keep from getting fouled with the seine itself, and ready to tow the seiner beam-to-the-wind once pursing is finished and the rings are up. The bug boat does this all in total darkness. Once he hears via radio that the seiner has finished pursing, the bug boat operator then begins to take a strain on the tow line and pulls the seiner out of the center of the fully-pursed seine, all the while the crew hauls back the net through the power block. If you have no bug boat, a carrier can tow the seiner, too, but this can be an awkward maneuver because a carrier is an eighty-foot boat, not a twenty-five-foot bug boat and all of the hook-ups need to happen in total darkness, or red light conditions. An experienced carrier skipper can make it work, but it is not easy.

Our carrier skipper was not experienced — not by any stretch of the imagination. Oscar Benson was a young guy from Rockland who had been around boats all his life, but had never run a carrier. The packing plant had previously bought all their herring through brokers delivered via tanker truck, but a small sardine carrier named the *Paul Frederick* had come up for sale down east. The factory wanted a steadier supply of herring, and had picked her up and renamed her as the *Capt. Ed* after Normie agreed that he would fish exclusively for them. In the end, Oscar got the nod to run the *Capt. Ed* because he had worked at the plant for a while, and had supervised the recent refit of the boat at the shipyard. Normie was not happy with the choice but he needed a steady buyer. *Capt. Ed* had come out of the shipyard two days before, and this was Oscar's first night on the job.

That night Normie was doing a lot of thinking out loud in the wheelhouse as he circled the fish. He did this often when the conditions were extreme and he was trying to make a decision. Only two men were required on the stern to toss the buoy and heave the twine to get it started, so I would often stand in the wheelhouse door. Normie would ask my opinion, but I knew that Normie didn't really want suggestions. Mostly he was talking to think it through. Besides, at this point everyone had been told to get ready and we were all tense and trying to get pumped and alert after dozing in our bunks. The boys stood ready at the stern. I stood in the pool of the red deck light, chafing to get going.

I continued talking to Normie, mostly listening, through the Dutch door of the wheelhouse as he rattled on about the conditions.

"Awfully tempting to set to wind'ard so we don't get blown down into the seine...but there's still a lot of wind spilling over the top of them cliffs... hard enough to blow us out of the seine too fast, so'se we don't have any arms a'tall...and having no arms is a bad bad thing...and then pursing we'll keep on drifting and the wind will be getting stronger."

"Right, I think there's more wind than we think — we're better off getting pushed down into the seine, than out of it." I offered.

"Yes," Normie continued, "I say we set to le'ward so'se we have a good set of arms...as long as Oscar there can get his nose in here with the carrier and hold a strain so we don't get blown in too deep...yuh, yuh, that's it, we set down wind. This is a good bunch of fish...big bunch...but I think we can get all of 'em with this seine."

Having fully convinced himself, Normie stepped to the Dutch door and shouted aft, "Okay boys, get ready."

He knew that even setting in the lee of Monhegan, the wind was blowing hard enough to make a big difference once we closed the circle. Even in the lee of the cliffs, the further we drifted from Monhegan the harder the wind would push us. Setting upwind would leave the *Candy B* blowing out of the center of the seine once we had finished pursing, but we would risk losing the fish if the seine did not form arms.

Instead, Normie decided to set downwind. With the *Candy B* to windward of the seine when he closed the circle, the northwest wind would cause her to blow down into the seine, guaranteeing the formation of the arms. This situation, however, would put more pressure on the carrier to hook up quickly and pull us out of a mess if the wind drove the *Candy B* in too deeply.

What we didn't count on was the enormous number of fish in the set.

We let the end of the seine go a little after seven pm, starting across the wind, turning downwind and then back to windward as we closed the circle and picked up the end. As we began to purse we could already see that it was a monster set. With no moon, the water was firing especially well, and after hauling a scant few fathoms of purse line we could already see an amazing show of fish.

The seine was full. It was a rare sight — the whole seine was lit with fish.

Halfway through pursing, Normie pointed to the arms forming in the seine off the bow and stern of the boat. We had a red deck light on so I ran up on the bow where it was darker to get a better look. Rarely could you see the whole shape of the seine while you pursed. Now, the arms were lit up on both ends of the *Candy B* with a river of herring streaming back into the center of the seine.

The whole seine was lit by the flow of ghostly underwater shapes. They were adult herring, twelve or more inches. I could see individual fish as greenish streaks as they streamed by. Now they were beginning to break the surface and make a noise like rain on the water. When I got back to Normie at the purse winch, everyone was watching. No one spoke. We all knew what this meant. If the seine was full, we could load the *Capt. Ed* and then two, maybe three additional boats, if we could hold them long enough and the other carriers got there fast enough. Instead of making five hundred dollars in a night, we were looking at getting paid over two thousand dollars — a lot of money for one night's work in those days.

Normie and Ronnie were both hauling the purse line, each with two turns on a winch head. Normie used a soft polyethylene purse line instead of a wire cable that spooled on and off a winch, and he pursed the old fashioned way by wrapping the purse line on a winch head and pulling by hand. The plastic purse line crackled as Normie and Ronnie hauled slowly on the opposing winch heads, slipping the line carefully on the constantly turning head if they felt the purse line hang on the bottom. Normie always wanted to feel the purse line as he hauled. If you got hung up and were able to feel it, you could back off sooner and the seine usually didn't get torn up as badly if you could get free.

But we had a problem. Oscar and the *Capt. Ed* were nowhere to be seen. Either Oscar had been waiting for Normie to call him, or he hadn't been able to decode which direction we were laying and couldn't see a clear path to nose the *Capt. Ed* in to throw us a tow line. Either way, he had not hooked up to the bridle we had rigged for the tow.

To make matters worse, the combination of the northwest wind driving us down into the seine, and the size of the set — the sheer volume of swimming fish — had created two monstrous arms that stretched well behind the bow and stern of the boat. As I looked over the windward side of the *Candy B* the twine on the arms billowed underwater out beyond the

Shape of the purse-seine off Black Head

corks and the arms were beginning to close together behind the boat. In other words, the narrow passage for *Capt. Ed* to reach us was nearly gone.

Normie was furious, but was doing his best to hold it together. He calmly tied off his end of the purse line and told Ronnie to stop while he stepped into the wheelhouse to call Oscar on the *Capt. Ed*.

The seine was already pursed enough to keep the fish from running out, but with this many fish, we had to be careful not to dry them up too hard. With a gigantic set like this we needed time. That meant giving the fish enough room to breathe until we got more boats lined up. We definitely did not want them to smother.

Besides, even without completing the pursing, the herring were beginning to put too much pressure on the corks. With a big set like this, we needed to get a carrier to pick up the corks on the other side of the seine and lace them to the side of this boat. That way the weight of the fish could not take the corks down and allow them to run out over the top like water over a dam.

"It's too late to tow us out of the seine now," Normie said. "I'm going to warn him off and get him to lash up to the corks on the other side," and dashed into the wheelhouse.

Normie got off one call on the VHF. "*Cap'n Ed, Cap'n Ed. The Candy B.* Come back, Oscar." But it was already too late.

Ronnie tapped me on the shoulder and pointed to windward. We could see the red and green running lights of the *Capt. Ed* coming straight in.

Oscar was trying to thread his way between the two arms of the seine, but they were already closed. Oscar's deckhand was standing on the bow, one hand on the forestay looking over the bow. When he finally saw the corks of the seine closed up in front of him, he stood up and motioned wildly, waving Oscar back, and yelling to back her down. We heard one low-throated grumble of *Capt. Ed*'s Cummins diesel and that was it.

Capt. Ed slowed considerably but kept on coming. Quickly we saw Oscar run forward from the wheelhouse toting a large hundred-inch balloon bumper. At first I didn't know what he was doing, but then I could see that he was going to try and use the balloon as a cushion for the collision that was about to happen. *Capt. Ed* wasn't moving all that fast, but when she struck the *Candy B*, her bow brushed Oscar's balloon aside, shattered the cap rail, and broke the gunwale with a zigzag vertical crack from cap rail to deck. All the while, Oscar was shouting to Normie by way of explanation, "I picked up the seine in my wheel and I didn't want to back down and make it worse."

Now we were all in a pickle. We were still working in red light because we hadn't even finished pursing and couldn't risk spooking the fish. The seine was so full that it was only pursed at the bottom and the rings were nowhere in sight. It was blowing thirty-five knots, the *Candy B* was disabled by virtue of being surrounded by a seine full of fish, our carrier was also now disabled and fouled in the heaviest and most important part of the seine where the fish are normally dried and pumped, the bunt, the two boats had collided albeit with minor damage, and the northwest chop was beginning to push the *Capt. Ed*'s bow up onto the *Candy B*'s rail with a sawing motion.

I had never felt such dread. I think all of us took a look inside and found nothing but a leaden sense of despair.

No one was in any particular danger, but it didn't matter. The northwest wind was blowing us away from the cliffs on the backside of Monhegan Island, and from where we sat we could drift all the way to Ireland without running into a land mass. Danger was not the issue. Neither the *Candy B* nor the *Capt. Ed* had suffered any serious damage to their hulls. No one was hurt. Nothing was on fire. Nobody was taking on water. Nothing had parted and fallen on anyone. The hydraulics for the power block and purse winch heads were both working. And we were still close enough to be in the lee of Monhegan, so the sea action was hardly a factor.

But we were in a mess. A cluster fuck. A place where no one wants to be. A helpless place where nothing good comes to mind. A place where we wanted to disappear, where we wished we could be beamed straight home and give up fishing forever.

"Boys, boys, boys," Normie said as he rubbed his chin with his hand and then stood motionless. He stopped and held his hand across his open mouth like he was stifling a yawn. All eyes were on Normie.

Then he said, "Okay," and paused for a long time as he looked at the *Capt. Ed* gnawing on the rail of the *Candy B*.

"Okay, Ronnie, you go and get yourself aboard *Capt. Ed* and see how badly she is wound up — and don't let Oscar do anything until you tell me what's what over there."

"Paulie, you take the other side of the purse line with me. We need to get the rings all the way up so we can start hauling back. We may lose some fish over the corks but that is just too bad."

Ronnie climbed up over the *Capt. Ed*'s bow with a flashlight and proceeded aft with Oscar to get a good look at the wheel. Normie and I started hauling up the rings, which were not as far down as I thought. They broke the water with big sea herring rolling off the twine like water off of a circus tent big top. The fish were boiling at this point and we couldn't see the corks at all on the backside of the seine. The herring were heavy enough to submerge the corkline and were running over the corks, escaping. But we didn't have much choice. We tied off the purse line, I unsnapped the first ring and started the end of the seine up through the power block — beginning the process of hauling back the seine.

"I am going to make a call and see how far away the *Pauline* is," Normie said referring to a sardine carrier that he had been gossiping with on the radio earlier, and was on its way east. The *Pauline* was arguably run by the most experienced carrier skipper in the business. "If we can get her on the backside and laced up to the corks, we may be able to get some fish out of this situation — even as bad as it looks."

Normie disappeared into the wheelhouse and I went aboard *Capt. Ed* to see how Ronnie was making out. To get a good look at the damage done by the blades of *Capt. Ed*'s wheel, Oscar and his deckhand each had a death grip on Ronnie's oil pants and were holding him upside down to get his head down under the jowls of the hull to look at the propeller with his flashlight. After a minute, he yelled to lift him up.

Once he got his feet planted on the deck Ronnie just stood there saying, "Fuck. Fuck. Fuck. Fuck. Fuck. Fuck," and stomping his feet. "They are running out through a hole the size of a goddamned Buick."

Oscar said, "Jeez I feel bad about..." Ronnie whipped around to face Oscar and said, "You're fucking right you feel bad, you stupid little shit."

Continuing six inches from his face, "In fact right now, cappy, you just made the top of my list...top of the list of the absolute stupidest people I've ever known."

Oscar stood there. Ronnie stomped back to the deck of the *Candy B*.

With Ronnie's flashlight gone, I looked down in the water. I could see the fish streaming out through the hole in the seine like the outflow of a sewage plant. The herring may have missed the gap under the *Candy B*, but they were not missing the huge tear in the bunt end of the seine. They never do. Once the river starts, it is very hard to stop.

Like a single intelligent organism, the whole school was playing follow the leader, running out through that hole as fast as they could swim. Our only means of stopping them would have been to haul the bunt aboard the *Capt. Ed* high enough to get past the tear, but with such a large chunk of twine wound into the wheel we had no slack and couldn't haul past the tear.

Normie was calling me so I made my way back to the *Candy B*. Normie had reached the *Pauline*, but she was already on the other side of Matinicus Island, an hour away. The news from Ronnie was the clincher, anyway.

Ronnie was carrying on, "Normie, the bunt is fucked. Shithead's wheel over there sucked in a big chunk of the bunt and left a huge fucking three corner tear — it must have been where the blades first cut into the twine."

Interrupting Ronnie, Normie suddenly looked around, alerted like a dog to a sound no one else could hear. Then the rest of us heard it. The water had quieted down. The fish were no longer boiling. They were gone. The whole catastrophe had taken less than fifteen minutes.

"I guess they're gone, boys" Normie said. His jaw went slack for a few seconds as we stood watching him and waiting for instructions.

Then he looked up like he had just awakened from a nap, lit a cigarette, and after the first good draw, said, "Well okay, Ronnie, you get back over there with Mr. Numbnuts and see if you can get the bunt out without doing too much more damage. The rest of us will get going on hauling back."

"Let's go boys. That — as they say — is all she wrote."

We had witnessed a sight that many of us had only dreamed of seeing, a sight that had given us sweet thoughts of a multi-thousand dollar night. We had envisioned two carriers strapped on to the backside of the seine as we dried up the fish — crowding the fish into a smaller and smaller space by hauling back more of the seine — to a density that was thick enough for the carriers to pump the fish aboard.

We would stand there and watch the two boats pump the fish, all three boats with our deck lights shining on the iridescent and multicolored scales of the big herring roiling in front of us. We would light up cigarettes and smoke, basking in the knowledge that it was money that was flattening the two carriers, thinking that we had a smooth operation, that we could even do this again, that this was the beginning of a run, that Normie was getting hot again and that we were going to stick with him so he could stay as hot as he wanted to be with a seasoned crew that knew how to handle big sets.

But that was not happening. Instead, we were about to grind the rest of the twine out of Oscar's wheel, tearing an even bigger hole in the bunt, haul back the rest of the seine now empty of fish, steam home to Normie's wharf, drive home to sleep in our own beds, come back and spend all the next day putting the bunt back together — all this time deciding whether or not we wanted to fish for the Boothbay factory ever again.

FLOATING MUSEUM

A S A CREW, WE HAD ALL THREATENED to quit the boat if we had to rely on Oscar again. This caused Normie to call the plant manager, and offer to put one of his own crew aboard to run the *Capt. Ed* if the factory would agree to replace Oscar. Oscar was taken off the boat the next day. Normie knew I had run boats for other people and had asked me if I was interested in taking the *Capt. Ed*. I called Sam and, once I had convinced him to come on deck with me, we had a deal. Sam and I drove to Boothbay that afternoon and headed *Capt. Ed* straight out to Monhegan to meet Normie for another crack at the fish that night.

We were ready and willing, but *Capt. Ed* was in sad condition. Over the course of the next eight hours, we discovered that she was leaking somewhere between ten and fifteen gallons of water an hour, judging from the fact that her automatic bilge pump only shut off for five minutes at a time before the water rose high enough to trigger it again. To make matters worse, the bilges were a quarter full of engine oil. As our first night wore on, we began to understand why Oscar had stored eight five-gallon cans of oil on the floor of the engine room — so many you could barely walk around.

By our calculation, *Capt. Ed*'s beige-painted Cummins diesel was leaking almost a gallon of black engine oil over a four-hour period. As a result of the heavy bilge flushing caused by the leaking hull, *Capt. Ed* was almost constantly pumping engine oil overboard as well. Normie did not get on to any fish that night, and after talking to the plant manager on the radio and spelling out the details of the problems with the *Capt. Ed*, we convinced the factory to authorize a visit to the shipyard. *Capt. Ed* had just been refastened in East Boothbay so that was the logical choice.

Capt. Ed, later renamed as Kelani & Donna

As far as the leaking hull went, Sam and I both pointed to the refastening process at the shipyard. Our best guess was that the workers had drilled a number of holes to put in fastening screws, but in the rush to get *Capt. Ed* operational they had left more than a few holes empty. Since the engine room and the holds were all ceiled (meaning they had wooden sheathing on the inside of the timbers that prevented us from seeing the actual frames and outside planking), we couldn't locate the streams of water. The only way to find the empty fastening holes was to haul her out on a railway cradle and find them on the outside of the hull. When Normie gave up and headed for the barn at about 1:30 am, we pointed *Capt. Ed* to the shipyard at East Boothbay, a few miles up the Damariscotta River and directly across the river from South Bristol.

Sam and I spent the next day in the engine room looking for the source of the oil leak, while the shipyard worked on the ingress of water by filling the drill holes with fasteners or wooden plugs. After an hour of looking for the oil leak, we found the culprit — a hole in the oil filter canister. Unlike auto engines, which have disposable filters, diesels have larger oil canisters that hold replaceable filter cartridges. For some reason — and one that was to remain forever unknown — someone had drilled a hole in the oil filter canister and then plugged it with plastic wood. Now the oil pressure was pushing the hot black engine oil out in a small but steady stream and filling the bilge. The canister was cast aluminum so the solution was simple: screw in a self-threading sheet metal screw as far as it would go and snap it off. According to the chief mechanic at the shipyard it would never come out.

The broken screw never did come out, at least not during the winter that Sam and I ran the boat. As it turned out, this method of fixing things set the tone for solutions to many other problems on the *Capt. Ed*.

By late afternoon, we departed the shipyard and steamed across the river to the wharf at the Harvey Gamage Shipyard in South Bristol. Normie called on the VHF to say that he'd picked up a used bug boat and would meet us off the mouth of the Sheepscot River in two hours. He'd had reports of fish around Isles of Shoals, so we were headed south. The weather was turning disagreeable, a lowering sky with dark clouds scudding overhead and the wind swinging now directly out of the west, the wind direction for changes. The wind never stayed long blowing out of the west. It either veered to the northwest and got cold and clear, or backed toward the south. Since it had just screeched for two days out of the northwest, this was clearly a backing wind (headed counterclockwise on the compass), and a backing wind was never a good thing.

FIRST NIGHT

JOY DROVE DOWN TO PICK US UP once we were tied up at the Gamage shipyard. I remember the dark look on her face when I told her that Sam and I were leaving for the Isles of Shoals off of Portsmouth, New Hampshire, in an hour.

"The weather doesn't look very nice," she commented, slouching her hips forward as she stood looking down at us on deck from the wharf on high. It was low water.

"What do you want? It's almost Thanksgiving for Christ's sake," I said.

Joy was in her smoking pose — she put her left arm across her belly supporting her right elbow in the palm of her left hand. With her right forearm upright, she could hold a cigarette convenient to the corner of her mouth, close enough to suck a substantial draw without breaking eye contact. Her favorites were Parliament filters. She never smoked anything else. I think she liked the design on the pack.

Joy was beginning to lose faith in our lives in Maine. Our '65 Dodge Dart looked like a demolition derby contestant. Joy had gone off the road several times in two successive winters and I had endeavored to avoid the cost of a body shop by replacing the hood and left front fender with salvaged parts from a junkyard. The car was green, the hood was blue, and the fender was white — a metaphor for our patched-together existence in Maine to date. We needed to make some serious money to break out of our running line of poverty and were counting on Normie to break that trend. I told Joy about the debacle on Monhegan and that I would be taking the *Capt. Ed.* She knew that I would likely be gone for a while, but neither of us knew how long that would be.

"Well, that's good, I guess. I mean it is good, isn't it?" she asked.

"Yeah, it's good," I replied, "as long as Normie can catch fish, we all get paid."

Joy was right about the weather that night; it continued to blow hard out of the west. Normie met us abreast of the mouth of the Sheepscot River around four pm. I wasn't fond of traveling at six or seven knots — top speed for the *Candy B* — since the *Capt. Ed* could easily do twelve knots, but it paid to travel in pairs. Ultimately, we stayed inside and hugged the coast all the way to New Hampshire, instead of running straight across for the Isles of Shoals. By the time we got to the islands, it was just after two am.

Normie immediately found a good bunch of fish below White Island, in fifteen fathoms of water and on smooth bottom. He wrapped the twenty-fathom seine around them and by three am we were cleaned up and on our way with both holds full of adult herring. On the *Capt. Ed*, a full load weighed out at 57,500 pounds and filled a tanker truck.

Done for the night, Normie headed into Portsmouth, New Hampshire, to one of his favorite haunts, a restaurant across the Piscataqua River from the naval shipyard in Kittery, Maine. The Piscataqua is the second fastest tidal river in the U.S., second only to the Columbia River in Washington State. On an ebb tide, with the outgoing tide running in the same direction as the river, the current can run as high as six knots. Normie tied up at the floats in front of the restaurant, a very protected berth out of the current and convenient to the bar.

But Sam and I needed a fish pump to suck the herring out of the hold and into a tanker truck, so they could be sent to the packing plant in Boothbay. Since there was no such machine in Portsmouth, we were bound for Cape Ann and Gloucester. A fish pump is a giant vacuum cleaner mounted on a wharf — and it makes a great deal of noise for its size. For that reason, the City of Gloucester disallowed the use of the pump until eight am. As a result, if we arrived loaded at one am, we still had to wait until eight am to unload. Fully-loaded, we could make eight knots. With twenty-nine miles to Gloucester, running around Cape Ann instead of taking the shortcut through the Annisquam River, we could be there in a little less than four hours. Assuming no one was ahead of us at the pump, we could be unloaded and cleaned up by ten am, take a three-hour nap, refuel, and get back to the Isles of Shoals in plenty of time to meet Normie and crew by the edge of dark.

SHORTCUT BY THACHER

EVEN AFTER SIX YEARS FISHING, I had never been to Gloucester by water — and knowing that we might make this run the next night, I decided to write down times and compass headings to make life easier. We had not had enough time at the shipyard in East Boothbay to get the compass compensated, or accurately adjusted, but using times and courses on an uncompensated compass was better than nothing. I figured that I could redo the courses after we got the compass looked at, whenever that was.

By the time we got to the green buoy, a flashing bell buoy that marks the Dry Salvages off of Cape Ann, it was daylight around 5:30 am. I had recorded the straight shot from White Island to the green buoy in my book as "fully-loaded, heading 180 degrees at 1,400 rpm for 2 hrs 17 min." From the green buoy, the next leg ran to the southern end of Thacher Island to run between the southern tip and a big ledge called The Londoner to save a little time.

The course just brought us to within a hundred yards of the shore. A little close, but it was daylight and there was plenty of water under the keel, so I didn't think much about it at the time.

Capt. Ed drew six feet when light, but fully-loaded Sam and I guessed she sat close to ten feet. A lobster boat was ahead of us going directly over a sixteen-foot spot marked on the chart to the southwest, so I headed outside of him. Lobster catchers were always sneaking around ledges they knew by heart, and a sixteen-foot spot was not even close for him. But *Capt. Ed* was not a lobster boat. So I entered the heading in the book and made a note to split the distance between Thacher and The Londoner on the next run, but to not turn too quickly to the southwest in order to avoid the sixteen-foot spot.

From Thacher, we ran past Milk Island and straight on to Eastern Point, the entrance to Gloucester's Outer Harbor. The sun was shining through haze and there was a long swell developing out of the southeast. According to the radio, the wind would swing southeast then northeast during the night. Wind speeds sounded like they would be moderate when it swung to the northeast, twenty knots inshore. I had no reason to doubt it. NOAA was relatively predictable inshore.

Once past Ten Pound Island, we headed for the North Channel of Gloucester's Inner Harbor. The pump station was well up in the North Channel — within two hundred yards of the end of the cove. When we got to the mouth of the North Channel, I could already see two boats tied up under the pump ahead of us. Queued up first on the inside was Danny Todd on the sixty-five-foot *Joyce Marie*, a beautifully maintained wooden sardine carrier from Stinson's cannery in Bath, Maine. Outside of Danny was Bob McLellan's *Miss Paula*, a seventy-five-foot steel boat with a long southern shrimper wheelhouse. Bob was pair-trawling, a new way of catching herring with a huge mid-water trawl. Danny was flattened and I knew he could carry north of 120,000 pounds and Bob looked nearly full with 200,000 pounds. To get both of them unloaded would take at least two hours, maybe three. At best, that would put us on the pump at eleven am and noon by the time we were finished.

I eased in alongside the *Miss Paula*, but had trouble getting the *Capt. Ed* to back down. The reverse gear was slipping badly. Sam and I knew it was somewhat of a problem, but now it would hardly grab when I gave the engine any juice. I had to keep the engine at low rpm's — practically at idle — or risk burning up the clutch and having no way to stop. I was barely making way when I put the *Capt. Ed* in reverse, but even with the engine running at little better than idle I shot half a boat length past the *Miss Paula* and had to chug slowly back in reverse to get us tied up. It was clear from this experience that Sam and I would need to get someone to look at the reverse gear that day.

Even though she was fifty-five feet, the *Capt. Ed* had an ancient Paragon reverse gear with a manual clutch, probably the original equipment from her launching in 1951. I had seen manual reverse gears on a few small workboats, but never on a boat this size. Some items had been renewed when the factory purchased her, but installing a modern hydraulic reverse gear did not make the list.

Capt. Ed's manual gearbox was mechanically connected from wheel-house to engine room with a series of heavy bronze shafts and control arms — an arrangement that would have made Rube Goldberg proud.

To go forward, you lifted a hinged bronze arm the size of an axe handle in the wheelhouse, and pushed with both hands until you felt the clutch on the Paragon gear way down in the engine room thump into place. When you wanted reverse, you lifted the arm, put it behind the small of your back, and pushed back as you bent your upper body forward to reach the throttle and goose the engine. How this system had survived this long was a mystery to me.

I was convinced the *Capt. Ed* had the only manual Paragon reverse gear of this size still in operation — probably in all of the Northeast, if not the whole East Coast. And her steering mechanism wasn't much different. Modern boats used hydraulic steering systems, but not the floating museum of *Capt. Ed*. A great iron steering wheel three feet in diameter stood in the wheelhouse attached via chain routed through sheaves all the way back to the rudder. It worked, but her lack of autopilot made for some lengthy and strenuous watches when the runs were long and the weather was bad.

Then there was the matter of her canoe stern. *Capt. Ed* sported a stern shaped like a canoe, an ancient and beautiful double-ended design that left her with a number of drawbacks. Top of the list was her inability to support heavy loads aft.

Boats with square sterns have more buoyancy in the stern and carry more weight, but *Capt. Ed's* canoe stern regularly put her after deck ankle deep in water when she was fully-loaded and underway. In fact, we had to be vigilant about closing the engine room door, located on the aft side of the wheelhouse, because the water on the stern deck came two inches up on the eight-inch coaming.

Six more inches and seawater would pour over the coaming and run down the engine room ladder like a waterfall. With the door closed, the engine room bilge pump could handle any splash-through around the door, as long as a wave over the stern in a following sea didn't break the door. Either way, we always put the weight as far forward as possible on the *Capt. Ed* to keep her ass out of the soup.

More importantly, *Capt. Ed* couldn't turn worth a damn. Like a canoe, she always wanted to sail in a straight line. This made me dread turning around in a harbor. In Gloucester, for example, the North Channel where we tied up was a full two hundred yards across. But try as I might, I couldn't turn around without making five or six back-and-fill runs, forward with not enough turn, then back, then forward again, over and over.

Even when I drove the old girl forward against a spring line from a wharf piling to her bow, put the rudder hard over and patiently waited until I had swung her stern almost perpendicular to the wharf, then backed all the way across the North Channel, I still could not make the turn in less than two or three tries. I know I got more than a few laughs that winter from other boats watching my gyrations.

After we were tied up outside *Miss Paula* that morning, I sent Sam on the hunt for a mechanic while I went aboard the *Joyce Marie* to talk to Danny Todd, a very likable guy who looked a lot like Buddy Holly. He was tall, with black-rimmed glasses, very outgoing and funny. Danny talked nonstop and had a large repertoire of dirty jokes. He was also very helpful at figuring out how to fix some of *Capt. Ed*'s problems. Danny knew via radio chatter that Sam and I had taken the *Capt. Ed*, and he also knew that she was a boat with an ancient infrastructure that had only been partially renewed.

"Danny, I bow at the feet of the master," I said bending at the waist with my arms outstretched. I was in the forecastle of the *Joyce Marie*. Beautifully kept by the Bath cannery over the years, the galley table and the bunks were dark with many coats of varnish and the galley counter was a well-worn sheet of stainless steel. Danny was smoking and drinking coffee.

"Have mercy on us two kids from South Bristol, lowly South Bristolites who have never run a carrier before, and are trying to keep this hunk of junk afloat."

"Awww Gawd. She's not that bad is she?" I grabbed a mug off the brass hooks and made myself a cup of instant coffee.

"Well, apart from having a twenty-seven-year old reverse gear that doesn't work and has a linkage that looks like it was invented by some deranged plumber, a fish pump that I don't really know how to operate, and a hopeless diehard like Normie to follow around in the middle of the night, everything is fine," I said.

"Oh now, diehard is a *good* thing, Paulie. Jesus Christ, you don't want to be carrying for some fucking wimp, do you? You'd go broke waiting around for nothing to happen. Winter weather sucks and Normie brings home the bacon. He goes when other people won't. That's the deal, bucko."

"Yeah, yeah. I've got a wicked pain in my stomach all the time, though. You got any Tums or anything?"

"Over your head there in the cupboard," pointing over my shoulder.

Judging from his knowledge of its exact location, I realized that Danny likely had the same problem, and that it probably went with the territory.

"So what's the matter with the fish pump?" he went on. "She's got a wet pump, right?" he said looking over at *Capt. Ed* through the porthole.

"Yah, that fucking pump is an ancient artifact, too, and we can't seem to figure out how to get the thing to suck. You know, we're sitting there last night with the hose in the water and Normie's got the fish dried up and we couldn't get the fucker to pump. We turned it on and off, on and off, revved the engine. I could see Normie was chafing, you know standing there at the rail and then turning away. I'm sure he was complaining and muttering. Finally, the pump took the fish."

I took a gulp of coffee. "What the hell am I doing wrong? You've got a wet pump, too, right?"

Danny smiled. "Paulie my boy, we must think long and hard before we tell you the solution to your problem," he said looking over at his mate for twenty years, Manny Olsen. "This is very precious knowledge and Manny and I need to find something very valuable, something that will cost you in return," toasting me with his coffee cup. Then, speaking to Manny, "Besides, Manny, I just don't know whether Sam and Paulie, here, have suffered enough with the fish pump, do you?"

"Naw, Danny, I think they need another night fucking around with that pump handle, pushing it in and out, you know so they get themselves all in a lather and then they don't know who's fucking who," said Manny stifling a laugh.

Like many older carriers, *Capt. Ed* had a large centrifugal fish pump mounted in the engine room. I marveled at the huge cast iron housing shaped like the shell of a nautilus. To engage the pump, you needed to manually push an iron handle forward. This connected the pump shaft directly to the engine and started the impeller spinning inside the pump housing. The impeller worked on the same principle as a fan, spinning the water around the inside of the nautilus-shaped housing. The centrifugal force of the spinning water threw it out the output nozzle of the pump and induced suction on the intake — hence the name centrifugal pump.

In the case of a fish pump, the fluid being pumped was a combination of fish, herring scales, and water. Some of the herring scales were rubbed off in the process of passing up through the intake hose and churning through the pump. The rest of the scales were taken off in the scale box, a watertight plywood box on top of the wheelhouse equipped with two sets of screens to separate out water, scales, and fish.

Fish went into the hold, water flowed overboard, and scales poured into perforated baskets for further draining. These scale baskets were periodically changed out as they filled. Herring scales were a direct source of cash for the crew. It was customary, and I never heard of a carrier or packing house that didn't follow this custom, for the scales to be sold and the money pocketed by the crew. Called shack money, it was an understood part of the underground economy and was always paid in cash.

Herring scales were sold to small companies with names like Maine Pearl Essence and Mearl Corp. who somehow extracted the iridescent paint-like substance on the back of the scales. This extract, called pearl essence, was used in lipstick and eye shadow. In 1977, we were getting twelve cents per pound for scales. Mearl was so desperate for scales by midwinter, they would send a man down to Gloucester from Eastport, Maine — an eight hour drive one-way — to pick up as few as eight baskets of scales. Like many people in Maine, his sixteen-hour round trip to pick up the scales was part of his second or third job. Life in Eastport was very hard then, and probably still is. In November, when I asked him about the drive, he told me that it was a nice break from cutting Christmas trees and making wreathes.

After torturing me for a few minutes more, as I'm sure someone had done to him, Danny laid out the secret formula. The old fish pump would work perfectly as long as it encountered no air in any part of the system. Danny explained that this was the source of our problem. Most of the bigger seiners were using hydraulically powered pumps that were dropped over the side and immersed directly in the fish. This eliminated the problem of air on the suction side. The old fish pumps, like ours and Danny's, used a considerable length of ten-inch hose on the suction side and needed a series of steps to flush the air out of the hose. Otherwise, the pump would continue to cavitate, or lose pressure, while it tried to pump air instead of water. That is exactly what we were experiencing. It turned out to be sheer luck that we managed to get it working at all.

This is what Danny told me: After I put the suction hose into the fish, I needed to engage the pump and run the engine at five hundred rpm above idle for a full minute with the primer valve open. The pump's primer line would provide enough water to push a significant column of water into the output pipe above the pump, though at this point the pump would still be unable to suck the air out of the hose that had been dropped into the fish. After a minute, I was to throw the pump out of gear. This would cause the column of water that was held above the pump to rush back down through the pump and out through the intake hose — thereby flushing out the air in both the pump and the intake hose. Then it was simply a matter of slowing the engine to idle and putting the pump back in gear. The pump would then have a contiguous column of water between it and the fish and would pump like a bandit. I was then instructed to turn off the primer valve and watch money pour into the hold.

Danny had just finished when I heard someone thump on deck above followed by Sam poking his head into the doghouse of the *Joyce Marie's* forecastle. He was grinning as only Sam could grin.

"I found it."

"Found what?"

"The part for the reverse gear."

"No shit."

"And the guy from Gloucester Marine will be over in an hour to put it in."

I was amazed. In the space of forty-five minutes, Sam had found the parts to repair a twenty-seven-year old Paragon manual reverse gear and someone who would come aboard and install it. Only in Gloucester, Massachusetts.

Maine was a different story. I certainly had a strong sense of community in South Bristol. The extended family that fished out of Henry Jones' wharf was very clannish at a personal level. We shared information about what we caught, where we caught them, and how to rig your gear to catch them, information we would never share with anyone outside of the clan. In fact, lying to non-clan members about catch weights — particularly over the radio — was an important survival tool. If you were stupid enough to be honest about what you caught on the positive side, most of your neighbors and numerous people from afar were sure to land on top of you the next day to share your good fortune. Being honest about a small or moderate catch had no risk, obviously, so the default condition about your catch situation was pretty much in the "didn't do much" category.

The radio script went something like this.

"We're doing a little something here, but it is hard slogging, I mean if you put your time in you get a little something out of it, Wendell. What's a poor boy to do, I dunno. Jimmy says it looks the same over to the westward so I wouldn't waste your time and money burning up the diesel to go up there."

All were acceptable phrases from the lexicon of catch-assessment lies. Some clan members, if they were fishing for the same species, went as far as buying radio scramblers so they could talk to each other in private. Even at the wharf, if someone came down to eyeball your catch in person, see how extravagantly you lied, they never pressed you for your location. Gloucester was no different from that point of view. But when it came to rigging and repair, Gloucester was very different.

In South Bristol, in Henry's clan, each boat was pretty much on its own when it came to matters of rigging or repairing nets. Time spent on someone else's gear was time taken from your own problems. But in Gloucester, repair was considered a community project. No matter who you were or where you were from, if you tied up in Gloucester and were obviously working on repairing damage to your gear, if you had torn up a seine or your dragging gear, people would show up to help. Strangers would climb down the ladder and grab a twine needle and you would usually be done in a quarter of the time it would normally take. The only quid pro quo arrangement had to do with food. The community would swarm aboard to help you mend, but the boat was expected to supply food. A large chowder worked pretty well, or a stew.

Getting parts in South Bristol was also very painful. The nearest town was Damariscotta, twenty-six miles round trip just to get a hex nut. But if you wanted anything that vaguely resembled marine hardware, you needed to drive to Rockland, a three-hour round trip. Engine repair was by appointment and meant multiple days down. Twine and rope was a trip to Warren, two hours on the road minimum.

But Gloucester was repair and provision heaven — numerous marine railways accustomed to dealing with the raw and expedient nature of fishing

Capt. Ed underway

boat problems, had welders and boat carpenters on the payroll and engine
mechanics on call; marine hardware and electronics dealers were all over
town; grocery stores allowed charges to the name of the boat; equipment
repair shops kept parts inventories reaching back to World War II—all
within walking distance of the harbor. Imagine the most obscure part, and
the most arcane knowledge required to install it, and you could likely get it
done in Gloucester.

At eight am sharp, Danny and Manny on the *Joyce Marie* started up the
fish pump on the wharf and were instantly running their load up through
the giant vacuum and into the first tanker. The inescapable din stirred the
McLellan crew and a few of the boys came out on deck waking their souls

with steaming cups of coffee. With 200,000 pounds paid out at $150 per ton, the *Miss Paula* would stock $15,000. The boat would probably take seventy-five percent including fuel and food, and the crew of three plus the captain would share up the remaining $3,750 or $937.50 each. Not a bad night in 1978.

The Boothbay packing plant paid the same price, but it was split between the two boats. Normie was getting $120 per ton and the crew of the *Capt. Ed* was paid $30 per ton for freight work. With a hold-full, *Capt. Ed* carried 57,500 pounds or 28.75 tons, so Sam and I would split $862.25 from the factory and then $150 in cash from the scales for a total gross of $1012.50, or $506.25 each.

Thirty minutes later, a man with neatly trimmed pure white hair, wire-rimmed glasses, and dressed like a merchant marine engineer in khaki pants and shirt, was standing on the wharf with a cardboard box and a carpet bag toolbox. The mechanic had arrived.

Sam and I climbed over gunwales to greet him and take the cardboard box from him so he could get down the ladder to the deck of the *Joyce Marie*. His name was Wilton Avery, "Call me Wilt." Over the din of the pump, he shouted, "You're the fellow with the museum piece I take it. I thought I'd get over here before the day got too wild at the shop."

"I dunno, Wilt, it already seems pretty wild around here don't you think?" I said.

"That's how it is when you come to the big city," he said as he pointed to the *Capt. Ed*. "Is that the old girl over there?" I nodded and we started hopping across the rafted boats.

On the *Joyce Marie*, Danny had given his deckhand a break and was in the fish hold moving the ten-inch vacuum hose over the fish. Manny held a remote controller in his hand attached with a cable to an electric hoist overhead to control the height of the hose while Danny shouldered the big green hose around and sucked up the fish. It was noisy on deck and noisy down in the hold. At the sucking end of the hose, the noise sounded like someone slurping noodles, but very loud.

Danny and Manny were finished with the forward hold and in the process of moving on to the aft hold. Manny was raising the hose up out of the hold with the electric hoist while Danny washed down with the hose. I introduced Wilt and Manny with a shout. Manny kept a grip on the hoist controller, but reaching over to shake Wilt's hand, he let go of the vacuum hose, which immediately swung towards Danny's head. We heard Danny shout, "Hey, watch what you're doing with that thing."

I looked down just in time to see the hose suck the black baseball cap with the yellow word "Cat" off of Danny's head. "*Thwip.*" Danny's hat flew up the hose, into the juicy fish chute, and into the tanker truck standing on the wharf.

"Yo," Danny said as he reached up for his bald spot. I had never seen Danny without his ball cap. He had a farmer's tan on his face — ruddy brown — but his forehead and bald spot, where the cap had once been, were the color of a baby's bottom. We all practically fell down laughing, slapping our knees with our hats.

We took Wilt down to *Capt. Ed*'s engine room. "I always like dealing with you Maine boys. You ride around in antique boats and have a good sense of humor," he said.

I left Wilt with Sam and went up to the pay phone on the other end of the wharf. I called the factory manager and told him that we had fish, but probably wouldn't be able to get a truck rolling for Boothbay until noon, since it was already nine am and we had two boats ahead of us. I told him about the reverse gear and the potential miracle of getting it fixed, and he said he knew about the problem and was glad we were having it taken care of. I also told him that we were going to turn around after we unloaded and run back to Isles of Shoals.

Then I called Joy. She was using the front of our house as a studio and beginning to do a lot more painting.

"Oh good," she said, "I'm really busy. Steve Merriman called, you remember the guy from the Belmont Day School? He told me about a job at a boarding school in upper New York State. Isn't that great? Teaching art. Can you believe it? I am so, sooo excited." I thought she was going to jump through the phone.

I laughed, "This is good. This is good. Do you want to know about the fish?"

"What do I need to know about the fish? You got some? What do you do with them anyway, after you get them?" she asked.

"We pump them out. We're in Gloucester."

"You mean the place with the statue and all the men went down to the sea in ships on the plaque?"

"That's the place."

"Boy, that was fast. You just left. That's in Massachusetts, right? How'd you get way down there already?"

"It's easy. You don't sleep."

"Oh, you poor little Maine boys. Are they being nice to you there? What do they do? Do they tromp down to their ships with their big boots in the morning singing sea chanties?"

I laughed again, "Yah, that's right. But they sing them in Italian and Portuguese. Very operatic."

"Well, I just better get down there and see this myself. And to whip them into shape, that's all," she said.

"Okay, maybe next week, sometime. Next weekend the packing plant will be closed and we won't fish, so we'll need a ride home anyway. Maybe you can drive down and pick us up."

"I can do that, I guess."

"Listen, Joy, I've got to get some sleep because we've got to turn right around and meet Normie back at Isles of Shoals tonight."

"Why don't you guys just get a good night's sleep? You know, take the night off?"

"No can do. When Normie says go, we've got to go. Besides, when the fish are there you've got to be there, too. It might blow for a week or they might disappear. You just don't know. You've got to go."

"Okay, Paulie. Don't get hurt."

"I'll be fine." I told her I was off to my bunk.

We had been up for twenty-four hours. Finished at the shipyard the day before at one pm, departed South Bristol and arrived Isles of Shoals after two am, loaded up off of White Island, and on to Gloucester. Somewhere in there we had breakfast. My stomach was hurting and burning, though. I walked to the drugstore and bought some antacid tablets. They tasted like lemon creamsicles.

Back on board, I told Sam I intended to turn in and asked him to wake me when it was time to suck the fish into the truck. In return, I told him that I would take the first watch on the way out so he could sleep.

Down in the forecastle, I took off my trousers and socks and crawled into my sleeping bag. The inside of the bag was refreshing — the fabric felt cool on my feet and on my legs. I heard the small melody of water against the hull and the *churr* and *woosh* of a propeller underwater. Someone was backing down and rafting up with the boats tied up behind us as I zoomed away into sleep.

At 11:30, Sam shook me awake. Wilton Avery had turned out to be a magician and had been in and out of the reverse gear in less than an hour and Sam had gone up the street for groceries, since we had left home with sparse provisions. I was thankful for the rest but I was drunk with sleep and I stood on the forecastle ladder with just my head sticking out of the companionway, slurping coffee. Sam was working with the McLellan crew on the *Miss Paula* to slide her out and pull us into the wharf. Danny was already rafted up outside of us. When it was time to go, we would just pass the *Miss Paula*'s lines around our stern and onto the pilings while we motored out.

Unloading was uneventful and by one pm we were cleaned up and on our way. Sam turned in for a two-hour nap. With just two of us running the boat, we each stood two-hour watches: two on, two off. In bad weather, both of us used the wheelhouse bunk so we wouldn't have to go forward across a pitching deck — without someone watching us — to fetch each other from the forecastle. If you went overboard, the other guy would never know it and just keep sleeping with no one at the wheel. In good weather, we slept in the forecastle. We slept much better up there because it was quiet and far from the engine.

On our way back to Isles of Shoals, we had an eight-foot swell out of the southeast which put the wave action on our stern quarter, since we were steaming almost due north by the time we cleared Cape Ann. *Capt. Ed* was rolling heavily so Sam turned in behind me in the wheelhouse bunk. There was no door, just a bunk on top of the lockers with a foam pad and blanket.

The Cummins diesel had no turbocharger and was relatively quiet, a low thumping sound combined with the classic diesel clatter. No matter what, diesel engines sound like inside them are a thousand demons rattling pots and pans and beating on the cylinder walls with ball peen hammers to get out.

I spent two hours at the wheel and handed over to Sam, while I took a small kink. I woke when he throttled down the engine. We were off the backside of Isles of Shoals an hour before the edge of dark. Normie had already arrived and was scouting around to the eastward. Rubbing my eyes, I called him on the radio and told him that we were going to have some supper.

"Don't get too comfortable," he said coming back on the VHF radio, "things here are looking pretty good. I've got a nice bunch of fish in front of me. I just have to wait for them to come up a little bit."

"Whenever you get ready, we'll be there, Normie. Sam and I will just get a cup of coffee and a sandwich," I said. I turned to Sam, "Jesus, what a diehard."

Sam said, "No doubt about it, Normie likes to make the fish go up the chute and into the trucks."

"Next time I tell you that I want to carry for Normie, you know what to do, Sam," I said.

"Sure," said Sam. "Put a bullet through your head."

SECOND NIGHT

DESPITE NORMIE'S OPTIMISM, the hours wore on as we stood off the Isles of Shoals. After two hours of sleep in thirty-six hours since leaving Maine, we were entering the zombie zone. This night in November, the herring had made their move, but Normie couldn't find a decent place to set on them until after nine pm. He needed a spot with smooth bottom to set his twenty-fathom seine and the fish were not cooperating. Finally, at 10:30, Normie had them and we were coming alongside to pump.

Now that we had been given the secret formula by Danny Todd, we could pump fish to our heart's content. Sam engaged the pump in the engine room while I stayed in the wheelhouse and brought the engine to nine hundred rpm for about a minute. When I slacked it down to idle, Sam disengaged the pump, flushing the air out of the intake hose. He waited ten seconds, re-engaged, and the pump worked as advertised. It was a great feeling. Water poured out of the wash pipe on the port side, fish flew forward into the fish hold, and scales flowed out of a six-inch galvanized pipe thick as oatmeal, filling up the black scale baskets. When things were running smoothly, there was nothing better than loading a boat with fish.

As we neared the end of the fish, with the hold filled, we were pumping the remaining five thousand pounds or more on deck using pen boards to keep the load as far forward as possible. Normie and crew had cast off and were heading into Portsmouth. He was a half mile away and still had his deck lights on as the crew cleaned up. I had dropped the suction hose overboard and was pumping clean water through the system to wash out the scale box, while Sam dragged the full scale baskets forward.

Suddenly, Sam shouted at me pointing to our deck lights. They were dimming badly, like the bulb on a flashlight when its batteries are about to give out. I quickly stepped into the wheelhouse, opened the breaker box and turned off the radar (a power-sucking pig), the two radios, all the deck lights, the engine room lights, and the wheelhouse dome light. Sam went forward to get the lights in the forecastle and to shut off the little twelve-volt television Sage had given us as a going away present. Grabbing a flashlight I looked at one of the few gauges I had in the wheelhouse, an ancient volt-meter with a rusty white backing and black numbers. It showed zero volts.

Sam and I both went below to the engine room. I thought we might have lost the drive belts on the alternator, but they were intact and turning. The only conclusion we could come to was that the alternator brushes had worn down to nothing and were no longer making contact. Then we began to check the batteries. Like most workboats, *Capt. Ed* had a hundred amps worth of batteries ganged together, but when we started taking the water fill-caps off of them, about a quarter of them looked like they were dry. We had two problems: if the gauge in the wheelhouse was right, the alternator was not putting out any electricity at all, and the yellow deck lamps told us that the batteries were dead. We thought the problems might be related, but they could just as easily be separate issues. At that moment in time, it didn't matter.

Sam and I went up into the wheelhouse to take stock and think in the dark.

"Let me give Normie a call," I said.

At the very least I wanted Normie to know that we were having a prob-lem. I thought I might have enough power to talk for a few minutes, so I turned on the VHF radio and made the call.

"Candy B Candy B — Cap'n Ed, come back Normie."

Normie answered, but when I tried to respond the radio was dead. Apparently, we only had enough power to transmit once and that was it.

At that point we had no radar, no radios, and no bilge pump. Normie had no idea we were having trouble and was on his way to five or six rum and cokes at the restaurant up river in Portsmouth. The batteries seemed to have a small amount of power — enough for the small red compass light that was stuck on the glass dome of the compass, the red and green running lights, and the white masthead and stern lights. The compass light was essential since we didn't have autopilot.

The southeasterly swell was still heavy and would require a lot of manual steering compensation at the wheel, so it was important to watch the compass while we did that. Heavily loaded, *Capt. Ed* tended to run like a canoe more than ever. Running due south, the southeasterly swell would push her nose to starboard and she would suddenly start running on a new line and then we would be forced to compensate by steering to port. The result was a steering oscillation back and forth — and a whole lot of work.

Running lights and the masthead and stern light were useful. Since we didn't have radar, and we couldn't see oncoming traffic, the navigation lights could keep us from getting run down — assuming someone else was watching.

Having no bilge pump could become a serious problem but only if we sprung a major leak. When you loaded a boat with fish you always took on a fair amount of water as well as fish. Since the fish hold was not watertight, the water that came aboard with the fish eventually drained into the bilges. We would be okay as long as we didn't take on any more water.

Either way, the most important thing was to get under way for Gloucester. According to my book entries from the previous day the course was 180. I brought the engine up to fourteen hundred rpm and noted that it should be two hours and seventeen minutes to the green buoy and wrote down the time that showed on my watch. Then, I asked Sam to go down and check on the bilges. When he got back he told me that the bilge water was an inch or so under the engine room floorboards. More than I would have liked.

"Not much we can do about it anyway at this point. It'll just have to wait, I guess," I said.

I paused. It had started to snow. The wind had swung to the northeast as predicted and it was snowing steadily.

"That takes the cake, Sam. The first snowstorm of the season and no radar."

Over the years, I'd become accustomed to using radar to pick up buoys at night and lost my sense of what distance I could actually see lighted buoys in the dark — like the green buoy off Cape Ann. If it kept snowing all the way to Cape Ann, with this kind of visibility, I had no idea whether we would be able to find that buoy. I was way out of practice navigating at night with just a compass.

I turned to Sam. "Well at least we know that the engine won't quit. That's the great thing about diesels — they run without any power whatsoever."

"That's not really true," Sam said.

"What do you mean?"

"The fuel shutoff is electrically powered."

"So?"

"Well, the fuel shutoff is what shuts off the engine when you pull this knob here," he said pointing to a knob on the wheelhouse dash.

"I don't get it."

"When you pull the knob, it cuts power to the fuel shutoff solenoid. That's how you shut off a diesel, you cut off the fuel. Otherwise it runs forever. It doesn't really have an electrical system like gas engines."

"Yah, but I'm not about to pull the knob right now, am I? Especially since the engine is about the only thing working on this piece of shit."

"No, but if the fuel shutoff loses power because the batteries are so low, then it will shut down the engine."

"Shit! How the hell do you know that?"

"I used to work with my father in Wilkes-Barre on truck engines, mainly Cummins diesels, that's how I know. You just need to screw in a little thumbscrew on the side of the solenoid — the override — to keep the engine from shutting down when you lose power."

"Well, I guess you had better go down there and do it," I said.

That was all we needed. Fully-loaded with no power, no radio, and no engine, wallowing in the rolling troughs of a southeasterly swell, middle of the night, snowing.

Sam laughed and grinned widely, "Aye Aye, Cap'n."

But he just stood there watching me steer. I carried on tending to the compass and course and wrestling the *Capt. Ed* back to 180 as she was set off course by another eight-footer striking the bow and climbing aboard. I was so tired I could feel a kind of prickly sensation around my nose like I had a rash on my face, and I wasn't sure if I was making sense when I talked. Zombie time was in full swing. It was 11:45 pm on the second day. Each of us was going on only two hours of sleep in almost forty hours. We were in rough shape, heading toward behavior that featured stumbling and mumbling. Finally, I realized that Sam was still standing there grinning like a lunatic.

"Jesus Christ, Sam, will you get down there and screw in that little what-ever-the-fuck-it-is, so we aren't dead in the water in the next five minutes?"

He hid the grin on his face by putting his hand under his nose.

"Already done, Cap'n. I did it when I went down to check the bilges."

He paused, took off his cap and scratched at his thinning hair.

"I just wanted to see if you were paying attention," he said and started giggling.

"You are an asshole, Sam, you know that? God almighty, an absolute asshole," I said back to him. I was too numb to laugh but I was beginning to let go of something.

"What the fuck. Paying attention, my ass," I muttered, "Jesus, mother, Mary and Joseph.

"Okay, Sam. I get it. I just need to see if we can hit the green buoy now. Hit the green buoy, not go inside it and end up ashore on the Dry Salvages. Don't want to do that. Unh unh, don't want that."

I continued talking to myself while I corrected on the big steering wheel, then swinging back the other way. Corrected again, oscillating. Sometimes when I was that tired I slipped into a personality resembling a humorless mechanized autopilot, but Sam had gone in the other direction and was pulling on me to keep me from falling into the pit. Somehow, he never lost his sense of humor. He was one of the most passionate people I knew, but passionately optimistic, and absolutely imperturbable.

Even so, could Sam's optimism transcend the *Capt. Ed*'s propensity for failure, I wondered? This thing about the fuel shutoff override was so arcane. I thought, how is it that I have Sam as a friend, and that he is on this boat right now, right here, when this happens?

And how is it that Sam happens to know about the existence of the manual fuel override on the specific make of diesel on this boat? And how close are we to the next problem? And what if that solution only addresses the current layer of decay? Is there another layer?

Sam broke my train of thought, this time serious again, "Anyway, I think we're good. Or until something else happens, I guess. This boat has a troubled mind, I think."

Sam had this mystical thing about wooden boats and their life on the sea. It was as though he was watching *Capt. Ed* from a different place, if that were possible, from some spiritual plane. After all, it was wooden boats that had given Sam a new life after he had been poisoned by epoxy, so he tended to give the frames and planks attributes that others didn't. I thought, it does make sense that he would think that way, and hey, maybe he is right.

Standing in the dark now of the wheelhouse as we pulled away from White Island in a semi-crippled state, I checked our departure time in my book, 11:45 pm, and added the two hours and seventeen minutes running time recorded from the previous day. That would put us at the green buoy at 2:02 am. I told Sam that I would take the first one-hour watch and he turned in on the bunk behind me.

Staying awake at the wheel under these conditions was probably made easier because of the steering oscillation. It gave me something to do — wrestle with the big iron wheel for an hour — as I wondered whether or not we could hit the green buoy based on the course I had recorded from the day before. *Capt. Ed* was sitting very low, especially with the deck-load. For the hour that I fought with the southeasterly slop, we took water over the bow and foredeck on almost every swell. Nearly half of the deck-load of fish we had penned forward was washed overboard into the night.

At 12:45 am, I shook Sam's shoulder to get him up and take the wheel. I flopped on the bunk and listened to the clatter of the Cummins diesel down below. Any thoughts that I had were either unreachable or nonexistent. I remember only bracing my feet against the starboard locker as the boat rolled down away from the swell. She always came back smartly, though I have no idea what we would have done differently if she had started to list or act sluggish from rising water in the bilge. I was simply too tired to check and I knew that Sam would feel it well before I would. I was supposed to be asleep.

An hour later I awoke with a start. Sam had not called me but somewhere inside me a clock had timed out. I wanted to see what we could see. As I stood up up next to Sam in the wheelhouse, the green buoy was flashing through the snowy darkness directly off the bow.

"Wow, that *is* good luck," I said.

To this day I still do not know why I had recorded that course on the previous day from Isles of Shoals to the green buoy. Maybe I was just paranoid. Or maybe I'd just believed my intuitive sense that the *Capt. Ed* had the most fragile infrastructure I'd have ever had my hands on. Either way, I felt blessed that I had written the courses and times in my book.

"Not out of the woods yet," I said to Sam. "We still have to get past Thacher."

"Yeah, yeah, you've got the courses, right?"

"Yes, but there's a catch."

I told Sam that I was worried because I felt like I had taken the course too near Thacher on the previous morning. In the daylight it hadn't seemed important. But the more I looked at the chart now, the more it seemed that putting *Capt. Ed* as close to shore as a hundred yards might run her right over a sixteen-foot spot just to the southwest of the point. It wasn't rational; it was just a feeling.

I fought with my emotions as we steered on the course line for the island. I knew that I wouldn't have any trouble seeing the southern lighthouse as we approached, but I wasn't sure that I could see far enough in the dark and snow to gauge my distance from the shore once we were close. I had no searchlight to penetrate the snow. Too far west, and I could end up slamming into the rock face if I couldn't see it. On the other hand, if I corrected too much to the east to avoid the wall, I might end up on top of The Londoner.

So I reasoned on. We weren't loaded that much deeper this morning than we were yesterday, right? True, the additional deck-load of five or six thousand pounds had probably pushed *Capt. Ed* deeper than yesterday by another six inches, but that wasn't much. And half of that load had washed overboard, and today we didn't have much choice, anyway. We had no other course and no radar, so we needed to stick with yesterday's course and time from the green buoy to the flashing red lighthouse on the southern end of Thacher Island.

It was still snowing heavily. I felt stupid. To a local, running between Thacher and The Londoner was a wide enough berth — and deep enough — to run a two-hundred-foot vessel through. Shit, what's the big deal, I thought.

But with no power, no radar, no searchlight, heavy snow, only one course and time to work from, and a heavily laden boat, my stomach was clenched and stewing on its own acid.

As we got close in under the southern lighthouse I opened the starboard wheelhouse door, latching the hook-and-eye to keep it open, and stood in the doorway with my hand on the helm. It was the heavy wet snow of a first snowstorm. Big flakes were melting on my face and blowing into the wheelhouse while Sam and I shined our flashlights off the starboard side to see if we could pick up the rocky shore. When we did see it, we were close enough to throw a stone and hit the rock face of the cliff.

I swung off, away from the island a good forty-five degrees toward The Londoner for a full minute, and then started my course for Eastern Point at the mouth of Gloucester's big Outer Harbor.

Both of us were relieved. But I was numb. We had been too close to Thacher.

At Eastern Point we headed north into the Outer Harbor. It was 2:30 am and the day boats were coming out of Gloucester. Sam and I saw six or more boats abreast, twenty or twenty-five boats coming at us at full throttle, many of them with deck lights blazing as the crews cleared for the sloppy weather outside, all of them probably headed for Jeffreys Ledge or Still-wagen Bank. It was rush hour in Gloucester. Like unruly Boston drivers, barely awake and slurping coffee at the wheel, the Gloucester day boats were headed to work, pedal to the metal. We were the only boat headed in. To those guys, we were flattened and making money. In our minds, we were limping back in, glad to be in one piece.

When we tied up under the pump in the North Channel of Gloucester's Inner Harbor, it was just before three am. Sam lugged the big yellow power cable up over the wharf ladder and plugged *Capt. Ed* into shore power. The bilge pump came on and started pumping a stream that looked like a murky red Kool-Aid. It was bilge water rich with herring blood that was now sloshing two inches above the engine room floorboards. Sam stepped back on deck from the ladder and made his way to the wheelhouse where I was sitting on the edge of the bunk staring at the floor. He put out his hand. I shook it and nodded.

"If we stay up until eight, we can make this adventure a full forty-eight hours on three hours of pretend sleep. That would be a new personal record for me. But I think I'd rather conk out."

I stopped and looked up at him.

"I thank your father, Sam, for teaching you about the fuel shutoff bypass."

"Strange what you remember isn't it?" Sam said. I nodded.

When we went forward to turn in, we had to walk through the remaining eight-inch layer of fish penned in on the deck against the forecastle doghouse. Stepping out of our boots, we left them sticking up out of the fish, and backed down the companionway steps to the forecastle in our socks. Herring scales were sticky and ended up on just about everything, so we did our best to keep them out of our bunks. We slept like stones.

Five hours later, at eight am, we were awakened by the boom, boom, of boots on deck and Danny Todd stuck his head down the companionway and said, "Let's go, boys. Soup's on. Power up." *Joyce Marie* had a load on and was tied up alongside us. The tanker trucks were queued up and it was time to push the big red button to start the fish pump.

After we emerged from the forecastle and stepped into our herring-immersed boots, Danny commented, "You boys did well last night. That's good because we're not going anywhere tonight."

"What's going on now?" I asked.

"Going to screech out of the northwest."

"Can't say I'm sorry. Should knock down the southeast slop. It was very shitty getting in here this morning. And we lost our power."

"Blah, blah, blah. This is just the way it is with these old wooden boats, Paulie. You've got to spend a shitload of money to keep everything hung together," Danny offered. "Next thing you know there won't be any more fish and you boys will be crying about that."

"Yah, Danny. I know, I know." I turned to Sam. "Do you suppose you can get that guy, Wilton whatsisname before he gets too involved in the rest of his day over at the shop? We really need someone to get a look at the alternator and the batteries. I can get started on sucking out the fish, if you see if he's available. Besides, I don't even know where you found him."

Sam and Danny went up the ladder and pushed the button on the fish pump. The tanker truck was already in position. The big hose started hissing and slurping herring.

Down in the fish hold the vacuum hose was making a small canyon in the tightly packed fish. I stood on the fish hold ladder caving in the walls of herring by pushing on them with my boots. That was the easiest method. The fish walls collapsed like landslides, a bushel at a time, fresh and stiff but oozing blood to be slurped up the hose. Sam came back in twenty minutes with Wilt Avery in tow.

"What happened, did you miss me?" Wilt yelled down over the roar of the fish pump.

"Right," I climbed up the ladder, took off my juicy glove and shook his hand. Sam put on his oil pants and climbed down into the fish while I took Wilt aft into the engine room.

Wilt said it wasn't the first time he had seen it, but then he allowed that he had been around for a long time. He explained what had happened to our power system several times, but I was still not sure I understood it. The alternator was indeed kaput. But it only needed new brushes and a new ballast resistor for good measure. The real problem was in the batteries.

The six-foot long hundred-amp bank of batteries was only a few months old, but it seemed that someone had cut a few corners on the electrical installation. When the batteries were all ganged together by their lead connectors, the overall voltage output was thirty-two volts DC with a hundred-amp capacity. That was fine for some of the electronic equipment like the radar, but the bulk of the gear, including all of the deck lights, our TV, various radios, and bilge pump were ordinary stuff from the hardware store that ran on twelve volts DC. It turned out that the proper way to pull twelve volts from a thirty-two-volt bank of batteries was to install something called a step-down voltage converter. Since DC (Direct Current) can't be stepped down to a lower voltage using a simple transformer, delivering a twelve-volt stream from a thirty-two-volt battery required first converting the current to AC (Alternating Current), running it through a transformer, and then converting it back to DC. That made the converter unit a little pricey.

Instead of paying the money, someone had drilled a little hole in one of the lead connectors between two of the batteries and screwed a sheet metal screw into the hole to secure a homemade tap-wire. Making that tap-wire the positive lead and running another wire to the negative side had indeed provided twelve volts DC. But the voltage regulator, which sensed how much current from the alternator was required to keep the battery charged, had been completely fooled by this makeshift tap-wire arrangement. The voltage regulator understood — correctly — that the batteries were continuing to charge across the full thirty-two-volt bank, but was not aware of the twelve-volt tap, which was drawing off a lot more current than the thirty-two-volt equipment. To the voltage regulator, everything was hunky dory. But the section of the battery bank that had been tapped for twelve volts never got completely charged. It would get partially charged and then discharged and then only partially charged, and so on. Pretty soon, that section of the battery bank had boiled off all of its water and was completely dead.

Wilton Avery had solved the mystery of the dead batteries, the factory agreed that we could get it fixed properly, and the weather had given us a much-needed rest. It was not the end of our problems with *Capt. Ed*, but we were hoping we were clear of the worst.

HORSE PISSING

OUR NONCHALANCE ABOUT further problems was a good indication of how tired we grew over the following months. One morning in early December we arrived under the fish pump at three am with a hold-full. It was my routine to check the engine room before we turned in up forward in the forecastle. When loaded, *Capt. Ed* was kept afloat by the buoyancy of the engine room at one end and the forecastle at the other. But with a hold-full, both of these spaces were also significantly deeper in the water, and thus under much more pressure, than when the boat was light. This meant that some leaks that didn't show when the boat was light had the habit of suddenly appearing when the boat was loaded.

That morning as I routinely stepped into the engine room to inspect it before we turned in up forward, I was greeted with a stream of water as big around as my finger arching three feet in the air from somewhere near the shaft log. In most boats of that size, the shaft log is the place where the propeller shaft passes through the hull. As such, the shaft log acts as the seal against the outside water pressure. Some boats have wooden shaft logs (hence the origin of the name: a large piece of wood with a hole bored through it). Others have a steel or iron arrangement, more like a large pipe with bushed fittings at either end that lets the shaft turn but keeps the seal watertight. *Capt. Ed* had the iron pipe arrangement. But it was ancient, and it was crude. The iron pipe had been fitted with two ends that wrapped around the propeller shaft, and was filled with packing grease via a standard automobile grease fitting to keep it sealed against the water. The increased water pressure due to loading had been just enough to pop off the corroded grease fitting on the iron shaft log and now water was shooting into the engine room, arcing in front of me in a stream that looked like a horse pissing.

But I was very tired, so I was unfazed and unconcerned. At that moment, all I wanted was a good four-hour nap until the pump was ready to suck out the fish. I saw that we had a saw and a hammer and some scrap wood lying in the lazarette area by the steering gear aft. I picked up a piece of three-quarter pine trim, cut off about a foot, took out my jackknife, whittled down the end to a size that tapered to fit the offending hole in the iron shaft log, picked up the hammer and drove the stick of wood into the hole stopping the water. It worked; and I remember not being worried at all that the plug might pop out while we were asleep, overwhelm the automatic bilge pump, sink the boat, and drown us both in our bunks. I slept soundly, or at least I think I did. And I believe that I even forgot to tell Sam about the problem until after we had unloaded the fish.

PIGEON COVE

USUALLY, NORMIE DID not like to take chances with his infrastructure. He was scrupulous about repairs to the *Candy B* and always paid top dollar for maintenance; and after owning her for ten of her twenty-eight years, she still looked liked a new boat.

But he was very fond of taking risks to catch fish, which often meant going after fish in tight places and on occasion tearing up the seine. By December, some of the herring had started showing at Cape Ann and Normie found a bunch just outside of Rockport Harbor, in a place called Pigeon Cove. There was a sandy spot just big enough for a set, but when he got too close to the northern edge of this favorite hole, the seine would inevitably hang and come back ripped. It was probably part of a wreck sticking up out of the sand, something sharp enough to cut the twine. He had torn up so many times in Pigeon Cove he said that he could almost predict the shape and length of the tear.

That night, as anticipated, Normie felt the seine hang as he was pursing. He immediately backed off on the purse line and told the boys to let the end of the seine go free — thus losing the fish but minimizing the damage. Halfway through hauling back, as the seine was taken aloft through the power block overhead, the dripping twine showed a large open window of torn mesh. Rockport Harbor was right around the corner from Pigeon Cove, so we took the *Candy B* and the *Capt. Ed* in to tie up at the end of the town wharf where Normie and crew could mend the seine under the lights.

When we arrived at the Rockport town dock, it was past midnight and no one was around. As we passed through the narrow entrance in the breakwater, I suddenly realized the last time I had been to Rockport. I was eight years old and the harbor had looked huge. It had been a hot day on the weekend and my family had decided to go to the ocean, which meant going to Rockport. The harbor lot was full, so we parked our 1955 green Buick Roadmaster a mile away and walked along the long line of parked cars by the side of the road. The harbor was busy with people but I didn't really understand why they were there. Rockport was a place where people went to see a small red building out on the end of the breakwater called Motif #1. Several artists had set up easels along the breakwater and were painting portraits of the red house.

Motif #1 was still there as we idled into the stone wharf, an old red fish house covered with lobster buoys. Normie said the town of Rockport claimed it was the most photographed and painted building in the world.

Shortly after tying up, the harbormaster, Bud Atkins, drove out onto the wharf in his pickup truck and offered Normie a rum and coke. Bud was an old friend and Normie was pleased that the harbormaster had seen us tied up with the lights blazing at the end of the town wharf. Normie proceeded to recount the activity at Pigeon Cove.

"It's a tradition. I can't come down here without going to Pigeon Cove and getting the same ten-foot three-corner tear at least once a winter. Wouldn't be right," he said.

If we had visited in daylight and the pitch of summer, Normie would have enjoyed being painted into someone's picture, but it was past midnight in December and all the painters and photographers were in bed blowing through their parched lips of sleep. It was a calm night and we could have just as easily strapped the two boats together and lay out in Sandy Bay while we mended. But Normie liked to visit his old haunts—if only to keep his reputation as a traveling man alive.

There was something to be said for the scene. Snow was falling under the cone of lights. The seine was hanging from the power block overhead like a mountainous theater curtain thirty-feet in the air, shining black under the bluish mercury deck lights mounted on the end of Normie's main boom. The seine glistened with water and scales — and a few herring that were small enough to be meshed in the twine hung limp, distributed across the hoisted seine like the ornaments on a Christmas tree. Ronnie Crenshaw and Marshall Foster, the only two hands that Normie trusted to properly lace up the rent in the net, had white plastic twine needles in their hands while the rest of us held the purse-seine out like a bed sheet so they could easily see the course of the tear.

Twine needles had probably not changed for a century or more, save for the fact that they were now made of plastic instead of wood. In this case they were about eight inches long, and were shaped like a bullet with two prongs at the blunt end. In the center, a pointed tongue allowed the mender to load the needle with twine by wrapping it from the tongue to the blunt end of the bullet, back and forth. Ronnie and Marshall both worked bare-handed to lace quicker with the needles; the rest of us wore rubber-coated orange gloves. On a warm day with nothing else to do, Normie's perfectionism would take over and he would undoubtedly spread the seine on the dock, methodically taking apart tonight's lacing and knitting the torn net together properly, mesh to mesh.

Despite the natural beauty of the scene, I was not enjoying the way my stomach was reacting to this job and the crumbling hulk of *Capt. Ed*. I was eating a hundred or more antacid tablets a week to control my constant heartburn. They tasted like banana-flavored chalk. Thinking it would help, I had cut back on coffee and was mostly spooning down cups of peach yogurt and drinking chocolate milk. Even so, about twenty minutes after eating I inevitably felt a terrific pain in my stomach.

Knowing we would be fishing out of Gloucester for the whole winter, Sage and Joy had driven my truck down to Gloucester a few days earlier so Sam and I could drive home on the weekends. Joy had then taken the bus home, but Sage wanted to stay with us on the boat for a few days and see what it was like chasing Normie around all night in the dead of winter. She and Sam slept up forward and I bunked in the wheelhouse.

The previous night we had plucked out two nice codfish incidentally caught in the seine and Sage had decided to make us fish chowder. The recipe was simple. Render some small pieces of salt pork for flavor and oil, fry up a chopped onion in the oil, add three peeled and chopped potatoes and water enough to cover them, cook the potatoes until they are almost done, put the codfish on top so it steams for fifteen minutes, and then add a can of evaporated milk to the broth.

Sage's presence changed the tone of the whole trip. She cheered Sam, and was a partial antidote to my dark cloud.

"You've got to lighten up you know. This is the life here, guys. You just don't know it. Will you think about it for just a minute? Here you guys are — you've got your own boat to run, someone else is paying all the repair bills, you're following Normie who keeps finding fish and loading you guys. And it is the middle of the freaking winter. Will someone please tell me what's wrong with that?" she asked.

"I really don't know the answer, Sage," I said, "seems like a pretty good gig, doesn't it."

Sitting there in Rockport Harbor, I continued to ponder Sage's admonishment. As to why we weren't on top of the world, I finally said back to her, "I think it has to do with the boat not being in the best of shape. But honestly, I can't figure it out myself, Sage."

Then after some thought I added, "Running a carrier is something I always wanted to do. I guess I can blame Henry Jones for that."

I climbed across Normie's deck, then up the ladder and took a walk to the phone booth at the head of the wharf. It was just after 1:30 am. Joy answered after five or six rings, very groggy.

"Are you all right?" her voice cracking as she struggled awake.

"Yeah, I'm all right. I'm sorry it's so late, I had to talk to you. Normie got torn up and we're laid up in Rockport."

"You know me, I thought something bad had happened."

"No nothing bad. My stomach is killing me, though."

"Well you ought to go see the doctor, then."

"I know, I know. When things calm down, I will."

"When is that going to happen?"

"I don't know."

"I had a scare the last night, you know."

"What happened?"

"Well, you know how dark it is here some nights, can't see your hand in front of your face when you go to bed?"

"Yeah."

"Well it was late. I think it was around this time, actually." She yawned, fighting sleep. "There was a bright light shining in through the bedroom window, you know shining in right above the bed."

"Yeah."

"Someone had pulled into the upper driveway in front of the shed, in a pickup I guess, and the headlights were lighting up the bedroom. It was so bright, it woke me up."

"Who was it?"

"I don't know who it was. That was the thing. Whoever it was just sat there in front of the shed with their headlights on for quite a while."

"What'd you do?"

"Well, I got really scared. Because they just sat there. So I climbed out of bed and went out the back door and crawled under the house."

"Jesus Christ, that's not good."

"Well no. No, it's not good. I was there under the house on the ground in my nightgown for about fifteen minutes and it was getting cold."

"Could you tell what kind of truck it was?"

"I don't know. Aren't you listening?"

"Yeah, I'm listening."

"Well, I'm under the house scared that someone is coming to get me or something, so I'm not going to be able to tell what kind of truck it is and it was dark. It was very dark."

"I get it, I get it. I'm sorry. That is bad. A bad situation."

I tried to take the edge off by telling her that it was probably just some guys out drinking and ranging around and they had pulled off the main road for a minute. But I told her to call Howard Plummer and tell him about it. He would be discreet, and as the constable he should know about it in case it happened again.

"Look, we'll be home this weekend because the factory won't pack, so I'll ask around town, too."

It was stupid to tell her not to worry. I didn't like it, and we both had plenty to worry about. But I should have seen that the writing was on the wall with Joy. We had been in South Bristol for more than six years. She had gone from waitress to teaching elementary school art out of a car, and was now at a dead-end job doing paste-up for the county newspaper. She was an artist and a teacher and was determined to find a place where she would be honored and paid for what she loved. I was gone all the time and she was already getting calls about teaching art in boarding schools. I knew that if something good came along she was going to jump.

ANNISQUAM

NOTHING IN THE WORLD COULD STOP Normie from setting on fish. I found that out a few weeks later one night off of the bell buoy at the mouth of the Annisquam River in Ipswich Bay.

It was the latter part of December and we had taken a run to Isles of Shoals and nosed around for several hours before giving up. The weather forecast that evening called for a bad southeast blow — gale warnings were posted and rain was part of the prediction. Wind can build gradually or come on suddenly, depending on the approaching speed of the storm itself. That night the wind came on very quickly. When we left the Isles of Shoals at 10:30 pm, heading back to Gloucester, the wind was blowing a steady twenty-five knots out of the south. By the time we were within five miles of Cape Ann, it was over forty-five knots.

At that point, all the herring boats out of Gloucester had chosen to head in and were saying that rounding the cape to head for Eastern Point was getting ugly. The largest boat in the fleet, the 135-foot *Barnegat*, reported that she had cut back on the throttle and was slowing down. When that news came over the radio, Normie called me on the VHF and suggested that we forgo trying to steam around the cape and instead enter Gloucester via the Annisquam River, the mouth of which was marked with a red and white bell buoy on the north side of Cape Ann. The Annisquam is a very effective short cut from Ipswich Bay to Gloucester — and that night the river had the added feature of putting us in the lee of the entire land mass of Cape Ann and completely out of the wave action currently crashing on the windward side of the cape.

By the time we reached the red and white bell, it was raining hard and the wind was driving the rain horizontally. Normie was ahead of us. I had planned to follow him through the canal since I did not know the

Annisquam well enough to navigate solely by radar, and my spotlight was absolutely useless.

When rain is blowing horizontal at fifty knots, you need a spotlight to pick up the reflective tape on the cans and nuns. But what the *Capt. Ed* had on board was a humorous imitation of a spotlight, another cruel joke perpetrated by the previous owners that literally looked like something salvaged from a vintage police cruiser. In fact, Sam had pointed to it once and said, in-character as one of the Blues Brothers, "What do you think Elrod?" It was that kind of spotlight. Worse yet, it was mounted on the wheelhouse, which was aft. When I turned it on, all it did was light up the bow. Fortunately, Sam and I had never had occasion to need it.

We were half a mile in the lee of Halibut Point, about a mile and a half from the bell when Normie cut back and stopped. Before I knew it, I was on top of him. I took the *Capt. Ed* out of gear. Guessing what had happened, I dreaded his call on the radio. "There's a good bunch of fish here," he said, "Right outside the bell buoy. Good bottom, too."

"Un hunh," I said, trying to mask my lack of enthusiasm.

"You think we should take a crack at them?"

I paused. It was definitely not a good idea to stand in the way of one of the best shoal seiners on the planet, even when he was acting crazy. A carrier crew was really just crew when you got right down to it — working for the factory and working for the seiner.

"If you think you can handle taking the seine back overhead in a full gale," I said.

"Not a problem," Normie said quickly.

I could tell where the conversation was headed. So could Sam. He had been checking the chart for the Annisquam River and was now telling me that he was alarmed about some of the depths, especially if we were going to attempt going through fully-loaded. I asked him what the tide was doing. Sam told me that the tide was ebbing and would be almost half gone by the time we were loaded.

I call back on the radio, "Normie, you think you can get me through the river at half-tide, fully-loaded? I'm sure as hell not going around Cape Ann in this shit."

"It'll be close but it should be okay at half-tide. I've done it loaded at half-tide. I can get us through there."

"That's good, because my puny spotlight only shines about ten feet in front of the wheelhouse and the radar is no good on close range."

I turned to Sam, off-radio. "Do you believe this shit? This guy is a fucking lunatic!" I was very loud. I was probably shouting.

"He is going to set that fucking seine in a full fucking gale and take us though the Annisquam drawing fourteen feet at half-tide." I was wildly exaggerating about the carrier's draft but Sam knew what I meant.

Back on the radio I said, "Okay, Normie. Give 'em hell."

"Better get your rain gear, buddy," I said to Sam, "this is going to be a freaking circus act. Normie's acrobatic seiners."

We didn't have to wait long. Watching the lights on the *Candy B*, I saw the red light on Normie's bug boat pull away from the seiner. He was setting, the seine bumping and rumbling as the leads skated over the stern of the *Candy B*. Most nights the big pile of twine was reduced quickly and the lower part of the seine inevitably smoked like a pile of compost. New layers of warm decomposing small fish that had been meshed three sets ago were exposed to the cold night air. That night I'm sure no one on deck watched anything but the weather, as they kept their hoods turned against the rain driving horizontally out of the southeast.

Normie rarely missed when he set, and that night was no exception. Missed sets were worse on crew morale than the boredom of waiting for the right bunch in the right place. The bottom Normie was setting on was all sand and flat as a tabletop. It was also, according to the chart, only fifty feet deep, which meant that a twenty-fathom seine would definitely be sitting on the bottom when the purse line closed. Once Normie circled the fish, they would not be able to dive under the seine to escape before he pursed. It was interesting that fish would stay bunched in that kind of weather. I'm sure wave action and wind have a lot less to do with the herring's schooling behavior than ambient light. But somehow I imagined them to be in an every man for himself mode, scattering into a diffuse cloud. Certainly in only fifty feet of water, they must have felt some push and pull from the wave action. If they were bunched in this fury, they would not be startled by the clatter of a seine being set around them. In truth, I was hoping that they would escape or that Normie would miss them, but that was very unlikely, even in a situation like this. If he did screw up, Normie would not likely set again in this weather.

To my amazement, Normie and crew hauled back in record time. It was clear that Normie was not applying his usual go-slow, feel the purse line for snags on the bottom methodology. He had wailed on the purse line and hauled it as fast as he could, knowing the ground was smooth and that his rings and leads were certain to be securely on the bottom. He also didn't give a damn about the white deck lights spooking the fish and snapped them on halfway through hauling back. That also eliminated the need to interrupt the hauling by stepping into the wheelhouse to call me, since snapping on the deck lights was a signal for the carrier to come alongside. Sam and I were already queued up, and when we saw the deck lights we came in quickly to pick up the corks.

After we strapped on the corks of the bunt, Normie's bug boat pointed up into the wind, towing the *Candy B* and the *Capt. Ed* broadside to the southeast gale. The bug boat's towing would keep both boats stable against the chop and prevent us from being blown down onto the beach at Wingaersheek.

We strapped the *Capt. Ed* and *Candy B* tightly together, pressing against the five or six hundred-inch balloons we had between us, but even with the bug boat towing us upwind the two boats were eager to chafe against each other as they went up and down on the steep chop in a counter-tempo like horses on a merry-go-round. Pumping was quick and we filled to within 5,000 pounds of our 57,500-pound capacity. We cast off as quickly as we could and hauled out the chart again to get situated.

The chart showed a channel at the mouth of the river that was marked as "6 ft. for width of 200 ft." in block letters. All depths were "mean low water" and it was coming up on half-tide. As we had previously estimated — by adding three or four feet for the load to the six feet that she drew light — we were probably drawing nine or ten feet loaded. Of course, that was a guess. The channel started just inside the first marker after the bell, which was "G C 3" (Green Can marked with the number 3) and ran for a half mile. Normie had warned me about this stretch and had advised me to never try entering it in a northeast blow as you could easily strike bottom in the trough of a swell. But with the wind out of the southeast, and in the lee of Cape Ann, we had nasty chop but no deep swell. Even so, adding six feet for half-tide to the six-foot mean low water depth of the narrow channel only gave us twelve feet of water, just two feet of clearance with *Capt. Ed* drawing ten feet loaded.

After this shoal channel, the river was reasonably deep until just before entering the Blynman Canal at the end of the Annisquam. Just before the start of this long dredged canal, was a length marked "7 ft. deep" between Wheeler Point and Thurston Point. That was the only other spot that looked particularly bad on the chart. Once we were past that, the ambient light from the town and the marina would be enough to let us see what was going on all the way to the Blynman Bridge, one of two drawbridges along the waterway.

"What's the point of even thinking this through," I said to Sam. "The only alternative to going through the river is to throw out the hook and wait six hours for daylight and then another three hours for high water. I don't know about you, but I don't want to hang on a hook in this sand with this wind for the rest of the night."

Sam peered out at Normie's lights pulling away toward the mouth of the river, "Looks like Normie's headed. So if we're going to decide, it had better be now."

"We just need to do this," I replied.

Over the radio I told Normie to give me a chance to get a little closer so I could follow his lights. Once we got past the entrance buoys, my radar screen would practically wash out, showing only two greenish blobs on either side of a narrow black thread in the center — the Annisquam River. We wouldn't be able to distinguish marker buoys at all.

I didn't bother with the spotlight. In fact by lighting up the bow, the spotlight would have made it harder to see Normie's lights ahead. Confident that Normie knew the river well, I stayed as tight as I could on the *Candy B*.

My biggest concern was that I would miss a buoy or lose sight of Normie and drive the *Capt. Ed* ashore in the narrow river. As I look back now, I realize that the larger risk was actually getting into the river through the six-foot channel — a danger that I all but ignored in my rush to close the distance to the *Candy B*.

The entrance channel ran through a sandbar that shifted on a regular basis. Sand was softer than rock, but with a load like we were carrying, anything other than a rub would have been a problem. I was so intent on staying within a hundred yards of Normie, that I had no sense of how close we had come to either spending the night aground on the sandbar or sinking the boat in the channel. We felt nothing as we passed into the river. Silence of the keel passing over sand with the wind roaring overhead.

The rain was very heavy. I remember the water-stained wood of the wheelhouse and the leaky windows. When it was cold, ice would form and melt down onto the sills. The wheelhouse interior had never been painted and the water stains showed like dark spills on the old delaminating plywood. The rain was driving hard enough to sound like someone throwing sand onto the windward windows.

After the entrance channel, the next bad spot — I think the only place with actual rocks — was off of Babson Point. Normie called me on the VHF and told me what to do: After Red Nun "8" I needed to stay right and give Babson Point a wide berth without going into the mud on the right, then almost run down the Red Nun "12" to avoid another seven-foot spot that reached out from Babson there. I favored right and rubbed "R N 12" as prescribed. No bumps past Babson.

Nearing the next bad stretch between Wheeler and Thurston Points, Normie slowed way down and we glided through the two hundred yards marked on the chart "7 FEET NOV 1971–MAR 1972." This description was likely from the last time the stretch was dredged. Sam and I were not speaking much with the exception of Sam noting the numbers of the cans and nuns after he had shined the flashlight on them. Silence was good. No rubs, no unexpected noises.

That put us at "G C 21" after which it was hard to get into too much trouble. Beyond it was mostly dredged canal and narrow enough so the shore loomed close. With more and more light pollution from the City of Gloucester, passing through the narrow canal was like walking in a dark canyon. The walls were shiny, sticky mud lashed with rain.

The only other obstacle was what we called the Train Bridge, a drawbridge shown on the chart as a bascule bridge, a counterweighted bridge where the commuter train from Boston passed over the river and into Gloucester. The bridge tender usually left the drawbridge open after the last train somewhere around eleven pm to avoid having to get up in the wee hours. Normie radioed, "Train bridge is open." It was a black trestle standing upright like a pair of iron jaws silhouetted against a sickly greenish sky.

The last leg was the Blynman Canal and the Blynman drawbridge. We backed down in front of the Cape Ann Marina. Normie and crew would tie up there for the remainder of the morning at a long run of floats twenty yards from the channel. We still needed to go through the Blynman and into the Inner Harbor to get under the pump at eight am. The Blynman drawbridge was closed. I radioed the bridge tender who was surprisingly quick to open it. It was two am. The gut is very narrow, one-boat-wide at the bridge, and that morning it was flowing hard as the tide emptied into Gloucester's West Harbor. For some reason I thought of Sam and me as two bugs riding a leaf down a storm drain and finally dumped into the harbor.

We didn't hit anything, didn't rip the bottom out and spill the guts of the boat in a glittering pile of fish. But we were nothing more than lucky. Proof of that came two years after I had left. Normie was trying to get through the Annisquam at half-tide loaded with herring for the lobster bait market and put the *Candy B* ashore. Despite his skill and knowledge of the river, he hit the seven-foot spot opposite Red Nun "12." She sunk on the spot but was only partially submerged. No one was hurt, and once Normie got past the hassle of dealing with the City of Gloucester's restrictions over dumping fish and was able to offload the bulk of the herring from the hold, he righted and raised the *Candy B*.

THRESHOLDS

F EAR IS ALWAYS READILY accessible on the water. Anyone who stands watch underway on a sailboat or workboat overnight becomes familiar with it, particularly in Maine or Nova Scotia where there are plenty of rocks and long periods of fog. It is part of the process of learning. Often you encounter a situation that you have never experienced before — a situation that causes you to question whether you're taking the right action to deal with it. But you can't get the experience and the understanding of the situation without being in it, face to face with the stark reality.

And since you can't imagine every possible screw up or weird combination of events ahead of time, you often can't get the experience of learning something new on the water without feeling a certain amount of fear and anxiety.

And once you've experienced the new situation — say, running between buoys in heavy fog without radar, in some relic like the *Capt. Ed*, with no radio, no lights, using only courses and times — the fear begins to fade. Often you find that, after ratcheting up your tolerance of fear and your experience, the things you were worried about were not actually very dangerous. But equally often, you might find that a combination of naiveté and luck has caused you to miss the real danger of the situation.

When I first started searching for herring with Henry and Gladden, Henry asked me one night to take the workboat in to Pemaquid Beach to have a look. It was high water and I skirted along the beach watching the sound machine scratch its marks on the roll of chart paper. Seeing no sign of fish, I throttled up and headed straight back out to Henry at full speed, running straight over the half-tide ledges in between. After I had passed over the ledges, I noticed that the depth recorder showed no space between the bottom of the boat and the jagged ledge. With a lump in my throat, I realized that I had missed ripping the bottom out of the work-boat by inches. I tore off the depth recorder chart paper and stuffed the evidence into my pocket, embarrassed by my mistake and chilled by how close I had come to wrecking Henry's workboat, the *Frances*.

Picking deckhands or crewmates was about tolerance for fear, too. Without question, the best shipmate I ever worked with was Mel. His real name was Bob Ryan, but everyone called him Mel because he had grown up in Melrose, Massachusetts. Nothing ever bothered Mel. When bad shit happened — which it always did — Mel was the coolest of the cool. He didn't yell and he didn't freeze. He just carried on. Whenever I had a say in choosing a shipmate or fellow deckhand, I never voted for the loud extrovert, life of the party. I always opted for the calm, quiet guy like Mel.

The other threshold often tested was my tolerance for disappointment and uncertainty. I might make two thousand dollars in one glorious and exciting night and return the hero. But that happy event might immediately be followed by no income for six weeks. This often meant working the same long hours, suffering through interminable and boring days and nights catching nothing, or tearing up gear on wrecks and rocks because of bad decisions, or wrestling with equipment breakdowns because maintenance was neglected. This list of misfortunes would then ultimately lead to wrestling with my own thoughts of moving on to something better, or finding a skipper not so pigheaded, or finding a better boat that was more comfortable or better equipped, all the while watching my bills pile up, and hating my life.

Deckhands had a bit of ritual dialog we would use to check in on our tolerance when things were going south — we would ask each other, "How's your courage?" The implication being that if your courage was not good, you would ultimately become dis-couraged and quit.

"How's your courage?"

"Truth be told, it's not so good, right now. Not so good."

Normie Brackett said he could predict these events. Out on deck alone, a deckhand would sit on the fish hold hatch coaming and stare at the horizon. Normie said when he saw this happening it was almost certain that within two to three days the guy would be gone.

HERE COME THE PAIR-TRAWLERS

SAM AND I CARRIED FISH FOR NORMIE in that '78–'79 winter from November through February. We freighted roughly 450,000 pounds to Gloucester, which added up to nine tanker truckloads of big sea herring sent over the road to the packing plant in Boothbay, Maine. For this the factory paid us $3,375 each, before taxes, and we each made an additional $675 from the scales (cash money in a brown paper bag). On the weeks that Normie went dry and we had nothing to carry, the factory paid us $120 apiece. In January and February the weather was horrendous, giving us only a handful of windows to fish in.

During this stretch of bad weather, I went back to my doctor in Damariscotta. It was an ulcer, he said, and prescribed pills that would shut down all my stomach functions for eight or ten hours at a stretch, stopping the flow of acid. They did that job, but I would wake up feeling as though I had eaten a small sack of concrete. My intestines felt stiff and twisted, petrified. Night fishing with Normie had turned my guts into a river of acid, now the pills were turning them into stone.

Even on the nights we did get out, the fish were too spread out and too deep to reach with a purse-seine. It was perfect fishing for the pair-trawlers, though, and they were slaying the big herring.

Some years before, it had been discovered that a pair of eighty-foot boats working together provided enough power to tow a mid-water trawl. This kind of net had been around for a long time, but it required the kind of power only found on much larger vessels — usually factory trawlers — just to pull it through the water. The concept is simple. If you can control the direction and the depth of a very large net, one that has an opening roughly the size of a football field — on average three hundred feet wide — and if you can tow it faster than the fish you are trying to catch, which is about four knots, then two boats can reach fish like herring when they are either too dispersed or too deep for a seine.

First, the two boats survey a number of relatively small bunches, or pods, of herring, too small to bother setting a seine on, and mark each pod on their electronic plotters. Because the electronic plotters are connected to their autopilots, the two boats can go back to the beginning of the plotted course, set the trawl between them, turn on the plotters and autopilots and tow the mid-water trawl through each one of the pods of herring.

Setting this large mid-water trawl in the water is not a trivial exercise. One boat sets the trawl trailing off its stern, then fires a line gun to the other boat to transfer one of the two bridles, so the two boats can tow the trawl together. The second boat must hook up the bridle line while carefully maintaining a constant distance to the other boat so as not to stress or tear the trawl. The two boats then reel off their cables at exactly the same rate and to the same depth, maintaining constant distance between them and the same course and speed. At that point, hopefully the two skippers have allowed enough time and distance to get the mid-water trawl to a stable depth before starting their run through the plotted courses. And hopefully, the pods of herring have not moved significantly from their original plotted locations.

When fish are spread across a large area, this turns out to be a very successful way of catching herring. If the two boats are rigged for pair-trawling but find a single whopping big bunch of herring, they can vacuum that up, too. The only problem in either case — thin and spread out fish, or large and concentrated schools — is gauging how many fish have actually been captured in a single tow. If too many fish are collected in the trawl, the weight of the fish and the water pressure applied by the power of two boats towing a great wad of packed fish at four knots can be great enough to burst the cod-end of the mid-water trawl, killing upwards of three hundred thousand pounds of herring and badly tearing the trawl.

The introduction of pair-trawling in the mid-'70s has radically changed the inshore herring industry. Since that time, the stop-seine sardine business that had instantly captivated me when I took a ride with Henry Jones, has all but disappeared from the Maine coast. Great shining schools of small herring no longer nose their way into the still coves of mid-coast Maine at the edge of dark. Stop-seining and weir fishing survive only in the remotest stretch of the Maine coast near the Canadian border, and only for lobster bait.

By February, Normie, Sam, and I had reached the end of our season. The fish were in deep water, and when the weather was decent the pair-trawlers were loading up their tanker trucks. There was little left for the likes of us. We made one last circle from Gloucester to Boston Light, on to Plymouth, halfway across to Provincetown and then back to Gloucester. Finding nothing that was reachable with a seine, we turned in early at midnight on February 15, 1979—a beautiful calm evening with the water on Boston Bay as flat as a millpond. We were done.

The next morning we pointed our boats to the northeast and steamed home. After four months of night fishing, it seemed almost summer-like to see the bleached rock of the shoreline again. We put *Capt. Ed* up to 1450 rpm. At that speed she gave us twelve knots, but blackish smoke came from the exhaust stack—a sign that the Cummins diesel was laboring. The propeller had too much pitch, was pushing too much water with each revolution of the blades, another thing that needed to be looked after. We would not be tending to this problem, though. Both of us were through with the *Capt. Ed*. The decision wasn't hard. I knew that keeping the old girl afloat was eventually going to land me in the hospital, and Sam knew that he wanted to get back to the sanity of shaping wood into boats.

After nine hours of clattering diesel travel, Sam and I tied the *Capt. Ed* up in Boothbay. Numbed by the throbbing monotony, we threw our duffels and sleeping bags in the back of Sam's pickup and drove home with Sage. We hardly talked during the hour-and-a-half trip to South Bristol. Sage said we were about as much fun as two cadavers. I told her that we had nearly reached that state of stillness. Bodies waiting for embalming fluid and no longer subject to the dangerous forces of the universe. Nothing much could go wrong driving in the pickup. Head-on collision—too quick and traumatic to feel anything. Other nominal risks all had the same sense of calm resolution. Flat tire—get out and change it. Engine loses coolant, overheats—pull over. Truck catches fire—pull over, get out, and watch it burn. Really, no risk. The only sensations we experienced were the feelings of inevitable decay throughout our once youthful flesh, and our longings for the cool sheets of our beds.

MACKEREL *(Scomber scombrus)*

Part Four

ALL ANYONE NEEDS

THE LIGHTED BOX

WHEN SAM AND I RETURNED from Gloucester, Joy had driven to a job interview at the Darrow School, a country boarding school in upstate New York. I thought about going, but I was too exhausted. Instead, I flopped and saw no one for two days. Just lay around with the cats in front of the big windows with the sun streaming in.

Finally, Joy called from New York. "They want me," she said, "This is so much the right thing. I can feel it."

I was quiet.

"I accepted the job. I'll start in the fall."

"Look, you can give up winter fishing, Paulie," she carried on cheerfully, "You'll see. This is a good thing."

"This is a big change, Joy," I said.

"I know it's a big change, but I'll be home for the summers and you can come down and live with me for the winters. It will be great, you'll see. Besides, you're too smart to keep this up forever. You need to get out."

After the call, I went back to the cats and sunlight. Dozing, I remembered a strange offseason experience. Gladden had told me about an Austrian marionette troupe, the Salzburg Marionette Theater, coming to perform at Bowdoin College in Brunswick. In return for helping the troupe hump their gear on and off the rental truck, we had free tickets to their performance, a full-length rendering of Mozart's opera, *The Magic Flute*.

We unloaded crate after crate of marionettes, props, and scenery, then set up the small stage — a wooden box, six by four feet. The miniature stage was decorated with elegant gold leaf scrollwork like a lifesized stage, but was open at the top so the puppeteers could manipulate their actors. The box stood in the center of the theater stage carefully masked with a curtain. As I stood halfway to the back of the theater, the marionette stage looked really tiny—too small—and I wondered how the troupe was going to perform a full-length opera in this little box and keep the audience engaged.

As we were setting up the stage, the troupe prepared an offstage framework of long poles from which the entire collection of two-foot high, and beautifully costumed, marionettes was suspended. Papageno the bird catcher was clothed in brilliant bird feathers. On his back was an intricate birdcage, and in his hands he held a struggling bird. The long black snake hung ready to display lifelike slither, and the Queen of the Night's face was proud but plaintive. On another frame, the scenery was stacked in the order in which it was to be used, the sound system was hooked up, and they were ready to perform.

For the first act, I stood backstage and watched them work. The puppeteers, squeezed tightly together and hunched over the tiny stage, were reaching over and under each other's arms, passing levers and strings over their heads, as the characters interacted on the stage below. They managed what looked like a tangled mess of strings and levers, but like musicians they were seemingly unconscious of what their hands were doing as they made the marionettes perform.

Peering intently down into the lighted stage, sometimes handling two characters at once, the music was loud enough so they could talk easily to each other in low voices without being heard by the audience. But they hardly ever talked about the logistics of what was coming next. They had no need, as they had performed this so many times and everything was neatly arranged and in the right order of appearance. Instead, they mostly talked to each other in-character, using different voices for each of the players in the opera. Speaking in German, they spoke to the other characters in their assumed voices—a man making the Queen of the Night plead with the hero Tamino for help talked to his human colleagues in the voice of a woman, and a woman puppeteer spoke low as the dark villain Monostatos. They were like children, totally engrossed by the story, completely given over to the dream. This was what they loved. Performing the opera was joyful play for them.

The performance was unforgettable. After the first act, I left backstage and sat in the theater. At first, the tiny stage looks absurdly small, a lighted box suspended in the dark. But in about ten minutes it grew larger. Soon it appeared to me as somewhere between a little box and a full-sized stage.

After a half-hour of watching I gave it no more thought. I was completely immersed in the dream of the opera. I was inside the lighted box.

As I continued to doze and walk through my memory, I began to realize that I was living inside the fishing life, just as I had dreamed myself inside the lighted marionette box. I saw only fishing gear and boats and dreamt only about new ways to make money and better ways to catch fish. I thought about what fish might do next and why they have just done what they have done. My sole intent was to make as much money as I possibly could make by fishing faster, harder, smarter, and more in touch with the underlying nature and movement of fish. Like the rest of my fishing friends, I read *National Fisherman* magazine and looked for stories that would give me a clue for where to go next. Should I run a bigger boat for a company, or should I keep my overhead low by fishing in my backyard?

If you asked me what I was going to do next year, or in ten years time, I wouldn't have an answer. I could see no way out. Why would I want to see a way out? I was thirty years old. This was my life. Why would I want to see a way out?

But my living inside the fishing life was also gradually distancing me from Joy. She lived in another life, the world of art and teaching. When she asked me what had happened that night or that day — when I arrived home beaten up by the fishing life — I often said the same thing a child says when you ask them what they did today. Nothing. Or I said, you know how it is, we caught a bunch of fish and we'll get paid some money, and it was a little rough, or we didn't get a lot of sleep, and so forth.

I knew that Joy was right. I had to get out, eventually. I sure as hell couldn't stay in the lighted box, the imaginary world I was living in. My body had already proved to me that I couldn't keep running the *Capt. Ed* and chasing Normie. The evidence was a stomach ulcer. Although I knew Joy was dropping breadcrumbs for me to follow, still, I wasn't yet ready to step out of the box. This new gig was hers, and I was not ready to give up on the dream of catching fish in my backyard.

THE CRYSTAL BALL CLEARS

WHEN SPRING ARRIVED IN 1979, Sam and I decided to try a second season of mackerel trapping. Joy would be off to her new job in the fall and I would join her at the school after my season ended, at least for a while. I sold my old Novi boat and bought a rebuilt marina tender, an open boat with plenty of power, and started getting ready in earnest in April.

Sam and I were aboard the *Alice M* with Henry for early coffee one morning telling him some of our Gloucester stories from the previous winter. One tale included a very cold night with a lot of wind, a propane heater with no thermostat — sort of like the burner on a gas grill, stuffed inside a sheet metal housing — and Gloucester's historic Blackburn's Tavern.

Sam and I are in the wheelhouse of the *Capt. Ed* listening to the NOAA weather and have turned up the propane heater to take the chill off. After hearing a forecast for more cold and wind, and checking in with Normie, who is tied up in front of us, we go to dinner and drinks at Blackburn's with the heater still running on high.

When we return at midnight, the wheelhouse is roasting hot. We quickly turn off the heater and open both doors, but the woodwork inside is hot to the touch and the fluid in our large old compass has turned a milky white.

Both of us are pretty tight. Sam hovers over the compass. "Hunh. Looks like the crystal ball in the Wizard of Oz. You know, the one the Wicked Witch of the West used to track Dorothy and her friends," he offers. The difference, of course, is that we can't see anything at all, let alone Judy Garland.

"Yah, the green face, and the big long nose, I remember that. Shit, it looks like we pooched the compass, Sam. We'll have to call the factory in the morning," I say. I am not looking forward to the phone call and already feeling for the threads of a credible story.

Both of us go to bed knowing that we have come close to setting the boat on fire and it looks as though we have ruined our beautiful vintage compass—probably an antique.

We wake feeling guilty. The northwest wind is still strong enough to buffet *Capt. Ed* and make her pull against the floats at the marina like a spooked horse. Sam puts on his boots and dodges out quickly to the wheelhouse. We feel like kids who have broken a family heirloom.

As I stand at the stove making coffee, I hear him thump back across the deck. "She's clear," he says as he backs down the forecastle ladder. The compass fluid has turned clear again. The cold has mended our crystal ball.

Henry chuckled. He said that traveling always produced good stories no matter how small. Crews were always stepping over some line of behavior and that always made for revealing tales. We spent a lot of time that day with Henry talking about the impact of pair-trawling and huge purse-seines on the inshore stock. Listening to Henry, I became more willing to subscribe to belief in a dark future where the present is never as good as the wild days of the past. Henry had lived through the heyday of Maine's herring fishery—glittering shoals for the taking and fifty canneries where thousands of women snipped the heads off herring and packed them into cans. The more we talked, the more I convinced myself that it was all bound to get worse. Pair-trawlers would put the purse-seiners out of business. How could they not? They could cruise over ten or fifteen bunches of fish, program up the plotter with a waypoint for each bunch, tow the big trawl through the plotter points, and load the boat. Hell, you could even fish in full daylight so you could see what you were doing. It was game, set, and match. Purse-seining loses, pair-trawling wins. This crystal ball wasn't cloudy at all.

WATCHING THEM GO IN

D URING OUR SECOND TRAPPING SEASON, Sam and I developed more patience around the arrival of bluefish and pogies; we took the trap up for the better part of August hoping life would change when the weather cooled. Joy was getting ready for her trip to the Darrow School. She was a woman on a mission, not looking left or right, but I was as stuck as ever on making my life in Maine work out.

"Just come down and see what it's like," she said.

"Yeah, yeah, I know. I may not stay long, that's all."

"Well you don't have to, but I do. A dorm full of teenage girls will be high drama."

"I know, I know."

"Just try to keep an open mind. If you don't like it you can go home and drive down to see me when you get lonely."

I had no idea which end was up, but Joy had made a decision and for her there was no going back.

By September the weather had broken. Northwest winds were beginning to tear holes in the heat and the pogies and blues had moved on. Mackerel had returned and were beginning to bunch and be visible in schools. Sunrise was much later — and one morning Sam and I decided to wait and get to the trap for the high water slack around five am. With not a breath of air, the water was very still. As we looked north up along the shore we saw bunches of mackerel breaking the surface for at least a mile, and none of them more than fifty fathoms from the shore. We shut down the workboat and tied up to the corner of the trap, stepped into the dory with the skiff in tow, and hung on the corks to watch.

Author and Sam Jones preparing to haul mackerel trap

We stood there in the dory as quietly as we could as two large bunches of mackerel worked down the shore. The tide was just starting to ebb, and they chattered their way along at a speed somewhere between walking and running. The first bunch hit the leader, heads poking out of the water and kicking up a good strong rip as they turned and ran along the leader and in through the door. The second bunch was about thirty seconds behind and did the same. Our hearts were thumping.

"Sam, this just doesn't happen," I whispered, "you know, actually seeing them run in to the trap like this."

"Look at them," Sam hissed looking up the shore, "there are three more bunches coming down behind them."

"Sweet Jesus, Sam, I don't think Junior has ever seen them go in, you know just standing there and watching them. This is like some holy moment or something."

"Yeah, this is the look of a lifetime."

Author and Sam Jones hauling mackerel trap

We had built a small pocket net in our August downtime to make life easier drying up the fish and had hung it off of the backside of the trap. And the day before, I had noticed that we were out of ice and had borrowed a pickup to fetch a full load from Boothbay Harbor in case we had fish the next day. It was almost like we knew this was going to happen. It was spooky.

After scraping by all season, we now had close to twenty thousand pounds of mackerel swimming in the trap. Lately, the price had been high, between sixty and eighty cents in Boston, and we stood to gross some good money if the Canadians didn't flood the market with their government-price-subsidized mackerel. When that happened, the price would inevitably drop to ten or twelve cents for a week or more.

In the end, we took out 21,770 pounds over the course of two days, shipped them to Boston, and were paid an average of seventy-five cents per pound. Grossing close to sixteen thousand dollars in two days took some of the sting out of a terrible season, but it was over. After our brief moment of glory, the mackerel slowed to a trickle and we took up the trap in late October.

Joy was in full swing at the Darrow School and loving her new job.

"The school is on the side of a mountain and I've got a huge apartment in an old Shaker dormitory," she said when I called.

She went on to tell me about the long day—dining hall supervision, classroom, then coaching, then supervising the dorm full of girls until her head hit the pillow. The kids were lively, in fact, very lively. She was living on teenage time now.

"Can you sleep all night?" I asked.

"Sometimes, "she said. "Look, you can come and go as you please. Come down and see what you think. I'm here."

I told her that I had just thrown the mothballs on the mackerel trap to keep the mice out and stowed the anchors and would probably come down to stay from December to late winter. I didn't know if I was ready for teenagers, but I missed Joy. She was tough as nails and full of life. And she was happy.

WALKING IN FROM NOWHERE

A RRIVING HOME FROM COFFEE with Henry one day in November, I lounged around and finished reading Edward Lansing's *Endurance*, the survival story of Ernest Shackleton and his crew, all of whom were rescued after being lost for almost two years in the Antarctic and Southern Oceans. At the end of their ordeal, Shackleton and two of his party enter the remote whaling station at Stromness, South Georgia Island in 1916 traveling on foot. They have finally reached help after hiking the length of the island. In the process, they have climbed a forty-five-hundred-foot mountain range and slid thousands of feet down an ice-covered rock face on the remaining tatters of their clothing. When workmen at Stromness see the wild-looking men walking into the port from the interior of the island — a direction no one has ever come from — the three men are escorted to the station manager's house with many curious onlookers in tow. There, the station manager, who has met Shackleton before, stands in the doorway of his home to meet them. But because of their shocking condition, he recognizes none of them. Then, after a brief conversation and few moments of shocked silence, he realizes who they are and begins to weep.

As I read that passage, I remembered the same incident as described in Robertson's *Of Whales and Men*, a book about the height of modern whaling in the 1960s. The book was written by a medical assistant on one of the factory ships that were routinely carving up the largest creatures on the earth. Robertson had met one of the men from the whaling station at Stromness and found that even forty-five years after the incident, the story was told with the same detail of the station manager's reaction.

The men at the whaling station had some idea what Shackleton and his party had been through. But I thought about Joy and how little she knew about what Sam and I had experienced. Our four months was the routine life of a carrier crew at the winter end of the season and laughably lightweight in comparison. But I was struck by the community of understanding in the insane world of the Southern Ocean, and the lack of it in our relationship. I certainly held the responsibility for the paucity of communication. I had told Joy almost nothing about the fishing life. I had acquired a new vocabulary but only knew how to use it with other fisherman. Again, what came to me was the image of the lighted box with me inside it telling a story in a language she could not understand.

Not only that, I had been so wiped out when I got home that I simply didn't have the energy to explain anything, nor did I particularly want to relive the experiences. I wanted to sleep and put them behind me.

I remembered now the visits to her parents at their sweet cottage in Tenant's Harbor — the massive black cookstove, beds with bright quilts, simple Yankee furniture scattered throughout the house. In the summer we would go there for Sunday lunch, mostly lobster feasts with Tabasco-heavy Bloody Mary's. I would curl up afterwards on the couch, shed my shoes, and sleep for two hours, neck throbbing with fatigue, usually my hands and feet aching, then wake feeling swollen as if I had been on a binge.

Joy's parents had no way to enter the maze of my life, either. I had no words for them, and their questions would often probe from the wrong angle and burn up in my furnace of untranslatable experiences.

Now Joy was intent on developing another life while I had no idea where I was going. Thinking through the calendar, I knew that I could keep fishing in the summers. We would be separated for a few months, March to June at the beginning of the season and September to the end of November. But it wasn't clear that mackerel trapping would sustain us. It was a kindly and romantic idea from the past, but it was not a business.

Moreover, our life together pitted Joy's passion against my passion, and now I was running out of gas. Hers for art and for teaching had grown, while mine had been drained by years of heads-down, pure execution. Though I loved the highs of catching fish and the intense family of South Bristol fisherman, I was barely making a living. And the previous winter, because I couldn't make it with my own mackerel trapping business, I had turned myself into an itinerant deckhand to make ends meet.

I also knew that I was powerless to stop the change that Joy had initiated. I had been strapped down, medicated with my own exhaustion, and shocked into a blank state. Now I was in a new world and would have to change.

A week later, I made my way to the Darrow School in Mt. Lebanon, New York, to live with Joy for the winter. As with most teachers, living in the dormitory brought many a near-crisis, and at any hour the evening might be punctuated by a knock on the door. But the countryside was beautiful; the woods were all hardwood, mostly black walnut and hickory so they became very open when the leaves were down in the winter, especially compared to Maine's dense growth of spruce and pine. That December I saw my first herd of deer, twenty-five or thirty of them, crossing a hillside. I spent the winter reading and running errands, and in late February of 1980, I headed back to Maine to get ready for trapping again.

DOING THE MATH

JUNE OF 1980 CAME SOON ENOUGH. Sam and I set the trap again on the Pemaquid shore, and Joy was home for the summer, but we had a dismal season. The mackerel were sketchy and did not resurge in September. We were truly discouraged. All told, we had pursued mackerel trapping for three years, but that fall I told Sam that I planned to give up trapping for good.

The first week in October, I sold my trap, anchors, and dory to one of only three remaining mackerel trappers on the coast of Maine, a guy from Small Point. I called him on the advice of the rigger who had built my trap, and he was happy to take the gear off my hands.

Sam Jones and the author, South Bristol

I packed for another winter with Joy at Darrow, though I had no idea where to go from there. As far as she was concerned, we were living and working in upper New York State and summering in Maine. From my point of view I still lived in Maine and was visiting her in the winter. To those who asked, I described it as a long-distance marriage.

After getting settled at the Darrow School, I started tutoring students privately in mathematics. It was something to do, and I was able to help some of the hardest cases. Most of them just needed someone to talk to outside of the public spectacle that constituted the classroom. Many were crippled by a strange visual sense of what algebra symbols actually did and what they meant — but they were simply too ashamed to bring it up in class. One girl subscribed to the notion that X was more important than Y because it looked like it had two feet and could get around more easily — whereas Y looked like a bird standing on one leg. Business was good and they all paid in cash, plus I loved talking to them. Though I was an adult and not to be fully trusted, I was clearly an outsider. I must have had a certain look in my eyes, that indicated I was from a wild place and to some extent not like other adults, because they were unabashed about their problems and wore their hearts on their sleeves. Though they didn't know it, talking to these kids was very soothing for me.

I had no idea what was next for me and hovered in a state of uncertainty every day as I explained algebra to the lost children of Darrow. All the while I harbored a desperate fear of giving up my connection with the sea, of no longer being able to lick the salt off of my fingers. And as hard as it was scratching out a life in Maine, my heart grew leaden at the thought of leaving. I felt like one of the scrubby spruce trees hanging onto the ledges outside our house in South Bristol. They were stunted and gnarled because they could barely extract enough nutrients out of the windblown soil in the cracks of the rock. Even so, they lived a wracking life in the incessant wind.

I felt like someone who had endured by scraping the dry green lichen off of the rock with his teeth, sucking the small meat guts out of periwinkles, chewing an over-dry scrap of salt cod for some trickle of nourishment.

But where could I find respect for the raw life I had led for the past eight years? Why couldn't I do something on the water, something where I could get paid for running a boat? A few of my friends had gone through maritime academies and had worked on tugs — one had worked for years on a tug towing an oil barge between Boston and Searsport, Maine. Six weeks on, six weeks off. But I needed merchant mariner's papers even to do the simplest of jobs on deck, so I went to the Coast Guard office, where I documented my experience running several boats under a hundred tons, the owners, the names of the documented vessels, the length of service. Soon I had a laminated plastic card in my hand—a U.S. Merchant Mariner's Document with my picture, fingerprints, and classification. I would start at the lowest position on the Merchant Marine hierarchy, Ordinary Seaman, and work my way up through the ranks—as it is said, up through the hawse pipe. I would put in sea time and study for the deck crew, attain Mate, eventually Master.

Next, I needed a plan to get a real job. For that, I reached out to Jimmy B., a fisherman who had been educated at Mass Maritime and was now back in the service with his Mate's license. I needed a plan because having the laminated plastic wasn't enough. The problem was simple: I hadn't served on a ship. No one wanted to hire a seaman who had never served on a ship, even at the lowest level. I couldn't blame them. But getting your first assignment was not that easy.

According to Jimmy B., the only way to get your first ship was to sign up on a day when no one else would go. The best day was Christmas Eve. He told me that the plan was sure-fire but somewhat extreme.

"Look, you go to the Merchant Mariner's Union Hall in downtown Manhattan on Christmas Eve."

"Okay, so nobody wants to go."

"Right. There are always several ships in and looking for crew but no one wants to ship out on either Christmas Eve or Christmas Day. If you have your travel bags with you and your laminated document in hand, you are almost guaranteed to get on a ship. Once you get your first ship, it's much easier to get another."

That was the plan.

By the first week in December, I had my bags packed and was working out transportation to Manhattan. I had decided to join the merchant marine and work on large ships. But I don't think I really knew why.

Monday evening just after dinner, the assistant headmaster at Darrow gave me a call. She was my contact for tutoring. A stern woman with the posture of an iron rod, she proceeded to tell me how the new math teacher had just drunk a case of beer with two students, one of whom had only recently started attending AA meetings. It was six pm.

"Can you believe it?" she asked.

"Yeah, well, I was an errant youth myself, once," I said sarcastically.

"He was from Dartmouth, for God's sake."

"I guess he was a well-educated errant youth."

She was not in the mood. She went on to tell me that she had fired him and sent him packing forty-five minutes before. Now she was calling to see if I could fill in for a few weeks or possibly take the job for the rest of the school year.

I thought of the merchant seaman's union hall in Manhattan. I saw green institutional paint and fluorescent lighting and me standing in a room with no one I knew. I saw me chipping paint on some old hulk, or working in the galley as a steward, sleeping in a bunk bed again in a steel room with five other guys.

After the new life I had planned for myself had sufficiently flashed before my eyes, I told the assistant headmaster that I would take the job on a trial basis — and that we could both see if it was the right thing to continue for the full year. Click.

The next morning, I bought myself two ties, two new shirts, a tweed jacket and started teaching that afternoon. In one phone call, the Darrow School had severed and cauterized the heartfelt connection to my fishing career and prevented me from stepping into the numbing drudgery of the merchant marine's lowest job. My disconnect from Maine had begun. My wailing and keening for the wind roaring like a train down the Damariscotta River had been roundly silenced by the frightening prospects of the moment. Like my grandfather in 1913 arriving from Northern Ireland at Ellis Island, I put the history behind me and focused on finding out how to survive in the new world.

I had entered commercial fishing with a jarring jolt, and now in the same fashion I had just stepped into another insanely different world.

The first manifestation of my disconnect from fishing was the experience of standing in the classroom. Linoleum well past its prime curled against the front wall under the slate blackboard showing a large crack in one corner, anthills of chalk dust hiding behind the lifted faces of the old tiles, a battered oak desk pockmarked with the gouges of several generations of steel compasses used to draw arcs, names worn in with blue ballpoint pens, desultory teenagers with legs stretched as far forward as possible and torsos slouched so deep the napes of their necks rested on the top edge of the chair backs, all of them signaling that this was a waste of time, and that they didn't want to be there. No more salt, or baskets of bloody hake heads, no boning knives to butcher pollock and leave their glittering hearts beating in a pile at my feet, no more translucent gillnets, heavy black piles of herring twine, hard clamped wire rigging dripping in the fog, and rusty hydraulic winches. Instead, I had little pieces of yellow and white chalk in my hand. Those bits of chalk, and an inspiring dramatic performance in front of twenty students five or six times a day, were my new tools and my new vocabulary. I had donned my tweed jacket and wool tie, and now I was walking the walk and talking the talk. I was a math teacher.

It didn't dawn on me to think about the speed of this chameleon-like transformation, why it was so easy and why I found it interesting. I was so fascinated with another new role and so relieved that I wasn't wiping down the steam valves on the boiler of some twenty-thousand-ton freighter in the North Atlantic, that I didn't pay much attention. I had jumped from murdering millions of God's creatures for a living and scratching for money in a small wood-heated house perched on the rocks of Maine, to convincing adolescents that mathematics would not give them cancer or cause them to suffer a life of sustained humiliation.

But I had developed a very small vocabulary for anything but commercial fishing. After ten years, Maine had put me into a primal state. The bulk of my thoughts, words, and explanations were an obsessive soup comprised of the comparative behaviors of fish, planktonic feed patterns, currents, the warming effects of wayward Gulf Stream eddies, prices in the fresh mackerel market, Canada's subsidized fleet and its impact on Boston prices, the bulk price of herring and its dependence on the uptake of large herring in the European market, consolidation in the sardine canning industry, diesel horsepower ratings, hydraulics, the expected behaviors and lifespan of diesel engines, the proper frequency of changing fuel filters and methods of keeping deck water out of the fuel system and other — now useless — everyday fishing minutia.

At the Darrow School my salty thoughts and vocabulary did not apply. No one at this school had the slightest need to know what a rudder gudgeon or a garboard plank was. Nor would they have the mildest of interest. The twitch and slather of sea creatures, wet boots, yellow oil pants with red clots of blood, foaming bow waves and roiling wakes were all irrelevant.

But my students were interested. I wasn't sure why, but I knew that I had their attention. I told them my story, that I was married to the art teacher, Ms. Vaughan, that I had just sold out my fishing business and that I had been living in a small house that I had built myself and was heated with wood in Maine. I emphasized that the life I had just arrived from was clearly a place where algebra and trigonometry were unimportant. I was obviously not what they expected. Without fully realizing it, I had taken the stage as a new character. And though I had stopped swearing like a sailor and in general cleaned up my language, I was still as raw and bristly as a slab of rough-cut spruce.

A year later, one of the students finally told me what had been really going on without me knowing it — an indicator of how different my personality appeared to them.

In eight years, I had never left the house without a jackknife in my pocket. It was probably the most important tool any fisherman carried, and it was always razor sharp. As an everyday tool, a jackknife was essential for splicing lines, mending twine, building new gear, and for getting out of messes. Not only was it used almost every day, but ultimately, if you got tangled up in some gear and went overboard, or if some line came unexpectedly humming taut and was going to cause some damage or kill someone, you always had your jackknife. As we used to say, you can always "out-knife-and-cut." A jackknife always gave you a fighting chance. For many years after I quit fishing, I never went anywhere without my jackknife. In fact, I only stopped carrying my knife when I began getting stopped at airport security in the 1990s.

There I stood in my classroom, intent on helping a very unhappy gaggle of teenagers wrestle their private math demons to the ground. The two most common ways to take a moment out of the misery of math class were going to the bathroom and sharpening your pencil. In the hall, a large and ancient pencil sharpener was bolted to the wall. It made a wonderful noise, the wood shavings and pencil lead dust had an interesting if not intoxicating smell, and you could grind really slowly to maximize your time away from class. Better yet, if you took too long, Mr. Callahan would need to come out of class to see what was going on and that would add to the time wasted.

I couldn't do anything to prevent them from going to the head, but I did figure out how to short-circuit the pencil sharpener routine. As soon as a student stood up holding a pencil and mumbling something about sharpening, my kind offer would intercept. "Here, let me do that for you," I would say as I pulled out my jackknife proceeding to whittle the pencil to a fine point in front of them, sending the shavings into the old army green steel trashcan next to my desk and then blowing the dust off the point.

By sharpening the pencil, I got to break the routine of the class for everyone, show them how to whittle, talk to the student for a minute, crack a joke, lighten things up. I didn't think much of it at the time. I had no idea that it would rapidly become known as an eccentric, lovable quirk. Pretty soon, I had three or four kids asking me to sharpen their pencils every day and in every class. They knew it would piss me off if they made the pencil sharpening thing into too much of a joke, so they were somewhat discreet. But they would all smirk and try to control their giggling when someone would come up. I didn't care. I needed some way — any way — to connect with them. And I was doing something for them. That was part of the novelty. It seemed like a shock to them that a teacher would perform something so ordinary, and for them — that a teacher would do them a favor.

Then there were the questions: they asked me where I learned to do that, why I carried a jackknife, and I began to talk about fishing a little now and then, and they were intrigued that I had ended up teaching math and wanted to know more about that. In the end, they felt like they could talk to me. And they would come for help. And they would ask questions even when it seemed stupid. It was all good.

I was a natural teacher and I actually enjoyed myself.

Later, Joy told me how amazed everyone had been. She told me how she had sat in the smoke-filled faculty room when I first started, listening to the other teachers talk about me. How they felt that the Assistant Headmaster was throwing me to the wolves, how she had given me the worst of the worst — the most unruly and most unteachable math truants in the whole school, the bad actors. But they were my new life. I loved them. I cared about them and they knew it. And that made them care about me. And that is all anyone needs, isn't it?

EPILOGUE

I DID NOT STAY IN TEACHING FOR LONG. Though I loved the job and the kids, the salary was less than what fishing brought in. I could not bear to be poor any more. After ten years of living a hardscrabble economy, I jumped at the chance of making money. In 1982, the head of Darrow's Math Department purchased a Radio Shack Model I, and I watched with awe as he typed in a simple program and issued the command to run it. The tiny plastic computer returned the result instantly. This was nothing short of a miracle to me, especially after spending countless hours in engineering school during the late '60s entering programs on punch cards, one line per card, only to find out the next day that the program had crashed because I omitted a semicolon. Seeing my first personal computer, this plastic Radio Shack machine, I realized that a revolution was underway. That summer I took a computer science course at Wesleyan University, and soon landed a job in the IT department of a commercial bank in Boston. I spent the next thirty years in the computer networking industry.

Shortly after I left teaching, Joy and I parted. At the time I was crushed, not understanding why she no longer wanted to be together, but I realized later that she had lost the person she knew so well. I had walked away from two things that were closest to her heart, teaching and art.

Fortunately for me, Kippie Kelsey turned out to be right. My unborn children were waiting in the wings. After marrying my second wife, Nancy Roberts, a woman filled with unreasonable optimism and an inexplicable surplus of good cheer, our son and daughter decided to come on stage in the '90s. For those three events, I am supremely grateful to whomever is responsible.

AFTER A LONG DECLINE, the sardine (juvenile herring) industry has disappeared from Maine. The Stinson Seafood Company in Prospect Harbor, the last U.S. sardine factory, closed its doors in 2010. Many of the employees, women who had packed sardines all their working lives, were in their eighties. When management announced the plan to close the factory, local newspapers reported that the workers wept openly.

As for adult herring, that market is now dominated by the demand for lobster bait. With ground fish stocks in decline, lobster fishermen can no longer rely on an ample supply of fish racks, the leavings of fillet houses, from cod, haddock, pollock, and hake as a source for bait. In the '70s, only the isolated islanders of Monhegan and Matinicus used herring for bait. Now the entire industry relies on herring. But the market, once supplied largely by purse-seiners, is controlled by the pair-trawlers.

Worse yet, the herring never get much of a break from hot pursuit. Back in 1976, we returned home from Gloucester after the bulk of the herring had migrated through the Cape Cod Canal and into Buzzard's Bay. At that point in the season, the fish were no longer schooling in tight bunches and were too dispersed to be caught in a purse-seine. The few pair-trawlers then in operation were able to put together a haul by towing through many scattered bunches, but purse-seining was typically over until the June of the following year.

Today, pair-trawling is by far the dominant method. In March of 2012, boats chased herring all the way to New Jersey. In one case, the herring were up against the shore, massed in only thirty feet of water. The boats towing through them were so close to the shore, the crew could see the traffic lights. And the water was so shallow, that when the huge mid-water trawl was stretched between the two boats, the head rope of the net was actually out of the water. It is hard to imagine how herring could be pursued any more aggressively.

JUNIOR FARRIN LIVED TO BE NINETY-TWO. In the final stage of his life he was diagnosed with multiple ailments and treated at the VA hospital in Maine. Told that he had only two weeks to live, Junior was sent home to die. The VA doctors instructed his daughter Jackie that if she weren't careful with his medication he would die in a matter of days. Because he had suffered several heart attacks, she had to thin his blood — but not too much, because that could increase the internal bleeding resulting from the cancerous growth in his stomach. Apparently, Jackie mastered the balance because Junior lived for two more years.

But a full year into his miracle "two weeks," the VA psychologist made a house call. Like her colleagues before her, she had come to inform Junior that he was going to die. As she sat with him, she hauled out document after document and chart after chart indicating that his end was certainly near.

"Mr. Farrin," she said, "you need to prepare yourself for death, because as you can see the evidence is overwhelming that you do not have very long to live."

Junior, famous throughout his life for playing the part of a bumpkin for strangers, showed his best shock-and-mock surprise expression, and simply said (in his best on-the-water Maine drawl), "Really? I don't feel that bad." Her message delivered, the psychologist departed, whereupon Junior lived for yet another year.

JUNIOR'S STOP-SEINE PARTNER HENRY JONES died in 1988 shortly after losing his wife, Christine. Raised on the bare island of Damariscove, a fishing community with a history reaching back long before the creation of the Massachusetts Bay Colony, Henry was far and away the hardest charging fisherman, and the best story teller I have ever known. He remains a legend in South Bristol.

Henry's longtime friend, Roy Vose, lived out the remainder of his life in his trailer on Boot Hill under the watchful eye of his kind neighbors, Arthur and Tricia Poland. Mr. P sold the *Miss Angel* after ten years of hard-pounding service and retired to the rural free delivery of mail. Arthur remains as generous and funny as he ever was.

SAM JONES REMAINS a consummate wooden boat builder and master craftsman. His long career includes construction of multiple period ships, most notably a working replica of Sir Walter Raleigh's flagship, the *Elizabeth*, and countless wooden lobster boats built with Peter Cass at the John's Bay Boat Company in South Bristol.

AFTER FORTY YEARS OF HIS METICULOUS CARE, Normie Brackett sold the *Candy B II* in 2002. Under new ownership, she was lost with all hands October 10, 2003, forty-two miles southeast of Nantucket dragging scallops. According to the Coast Guard's investigation, the vessel's stability had been significantly reduced by its conversion to scalloping; thus it may have rolled over in the process of taking the loaded dredge over the side. No trace of the boat or the crew was ever found.

Normie is eighty years old and still lives in New Harbor. Though he quit smoking some sixteen years ago, I asked him if he missed it. He replied, "If you gave me a cigarette right now, I'd suck that baby down so fast and so deep...yes sir, so I could feel it all the way down to my toes."

RECENTLY WHEN I WENT BACK to visit South Bristol, I saw the first man who had given me a job, ninety-five-year-old Lamar Seiders. True to form, he jumped up from his chair and said, "Boy, am I glad to see you. Now I've got an excuse to have a drink with my lunch." We talked about old times and he told me that he planned to live to be a hundred.

I left South Bristol thirty years ago, but I haven't stopped visiting there because my friends are still there and, evidently, so is my heart.

APPENDIX

KNOTS There were two interesting things about tying knots in fishing. First, there was the fact that it mattered whether you were left-handed or right-handed. If you were left-handed, I mean truly left-handed, you really needed to learn how to tie knots from a left-handed person. Why? Because it was all about the motion with the working end, the free end of the line. Like throwing a ball, there is a motion, a way you address the knot. If you are left-handed you hold the working end in your left hand and tie the knot with that hand. The motion becomes like a muscle memory. If you're right-handed, the motion is a right-handed motion. Seems simple, but I later worked on deck with a true left-handed guy who couldn't tie a single knot. No one he had ever fished with — and no one in his family for that matter — was left-handed and so no one had ever been able to teach him how to tie the simplest of knots.

Second, most fishing knots were not tightly tied. Over time, I learned that the mark of a true greenhorn, including myself, was to cinch up and yank on knots so they were tight and rock hard. On fishing boats, most knots at some point will need to be untied. There were exceptions, of course. The only knot that I ever saw anyone yank on — I mean stand on the line with their boot and pull up as hard as they could to tighten it — was the fisherman's knot used to join two lines. Once tied, it could never be untied. Lobster catchers used that knot every day to lengthen out pot warp, or when they had to cut apart snarls where they got tangled up in other people's gear, then re-attach the line. Most fishing knots were variants of regular knots with a kind of slipknot approach for easy untying. Instead of using the straight working end, the loose end of the line, most fisherman make a bight, a loop, with the working end and use that to tie the knot. The bight serves two purposes. Because it is bigger than the single working end, it makes the knot looser against the standing line. In other words, this doubled-up working end is harder to crush into a binding knot that is so tight it takes beating on it with a hammer to get it apart. The bight also gives you the ability to pull the knot apart faster when you're untying it. That's the slipknot aspect. In the last step of untying, you just pull the free end and pull out the bight.

I know that all seems a bit fussy, but it matters in fishing because most knots can come under terrific strain and you often need to get them apart to get yourself out of messes — and there are always messes — without necessarily resorting to "out-knife-and-cut." And all fishing gear is held together by knots and splices, whether it is the fundamental small knots in a net, that lace the mesh to a corkline or a leadline, a hawser used to hold a boat at a wharf, or a wire towing cable pulling two thousand pounds of dragging doors. Undoubtedly, the most useful knot ever invented is the bowline. No matter how much strain is put on the knot, you can always get it untied. On a regular basis, towing loaded dories behind a workboat, we would put a bowline in the line of the boat to be towed, and then tie another bowline through that bowline to join the two lines. Even after towing a dory loaded with two tons of mackerel, you could easily untie the two lines.

STOP-SEINING In North America, canned sardines are not really sardines. They are juvenile herring. The true sardine (sardina pilchardus) is a Mediterranean, not a North Atlantic species.

The ideal way to catch juvenile herring is to wait until they mass in a cove and then shut them off with a long straight net called a stop-seine. A very simple net, a stop-seine creates a fence in the water meant to stop the herring. It consists of a corkline (a line threaded through heavy styrofoam corks) that floats on the surface of the water, and a leadline (a line threaded through lead weights) that sits on the bottom. Sewed onto the corkline and the leadline, and stretched in between the two, is the twine, or mesh, of the net. Even though twine is the proper name for the mesh, the whole system is commonly referred to as twine, as in "go fetch that dory full of twine." Dories are unpowered open boats used to store twine and are usually anchored in coves to stake out territory.

Finding herring is a matter of visiting the likely spots every evening and sometimes involves a spotter plane. Herring make their move at the edge of dark. They seem to come from nowhere, up from the bottom, or scattered in the mid-water, and bunch up. If that happens in a cove, and you are ready with a dory full of twine, you've got them. But most of the time, you're not that ready. And then when the fish do make their move — driven by the fear that they could just as easily leave the cove as they came in, or by the fact that on this particular evening the right twine is in *another* dory in *another* cove, or because you have been watching and waiting for so long you have almost forgotten what to do — you tear around as fast as possible fetching a dory full of twine and all the remaining gear to set it out. All part of being at the mercy of the herring — wild creatures that are going to do whatever they want to do.

Here is a sample timeline. Just past edge of dark, say eight or nine pm in midsummer, you have fetched the twine and are ready to set. You put a man in the stern of a dory with a grapple or a small seine anchor tied to the end of the seine. Since the dory has no power, you nose it in stern-first against the shore using a small powered workboat, hopefully without putting the workboat on the rocks. Your man in the dory throws the grapple on the bank or jumps ashore and ties the seine end around a boulder, hauls a bunch of twine out onto the shore to give it some slack and to make sure the high water mark is covered, and hops back into the bow of the dory to keep himself out of harm's way as the twine is setting. The workboat then tows the dory out across the cove to shut off the fish, the seine setting out of the stern of the dory, corks softly clicking, twine hissing, and leads rattling like stones against the wooden transom. If the dory runs out of twine before the cove is shut off, the crew stops and brings another dory full of twine alongside, laces the ends of the seines together quickly and continues the set across the cove. Once the other end of the stop-seine is put ashore and made fast, the fish are officially shut off. This straight length of seine then becomes known as the running twine because the fish will run back and forth across it. Small seine anchors are then made fast to the corkline of the running twine, and the anchors are dropped in both directions inbound and outbound of the cove to handle the pressure from the ebb and flood tides and the pressure of the fish swimming against the twine.

If all goes well, it is ten or eleven pm. The set is likely to have been made by a skeleton crew since not everyone goes out every night, but now that the fish are shut off the call goes out over the radio and phone calls are made for the rest of the crew.

Next step is putting a pocket in place, a square corral to hold the fish. Another dory carrying the pocket twine — usually a measured length of deeper twine used to make a more permanent holding pen — is laid against the deepest part of the running twine. This is important. Herring will run for deep water at first light, so you need the pocket to be sitting on that deep hole, if there is one.

The first side of the pocket is tied on with short throwaway straps usually made from cut up old lobster pot line — the corkline of running twine is tied at intervals to the corkline of the pocket twine — for twenty-five fathoms (150 feet) to make the front side, or entrance, of the pocket. Next the dory is towed at right angles to the running twine for another twenty-five fathoms to make the second side of the pocket, a handful of corks are bunched and tied to make a corner, and a seine anchor is run off to hold it in place. Then, another twenty-five-fathom side is paid out, another corner made and an anchor run, and then the last side is set back to the running twine to complete the square. The pocket is then closed by lacing the two ends of the twine together top-to-bottom. This time the lacing is very carefully done using a twine needle from corkline down to leadline, since the pocket could be in place anywhere from a few days to more than a week and it must be fish-tight.

By now it is midnight or later, and preparations must be made to run the fish into the pocket. Herring won't usually run into the pocket until first light, around three am in the summertime, but it never hurts to be ready. To get the fish to flow into the pocket, heavy weights are put on at the entrance astraddle the laced-together running twine and pocket corks and over the deep hole so the fish will run over the sunken corks thinking they are escaping into deep water.

With the pocket ready, if there is an hour or two before first light, it is a good time to have a mug-up, something to eat and a cup of coffee. Nobody can sleep.

By three or four am the fish have usually run in, but sometimes they are stubborn. If there is another deep spot against the running twine, for example, the herring might bunch and settle there and you might need to drive them with the noise of the outboard. For the most part, they go into the pocket all in one wallop, which you can verify with a depth recorder.

By now, it is sunrise and you begin to clean up. With fish in the pocket, there is no more need for the running twine. You can haul the weights off the corks at the entrance to the pocket, cut away the running twine corks from the pocket corks, and start taking back the running twine. You strap an empty dory onto a seine boat equipped with a power block, and haul the running twine into the dory — evenly layer the seine, corks in the bow, leads in the stern — pulling and stowing the anchors in the workboat as you go.

There are a number of reasons to run the fish into a pocket. First, a pocket makes it easier to keep your twine out of harm's way. Many a set has been lost from boat traffic — sailboats and lobster boats can snag and part the corkline as they run over it. When that happens, the running twine opens like a zipper, top-to-bottom, from the pressure of fish and tide. Most lobster boats have cages around their wheels (the working term for propellers), to keep them clear of their own gear. But any boat can have an errant bolt or a jagged piece of worn zinc sticking out here or there. Some sailboats have rudders with no kedge or connection between the keel and the rudder so they hang down like a dagger. Second, the pocket serves to make it easier to purse-seine the fish when it comes time to pump them onto a sardine carrier. You just set the seine around the edge of the pocket or set halfway across if you only want a piece of them — shooting the proverbial fish in a barrel. Third, the pocket serves as a means to keep the fish for a week or more. By doing so, the fish clean up for the cannery. The herring were probably in the cove because they were feeding or chasing feed. If their bellies are full of feed, the cans will explode when they are cooked at the factory. Keeping the herring for a day or more allows the feed to move on while the fish stay put and starve-out a bit. Plus, the cannery may be busy with other fish and may not be able to buy them right away.

As with all fishing, if you've caught fish, chances are good that someone else has fish, too. In other words, the conditions that caused the herring to come ashore in this cove probably occurred in lots of other coves; and if another crew was ready, you have competition in the market. Feast or famine, all fish or no fish; pick your favorite aphorism.

COMING ALONGSIDE A PURSE-SEINE The ritual and the procedure of bringing a carrier alongside a purse-seine full of fish is simple, but not always easy. If it is a small set and there is no danger of spooking the fish with white light and driving them over the corks, the seiner usually snaps on his deck lights to indicate he is ready. By then, the seine crew has hauled back to the bunt end and has put a line on the corks and taken them aloft on a boom or strapped them up over the rail. The carrier snaps on his deck lights — and everyone can see what they are doing. The carrier comes in starboard side to the seine; both boats have lots of hundred-inch balloon bumpers out and the carrier can slide in at a slight angle and back down hard with little danger of getting his wheel afoul of the seine. The carrier's deckhand then picks up the corks and ties them through the scuppers in two or three places. In light summer weather, the ball of fish acts as a bumper between the two boats until the fish are almost pumped out. In the winter and in rough weather, the boats can be lashed together tightly — bow to stern against the balloons — as the carrier pumps.

MACKEREL TRAPPING A mackerel trap is an upgraded version of the ancient weir, a fish trap used by ancient people for thousands of years. Weirs are heart-shaped (like a valentine) fences in the water, with an entrance, or door, at the top of the heart between the two lobes. In fishing terms, the top rounded parts of the heart are called the arms. Most weirs have two heart-shaped chambers, the parlor at the entrance and then a second chamber where most of the fish end up. Ancient weirs were made from poles driven into the mud or sand, and then with brush woven between the poles. Modern weirs, many of which were still active east of Mount Desert, were made from poles but had herring twine hung on the poles instead of brush. Mackerel traps didn't use poles. They floated in the water with a corkline like a seine and were held in place by anchors at the corners to make a squared-off shape like a weir. Some traps had two or three chambers, but others, like Junior's, had just one large chamber, one door. Most floating traps were seventy feet by ninety feet on the surface and twenty-four feet deep on the sides, which, like a herring stop-seine, hung straight down like a curtain. But mackerel traps did not reach all the way to the bottom. Instead, the sides connected with the belly of the trap, to form a giant basket in the water. The sides were leaded so they hung relatively straight down. The belly also had leadlines running across it, so it ballooned down eight or ten feet deeper than the sides to form the bottom of the basket.

Junior's was an unusually large trap — eighty feet by one hundred feet — and built with double the leads along the seam where the sides met the belly so it wouldn't get swept up by heavy tides. Junior had also tied clusters of the leads on the bottom corners of the belly to hold them down. He believed a bigger trap was able to catch and keep more fish than a standard trap but he also knew that he needed much more weight to hold it in place.

Keeping the underwater basket shape of the trap was very important. If a trap was swept by a strong tide, the big anchors on the corners would hold the corkline in place, but the rest of the trap would lose its shape. The twine in the belly and the sides would get swept up to the surface and flattened out like a bed sheet in a breeze. If that happened, all the fish — if there were any — would get run out the door. And the trap would certainly not catch any fish in that condition, either.

The trap was held in place by five anchors, the biggest of which connected the backbone of the trap — a heavy line to the shore. The backbone could run anywhere from seventy-five to a hundred fathoms from the shore. It was tied to a buoy, usually made from a block of styrofoam sandwiched between two pieces of plywood and held together with a couple of big galvanized ring bolts. The backbone buoy was also then tied to the anchor rode, the line down to an anchor of two hundred pounds or more.

As well as being central to the framework that held the trap in place, the backbone also served to hold the leader, which guided the fish into the trap. The leader was a very big mesh net, usually eight-inch or ten-inch mesh, hanging down from the backbone like a curtain twenty-four feet deep as it stretched out from the shore. The leader was tied to the backbone with straps made from short unraveled pieces of scrap rope so it could be easily cut away when it needed to be taken up and cleaned. The leader was not meant to catch the fish, but to lead them into the trap.

The big basket of Junior's trap was attached to the backbone in various ways — and to the remaining four anchors at its corners — and was held in place anywhere from seventy-five to a hundred fathoms distance from shore. The offset of the trap from the shore depended on the depth of the water at any given location. And that was determined by how steeply the sea bottom dropped off as you moved away from the shore. If you set the trap in water that was too deep, the fish would swim under the trap, instead of going in. If you set the trap too shallow, the belly of the trap would chafe on the bottom at low tide, and if it was hard bottom, it could hang up or wear holes in the belly.

GLOSSARY

bight: a loop formed by a line or rope.

bull net: a large dip net used for bailing fish aboard.

bunt: the last length of a purse-seine, typically constructed with heavy gauge twine to withstand the chafing and wear of bailing or pumping fish.

cat's-paw: a brief but intense gust of wind.

ceiling: wooden sheathing fastened on the interior of a boat's frames; typically used to make a fish hold watertight.

coasties: members of the U. S. Coast Guard.

cod-end: the last section of an otter trawl or mid-water trawl where the catch accumulates.

deadwood: dimensional timber elements of a boat's backbone that do not carry frames.

doors: the heavy metal or wooden paddles used to spread the opening of an otter trawl when towed by draggers; usually supported by gallows frames, port and starboard, in the stern of a boat.

drying fish: the act of crowding fish in a net to facilitate bringing them aboard via bailing or pumping.

fathom: a length of six feet.

flaking nets: orderly storing nets in a manner to enable smooth setting or shooting.

freeboard: a measurement of the remaining distance between the level of the water and a boat's gunwale.

gang: a series of nets or traps tied together in a long string.

gantry: the metal framework used to support the hoisting of heavy loads.

garboard: the lowest plank or strake in a boat's hull, typically placed next to the keel.

gunwale: the topmost edge of a boat's hull.

gurry: the general mixture of leavings, (blood, juice, mud, or slime) from the cutting of bait or fish.

in the corner: full throttle.

kink: a nap or rest.

lazarette: the sealed aft chamber of a boat, typically housing the rudder post.

net hauler: an hydraulically powered capstan used to haul gillnets.

peavey: a form of leveraged cant hook used by lumberjacks to roll logs.

pen boards: the boards used to partition loads in fish holds or decks.

pot warp: common lines used to connect lobster traps to their buoys.

shacking: the act of cutting or butchering fish.

shoal seine: a purse-seine that reaches a depth of fifteen fathoms or less.

short lobster: an undersized, illegal lobster.

side-scanner: a form of sonar used to view fish adjacent to a boat.

speaking: bringing two boats in open ocean near enough to have a conversation.

stringer: on an open boat such as a dory, a board fastened to the interior side of frames; typically used to stiffen the sides and afford a working or standing platform.

twine: the knit mesh of any net, typically stretched between corkline (floatation) and leadline (weight).

water firing: a condition that occurs when concentrations of bioluminescent plankton are sufficient to make the sea appear to light up when disturbed by the movement of fish or boats.

ACKNOWLEDGMENTS

FIRST AND FOREMOST, I owe the existence of this book to my dear wife, Nancy Pattison Roberts, who brought with her a room full of angels and the work ethic of a stevedore; my son Owen who read numerous drafts and told me to cut the technical mumbo jumbo; and my daughter Sydney who reminded me to chill on countless, and necessary, occasions.

Thanks to my friends from South Bristol: Donna Plummer, Jackie Farrin, Bill Kelsey, Tina Alley, Chuck Plummer, Sage Eskesen, and Kippie Kelsey for their boundless generosity; Arthur and Tricia Poland for their trust in the mystery of this project; Bob Ryan for never losing his sense of humor on deck; from New Harbor: Normie and Sandra Brackett for their kindness and their honest memories; my sister, Ellen and her husband, John Nolan, for their open hearts and a quiet room in Maine whenever I needed; from Vinalhaven Island: Mike and Stevie Mesko for capturing what few have captured; Joe and Mary Lou Upton for believing I could do this; back home in Massachusetts Bay, Chris Baldwin for his clarity and undying support; Gary Vacon for his irrepressible enthusiasm; Michael Snell for his unwavering faith in what I had in hand; and my dear friend, D'Anne Bodman, for her proofreader's eye and poet's ear in this world of chaos.

Blessings to the Schrock family for their longstanding welcome: Gladden for his wise counsel and firm push up the hill; Jan for loving me like a son; and Kate and Nate for their accepting and generous hearts.

This book owes an important debt to Mark Pawlak for keeping and sending back my letters from the '70s and for introducing me to my editor, Dick Lourie, a man with nearly infinite patience.

In the final stages of producing this book, I received a wonderful gift. Jon Albertson, a friend and artist I had not seen for forty-one years, agreed to be my book designer. As he read and laid out the interior of the book, he also produced a magical set of ink wash paintings that became illustrations and the basis of the book cover.

Lastly, my deepest gratitude is reserved for Hugh Sam Jones, who stood by me through impossibly hard times, and to whom I owe my understanding of what it means to build and create.

Photographs

Pages 15, 79, 162, 232, 233: Courtesy of Joy Vaughan

Pages 22, 26: Courtesy of Mike Mesko

Pages 36, 41, 53, 92, 164, 238: Ann Hillis photographs, courtesy of the South Bristol Historical Society

Pages 59, 75, 127: Author's Collection

Page 109: Courtesy of Bob Ryan

Pages 135, 145, 147: Courtesy of Norman Brackett

Pages 177, 189: Courtesy of Glenn and Jackie Lawrence

ABOUT THE AUTHOR

P. D. Callahan lives outside of
Boston, Massachusetts and
has published several short
works in literary magazines.

This is his first book.

Visit the *Door In Dark Water* photo archives at doorindarkwater.com.

Made in the USA
San Bernardino, CA
24 November 2014